'A superb and energizing history of the professional
women who paved the way for gender equality
in law, medicine, engineering and many other fields . . .
Deeply moving at times, this book deserves
to be read by young and old.'
Dr Henrietta Bowden-Jones, President of
the Medical Women's Federation, UK

'A rich picture of the struggles and successes of
those amazing women who trod so quietly to leave
such a massive footprint and legacy behind them.'
Dawn Childs, President of the
Women's Engineering Society

'A book of huge interest both to me
and to anyone, man or woman, who wishes to understand
how far we have come in gender equality – and presented
in the most fascinating and appealing way.'
Professor Carrie MacEwen, Chair of the Academy of
Medical Royal Colleges

'Modern professional women will read this
with a slow burn of anger and heightened respect for those
whose actions, such a relatively brief time ago, made today
possible . . . We ride on the shoulders of female giants –
courageous, eccentric, clever pioneers. Robinson is a
wryly amusing companion and this is an entertaining
book, teeming with characters.'
Melanie Reid

LADIES CAN'T CLIMB LADDERS

The Pioneering Adventures of the First Professional Women

Jane Robinson

BLACK SWAN

TRANSWORLD PUBLISHERS
Penguin Random House, One Embassy Gardens,
8 Viaduct Gardens, London SW11 7BW
www.penguin.co.uk

Transworld is part of the Penguin Random House group of companies
whose addresses can be found at global.penguinrandomhouse.com

Penguin
Random House
UK

First published in Great Britain in 2020 by Doubleday
an imprint of Transworld Publishers
Black Swan edition published 2021

A CIP catalogue record for this book
is available from the British Library.

ISBN
9781784163990

Typeset in Bembo MT Pro by Jouve (UK), Milton Keynes.
Printed and bound in Italy by Grafica Veneta S.p.A.

The authorized representative in the EEA is Penguin Random House Ireland,
Morrison Chambers, 32 Nassau Street, Dublin D02 YH68.

Penguin Random House is committed to a sustainable
future for our business, our readers and our planet. This book
is made from Forest Stewardship Council® certified paper.

MIX
Paper from
responsible sources
FSC® C018179

For Dr Tammy Oxley

Contents

Introduction

Never let anybody guess that you have a mind of your own.

THIS IS THE STORY OF some of the twentieth century's most influential women, whose entry into the élite fields of medicine, law, the Church, architecture, engineering and academia shaped the personal and professional lives of working women today. A few of them are famous; most are barely remembered beyond their own families. Yet all of them were pioneers, adventurers in a forbidden land thicketed with centuries of prejudice and hidden danger. Not the sort of danger likely to cost lives (although that did happen), but the sort that put their roles and reputations on the line, threatened their moral integrity, their very identity as female members of society.

The history of progress is full of transgressors, and that's exactly what these women were. To sense just how alien they must have felt in the professional workplace of their time, at the beginning of my research for this book I took myself on a tour of London. I wanted to see what they saw; to imagine how daunting it must have been to attempt an invasion of the Establishment's strongholds a century ago. I was confident that little enough would have changed – in the buildings' fabric, at least – for this experiment to work.

I started out on Westminster Bridge, close to where I planned to set the beginning of the book. On the south bank of the Thames, beyond the modern tower block of St Thomas' Hospital,

I could see the long façade of the nineteenth-century building, for ever associated with Florence Nightingale. I had just seen her likeness in bronze in St James's, the heart of gentlemen's club-land, on my way from Piccadilly Circus. She was – still is – the caring profession personified.

Opposite the hospital stands the Palace of Westminster. Only one female MP sat in the House of Commons in 1920, but she can't have been lonely: in the Queen's Robing Room, for instance, William Dyce's frescoes of chivalric virtues are adorned with scores of women. In the tableau called 'Mercy', Sir Gawain swears (as Dyce puts it) 'never to be against ladies'. Ironic, given the vehemence of opposition to women's suffrage among MPs at the time, but comforting none the less.

I walked up Whitehall and turned into King Charles Street to gaze at the old seat of Empire, the Foreign and Commonwealth Office. Ordinary members of the public can visit it only on spe-cial open days, but several years ago a diplomat friend took me inside. Again, I remember swarms of women. Not real ones, of course, but extravagant figures representing entire continents, and a goddess-like Britannia surveying her subjects with a stern, blank stare.

It was time to move on. At Trafalgar Square I turned right to Charing Cross (named for Edward I's monument to his Queen Eleanor) and made towards the City of London. I passed the Central Criminal Court at the Old Bailey on the way, and saw the famous gilded figure perfectly balanced on the dome, wield-ing a sword in her right hand and the scales of justice in her left: the epitome of wisdom. Eventually I reached the heart of the financial district, presided over by the Old Lady of Threadneedle Street, the Bank of England.

Once I got my eye in, I realized that all over the place build-ings were festooned with bas-reliefs invoking women. There were statues of queens; of the Blessed Virgin Mary; of saints and patronesses. I walked by the river to photograph a visiting tall ship (she was beautiful) before crossing to Waterloo, where I was welcomed at the station's vast, arched entrance by yet another stony-faced Britannia. It's a pity I couldn't have gone home in a steam train, to complete my perversely feminine journey: they are invariably described as ladies too.

I'm glad I made that tour. I had not realized before how potent the image of idealized womanhood was in public life, and how ubiquitous. Her dominant presence in the Establishment of the nineteenth and early twentieth centuries made it even more difficult for flesh-and-blood women – half the human race – to gain access. A real Victorian lady's place was nowhere near the inner sanctum of the traditional professions. She was the 'Angel in the House', characterized by Coventry Patmore in his endless poem of the same name as utterly innocent, utterly selfless, utterly beautiful – and so graceful that she somehow seemed to float an inch or two above the ground.

The Angel's natural habitat was the drawing-room or the nursery. Her duty was to marry as well as possible and to make others happy. If she must work – as an unfortunately 'distressed gentlewoman', perhaps, or a chronic spinster – then let her teach or, at a push, train for nursing; but always with an ambition to stop as soon as she could. (These are 'ladies' we're talking about; 'women', on the other hand, were expected to labour in factories, domestic service, anywhere that would have them. Men had careers; women had jobs; ladies, like children, behaved nicely and did what they were told.)

The first faint cracks in this divinely ordained order appeared during the late 1860s, when women were admitted to a growing number of British universities, though not always awarded degrees at the end of their studies. The campaign for women's suffrage gathered momentum at around the same time, and with it the concept of women's rights. As access to higher education widened and collective confidence grew through political activism, women began to demand, politely or otherwise, to be allowed a meaningful role in public life.

The First World War gave them just that, but only temporarily. Afterwards, the Establishment expected them to strap on their angel wings again, go home and subside into domesticity. True, the vote was won in 1918, but only partially. The Sex Disqualification (Removal) Act was passed in December 1919, but its scope was limited and easily misconstrued. And the habits of the past were hard to break. Virginia Woolf, embarking on her career as a professional writer, may have refused to play the part of the Angel but was only too well aware of her influence:

> The shadow of her wings fell on my page; I heard the rustling of her skirts in the room . . . [S]he slipped behind me and whispered 'My dear, you are a young woman . . . Be sympathetic; be tender; flatter; deceive; use all the arts and wiles of our sex. Never let anybody guess that you have a mind of your own.'[1]

By 1920 that secret was out. As universities produced increasing numbers of educated women, a problem emerged. What were they to do, once qualified? During the period between the two world wars, fewer women (women as in females: forget the class distinctions now) were able or minded to marry, and more found themselves solely responsible for dependants. They needed to work, to earn their own and others' living. And of those who *didn't* need to, many chose to, being creatures of intellect, energy and ambition. Those who had graduated in professional disciplines such as law or architecture, or had practical wartime expertise in medicine or engineering, were no longer content to waste their potential. They had already proved the reactionaries wrong: females did not collapse if they thought too hard; cleverness and attractiveness were not mutually exclusive; it was even possible for them to overcome their 'physiological emergencies' and remain rational beings every day of the month.[2] To sympathetic men – and there were many – all this was welcome news; to others, it was profoundly worrying and rapidly denied.

The time had come, as Virginia Woolf rather brutally put it, to kill the Angel in the House – or at least, to furnish her with a stout pair of shoes and send her out into the world, feet firmly on the ground. Just as they had claimed a voice in Parliament, so women now claimed the right to exercise a vocation, not only for their own good but for the benefit of others. So, with dignity and daring, serious intent and high spirits, confidence and trepidation, they approached the Establishment ladder, and began to climb.

I suggested at the beginning of this introduction that you might recognize some of the names in the following pages. However, as a social historian I always like to avoid celebrities and concentrate on relatively unknown, 'ordinary' women. The corollary is that people you might be expecting to meet here could well be absent. If your favourite lawyer or doctor, architect or engineer, academic or churchwoman is missing, I apologize. The chances are that she is written about elsewhere. I'm sorry, too, if I appear to have short-changed all but the six traditional professions: I have concentrated on this hexagonal citadel because it stood – and to a certain extent still stands – at the heart of the Establishment. The adventures of those who scaled its walls were shared by pioneers across the professional workplace. The obstacles put in their way were familiar to them all.

They might even be familiar to you.

1

The Society of Outsiders

FIRST FEET IN THE DOOR

Bluestockings are not wanted here.[1]

IT WAS UNSEASONABLY cold on the evening of 8 March 1920. There was already a promise of frost in the air as small groups of women began to arrive through the gas-lit dusk at the Palace of Westminster. Three or four strode confidently, neat and slim in loose-fitting coats with hems well above the ankle and close-brimmed hats. The rest walked more slowly. Their costumes were structured on old-fashioned lines; their fur stoles dangled the limbs and snouts of long-dead foxes and their hats were as wide as their hips. It would be difficult at first glance to imagine what brought this unlikely company together.

Business was over for the day at the House of Commons. Its 700-odd members (all men but one) had grappled with the fate of a military mission in Soviet Russia; the employment of ex-servicemen; how children should be provided with medical care at school; and the parlous state of the House's ventilation system. Further afield, the country was struggling to come to terms with the aftermath of war and the recent pandemic of Spanish flu: a cruel blow to an exhausted people only just beginning to raise heads above the parapet and look to the future. No family was untouched by grief. Some reacted to personal loss by reverting to the *carpe diem* philosophy of soldiers and their lovers between 1914 and 1918, telling themselves that all that mattered was to live for the day. Others disapproved of such purblind hedonism, preferring to trust in the pre-war values that had built the British Empire. Those gathering in Westminster that early spring evening in 1920 represented a third way. Between them, they were changing the world for British women at home, in politics and in the workplace. Radiant with the (partial) success of recent crusades for the vote and the right to a career, they had come to celebrate.

Among the first to turn up at the banquet was Ray Strachey, a veteran of the suffrage campaign and a progressive champion of women in the traditional professions. Not that there *were* many women in the professions yet: a few score doctors and surgeons, seasoned by war work but unwelcome in most teaching hospitals; some pretend engineers and architects whose unfeminine ambition made right-minded people laugh; a handful of unorthodox priestesses, recalling Samuel Johnson's famous quip that 'a woman's preaching is like a dog's walking on its hinder legs. It is not done well; but you are surprised to find it done at all.' There were thousands of women teachers, but until the end of the Second World War they were expected to resign upon marriage, which meant their average working life was just three years. A couple of fully fledged professors had been appointed, one at a Johnny-come-lately modern university and the other at a medical school – and there were no qualified barristers or solicitors at all.[2]

Ray Strachey was something of a Renaissance woman. Her interests included mathematics, which she studied at Newnham College, Cambridge; cricket, which she played with aplomb; engineering – especially electrical engineering; and architecture. In 1921 she would design and build her own house in Sussex, where she brought up the family. Though constructed essentially of mud, it still stands. She was closely involved with politics, standing unsuccessfully as a parliamentary candidate in 1918,

1920 and 1922. As next best thing to being elected herself, she worked as political secretary to the first and for a time the only woman MP, Nancy Astor (1879–1964).

The venue of this evening's celebration was particularly gratifying to Ray's friend and mentor Millicent Garrett Fawcett (1847–1929). Walking into Parliament by invitation remained a novelty for her. Memories of past violence and despair still stirred in the corridors of power, and it seemed strange to be hailed as a heroine by other guests – the Lord Chancellor, Attorney General and Solicitor General among them. Mrs Fawcett was in her seventy-third year. Her face was instantly familiar, apple-cheeked and cheerful despite that slightly downturned mouth, though her once slender frame looked bulkier now. She had never enjoyed the easy elegance of her old adversary Emmeline Pankhurst.

Most of the other women at the banquet were younger, including the bespectacled Helena Normanton (1882–1957), who would become one of the first two female barristers to take silk in England; her almost exact contemporary Lady Rhondda (1883–1958), an extraordinarily energetic business magnate and political activist from Wales; Lucy Nettlefold (1891–1966), known as Nancy, one of the first women to apply to the Law Society for training as a solicitor (though she had now joined her father's hardware business instead); and a young wife and mother called Gwyneth Bebb Thomson.

It was an enjoyable evening, with speeches and high-flown compliments on all sides. And lavish: oysters were on the menu, followed by trout, mutton, chicken casserole, croquette potatoes, peas, salad and *poires belle Hélène*.[3] (When the suffragists of the Women's Freedom League had held a similar celebration on winning the vote in 1918, it had been an altogether more frugal affair involving ravioli, carrots and some jam tarts. Now rationing was almost over, things were looking up.) Officially, the occasion was to celebrate the passing of the Sex Disqualification (Removal) Act (SDRA) a few weeks previously on 23 December 1919, and to launch a loan fund for women students hoping to study law, now that the Act had made it possible for them to do so. But in many ways, it was all about Gwyneth.

Gwyneth Bebb Thomson was born in 1889, one of seven children. She was educated at home in Wales, then at St Mary's, Paddington, a modest but progressive boarding school in London, before going up to St Hugh's Hall, Oxford, in 1908. There she was one of the first women to study Jurisprudence, or the theory and philosophy of law. Why did she choose what was almost exclusively a male discipline? It was a rash decision: women were not permitted anywhere near the legal profession at that time and Gwyneth always intended to work for a living. And why Oxford,

Gwyneth Bebb Thomson.

which refused to confer degrees on its female undergraduates until persuaded to do so by the SDRA in 1920? Had she been a man, Gwyneth's exam results would have pocketed her a first-class degree – and, more than that, she would have been acknowledged as the highest achiever of her year. As it was, she left university with nothing more tangible than a warm glow of achievement – not particularly helpful when applying for professional posts alongside men with letters after their names.

In 1913 Gwyneth sued the Law Society for refusing to admit women to train for the legal profession. She lost both the case and a subsequent appeal, on the Alice-in-Wonderland grounds that as women had never been admitted before, there was no precedent, and without a precedent they could not be admitted. This was a common argument against allowing women into any of the six traditional professions (academia, architecture, the Church, engineering, the law and medicine): 'the law of inveterate usage'.

During the First World War Gwyneth married Thomas Weldon Thomson, a solicitor, and worked for the Ministry of Food before the birth of their first child, Alice Diana, on the very day the SDRA was signed off in 1919. By now she had changed her mind, and wished to read for the Bar. Her application to Lincoln's Inn was accepted the following day, on Christmas Eve.

Gwyneth was asked to propose a toast at the House of Commons celebration. It was 'quite a lark', she reported in a letter to her sister afterwards, 'but very alarming' as 'all the legal nuts' were there, and she never much enjoyed being in the limelight.[4] She did brilliantly, though. In her speech she promised that if ever she were required to wear a wig in the course of her legal duties, she would try to arrange her hair so that it didn't look too ridiculous. Not for her own sake, mind, but to preserve the dignity of her new profession. 'Hear, hear!' chuckled Lord Birkenhead, the Lord Chancellor. Then she repeated a comment made to her by a fellow (male) trainee: unless she could drink a pint of ale and a bottle of port at dinner it was useless to expect to be admitted to any of the Inns of Court. No 'Hear, hear!' this time. An uncomfortable pause was adroitly broken by her admission that she had got away with quaffing ginger beer instead. She was grateful for the welcome she had been given at Lincoln's Inn, she added, and looked forward with confidence to the future.

Perhaps she was naïve. Stodgy arguments against women in the professions had been circulating for years, and were no less popular now than they had ever been, despite the passing of the Act. Gentlemen would never stoop to taking orders from women: it was degrading and flew in the face of nature. Women were unsexed by gentlemen's work; old-school doctors warned that thinking too much withered the womb. Some were refused high-calibre posts on the grounds of being plain; others because they were distractingly pretty. And then there was the perennial claim that women could not possibly work in a man's world, as there were no ladies' lavatories there. The smoking-rooms of professional societies, associations, institutions and clubs rumbled with self-righteous discontent at the thought of a petticoat invasion, while senior common rooms in the ancient universities refused to appoint women whose mercurial teaching methods might 'interfere', as they put it, with the proper education of young men.

The SDRA did prompt action in some quarters. Not only were the Inns of Court minded to admit women; in October 1920 Oxford decided to award its female students degrees for the first time, though Cambridge infamously resisted until 1948. Despite the Act, however, this was in many ways the worst time for women like Gwyneth to think of entering the professions. Though they had won temporary respect and valuable experience by metaphorically donning bowler hats and pinstripes or grabbing overalls and grease-guns during the First World War, priority was now being given to returning servicemen, while their wives and daughters, sisters and mothers were expected to unfold their pinnies and withdraw once again to the kitchen.

It is a myth that the First World War liberated women in the long term. Expediency meant that they were given the taste of independent careers, but socio-economic pressures ensured that in peacetime the old order was reluctant to change. Lip-service was paid in the form of the SDRA, but the professional world was still sclerotic in the years that followed, hidebound by convention, defensive – and, frankly, scared of competition.

None of this daunted Gwyneth. As a young mother still employed by the Ministry of Food she dutifully ate her regulation dinners at Lincoln's Inn and passed the necessary exams by studying in the evenings during her first year. The future did indeed look bright, and she was already a dignified role model for her companions embarking on a working life in the professions.

We might consider Gwyneth's story unusual. The popular image of the pioneering career woman is of a loud eccentric, set apart from mere mortals by genius and grim determination; a modern Boudicca riding roughshod over convention to lead a growing army of formidable females to storm the citadels of the Establishment and shatter the glass ceilings within – which in the case of the élite professions one imagines more as crystal. Gwyneth, by all accounts, was gentle, quietly humorous, a proud wife and mother, and very ordinary. Clever, certainly, and charismatic, with a strong sense of vocation, but no doyenne. She was just one of a small but bustling company of assorted pioneers who linked arms and went about their business: you and me, only braver, more intrepid and with none of the career advantages we now enjoy because of what they did. Virginia Woolf called them a society of outsiders.

When I asked a group of professional women recently whether they still felt like outsiders, the response was varied. Some had recently qualified; others were at the end of illustrious careers.

Many considered themselves beneficiaries of a battle already fought and won; others were not so sure. A professor of medicine told me that whenever she visits a hospital ward in company with male colleagues, even if those males are obviously her juniors, patients assume the men are in charge. There is a well-worn riddle about that. A doctor is driving along a road at night with his son. They are involved in a collision and taken to separate hospitals by ambulance. When the boy is wheeled into theatre there is a problem. 'I can't possibly operate on him,' says the surgeon, 'he's my son.' How can this be?

It can still make the newspapers – local, if not national – when a young woman is appointed to a post we persistently associate with men. The chief of a nuclear plant, perhaps; a naval commander; the pilot of the biggest and best aircraft in the fleet (provoking sardonic remarks about lady drivers when she introduces herself over the tannoy). The first female bishop in the Church of England was consecrated in 2015. Can you name more than two leading women architects?

It takes courage for a woman to admit an ambition to join the professional élite. The senior partner in a high-profile firm of London solicitors confessed that she had to be pushed by a male colleague into applying for the position: she was too modest, feeling herself to be an impostor despite years of training and decades of experience. 'Women still have to be asked to dance,' she remarked, a little sadly.

A century ago, women certainly weren't being asked into the professions. Apart from the lack of precedent and lavatories, Masters at the Inns of Court were appalled at the idea of girls joining them at dinner: they might eat all the cheese. Pioneers in engineering were warned that their stomachs were not robust enough to cope with the irregular meals that were an inevitable part of life for any busy professional. They would fade away. When discussing the threat of feminine infiltration at RIBA, the great and the good comforted themselves with the unassailable truth that ladies can't climb ladders. And if one or two do manage to work out what to do with their skirts and frangible ankles on all those rungs, they are bound to lose their heads on the scaffolding and plummet messily to the ground, possibly displaying their under-clothing as they do so.[5] Don't worry, said the Establishment, hunching cosily around the boardroom table with the door firmly closed; it'll never happen.

This book is the story of how it did happen, and who made it happen. It's about the first-footers, most of them long forgotten; about the personal cost of ambition and its rewards. Most of all, it's about a group of highly spirited individuals who worked with determination, tact, courage and good humour to earn an inde-pendent living for themselves, and to make it easier for those of us who have followed to do the same. They are people with whom we can identify, from whom we can learn; people fighting real battles for a variety of complex reasons and with mixed success in a crazily changing world.

Many blamed them for the craziness; and, as the professional woman grew more visible, the Establishment (hearing ever more insistent knocking at the door) began to panic. Correspondence columns bristled with indignation at the uppity 'modern girl'. Polit-icians warned against the dangers of letting air-headed flappers loose in the polling booth. Economists blamed the Great Depres-sion on women upsetting the labour market. We *told* you giving them the vote was a bad idea. At first, fashions celebrated the nov-elty of these women's masculine intentions (think of the cropped, flat-chested twenties) but then turned to the high heels and exag-gerated contours of thirties costumes as society became unsure whether it really needed a race of rapacious Amazons in its midst.

After the First World War, many of the teaching hospitals, having tantalizingly allowed women in as clinical trainees for a while, shut them out again, and professional firms declined to employ those who had fought so hard to complete their years of training: 'No bluestockings wanted here.' It was heartbreaking. Received wisdom would have it that once the weighty doors of the professional workplace creaked open in early 1920 with a rush of fresh air and light, all women had to do was trot inside – like those guests at the House of Commons dinner – and get busy. This is not true. While they watched each others' backs with a shared determination to live life on their own terms, their path was repeatedly obstructed, diverted, blocked. Fortunately for us, they persevered.

One might reasonably expect this to be a narrative of 'firsts'. The first women to do this, be that; the true pioneers. I have largely avoided well-known heroines, however. Famous names are important, of course; but so are the unfamiliar, whose stories too deserve to be told. Sometimes it took more courage to be the second or the tenth woman to achieve something remarkable, having witnessed the prejudice faced by the trail-blazer and appreciated that it requires industrial quantities of self-belief – an unbecoming attribute in a lady – to succeed. Everyone has heard of Elizabeth Blackwell (1821–1910), for example, the first British-born woman to be registered by the General Medical Council as a medical practitioner. And we all know about Millicent Fawcett's sister Elizabeth Garrett Anderson (1836–1917), the first to qualify as a doctor in Britain. But Welshwoman Frances Hoggan?

Frances was born in the vicarage in Brecon, and was educated first locally and then at school in Windsor before being sent to Paris when she was fifteen (presumably to a finishing school) and to Düsseldorf three years later. The curriculum at finishing schools of the mid-Victorian period was hardly taxing. A diary kept by a girl of Frances' age at another establishment in France tells us how the days pass.[6] She and her friends go for donkey rides, play charades, walk, munch their way through picnics, look at (and paint) endless identical chateaux, and occasionally go swimming. This means changing into elaborate bathing dresses in wheeled cabins on the beach and then, even worse, changing out of them again, all clotted with sand. They do gym, which involves hanging head downwards from the bars on the wall 'and other disagreeable things'. There are 'études' during which they must pay a forfeit of a centime if they lapse into English, and someone comes in to take music lessons and arithmetic. Sometimes, gratifyingly, it's a rather handsome young man. During holidays they can stay in bed until 11 a.m. before drifting to the salon for the rest of the day to gossip.

Frances Morgan was not a typical pupil. Two things distinguished her from her peers. The first was a fierce intelligence; the second, a shameful secret. In fact it is difficult to think of a more shameful secret. Frances had an illegitimate daughter. Elise (sometimes known as Elsie or Eliza) was born in Brussels when Frances was seventeen, still a child herself. For any respectable Victorian family — especially a vicar's — this should have been catastrophic. But Frances conceived and gave birth abroad. No one who mattered witnessed her pregnancy. With a little stage management, polite society might never know that the Reverend's daughter had been ruined; that beneath a façade of fresh-faced innocence lurked a fallen woman. A secret confinement was the obvious solution, followed by the baby's adoption or consignment to private care, and then complete denial. This was not an uncommon strategy. But the unconventional Frances had other ideas. Perhaps a narrative could be devised to explain the sudden appearance of a baby in the family, and a way found to keep her?

From Düsseldorf Frances returned to Britain, alone. She settled in London and volunteered at St Mary's Dispensary for Women and Children in Marylebone. Her clinical instructor there in 1866 was the hospital's founder, Dr Garrett (not yet married to James Anderson). Frances intended to follow briskly in her mentor's footsteps by working to gain a licence from the Society of Apothecaries, as Garrett had done in 1865, which would have qualified her to practise as a doctor. When Frances was halfway through the Society's course of exams, however, it abruptly closed its doors to all students except those trained at British medical schools. No women were allowed at British medical schools at the time.

The next we hear of Frances, it is the autumn of 1867 and she has enrolled in the university's medical school at Zurich. She excelled, completing the five-year course in three and defending her thesis on muscular atrophy in 1870 with such natural authority that the audience who had gathered to see this dog walking on its hinder legs was awestruck.

In 1874 Frances married fellow medic George Hoggan, with whom she set up the first husband-and-wife GP practice in the country. There was no time for a honeymoon. They shared the household with the young woman whom later research has revealed to be Frances' illegitimate daughter. Elise must have been smuggled home to Wales soon after her birth and looked after by Frances' family. The fiction was maintained that she was Frances' younger sister, which worked well enough unless one happened to know that Frances' father died in 1851, long before Elise was born. Ask me no questions, I'll tell you no lies.

Despite her successful practice, Frances remained an unqualified physician until 1877, when the King and Queen's College of Physicians in Dublin agreed to license women, making them eligible for registration by the General Medical Council (if they passed the appropriate exams, which, of course, Frances did). By then she had a position as Dr Garrett Anderson's assistant at the New Hospital for Women and her own consulting room in London. This suggests that there were enough female patients with radical sympathies to sustain clinicians like Frances, qualified or not.

Medicine is untypical of the traditional professions in that it began to accept qualified women a few decades earlier than the others; it is, however, typical in that they were not welcomed by its governing bodies. The climate for Frances was therefore much the same in the 1870s as it was for Gwyneth Bebb Thomson in 1913: cold and inhospitable. Frances succeeded because of an unusual degree of family support and because she was a natural nonconformist and remarkably self-confident. She had much for which to thank Dr Garrett Anderson; but when she noticed her supervisor's increasing enthusiasm for what Frances believed to be unnecessarily high-risk surgery at the New Hospital, she resigned in protest.

Frances' approach to medicine was more reformative; she was never a medical firefighter. In 1871, in fact, she and her close friend Elizabeth Blackwell co-founded an organization to help the public to take better care of itself. It was called the National Health Society: the original NHS. Its slogan was 'Prevention is Better than Cure', and it sponsored various pamphlets designed to encourage good practice. One of them was a *Penny Cookery Book*, published in 1884, full of wholesome recipes and remarkably modern advice. Never peel your potatoes, because the best part of them is just beneath the skin. Weigh or measure everything you eat, to avoid waste and over-eating. The section on 'sickroom cookery' is full of common sense:

> Try to put as much nourishment as possible into a small compass. Choose always those foods that are most digestible, and cook them so as to leave the least possible work for the digestive organs. Make everything look as pretty and as appetising as you can. Therefore, don't put a little broth at the bottom of a large basin, and don't serve anything with a plate or spoon that has been used before.[7]

Frances was a woman well ahead of her time.

The 1881 census records Frances, George and Elise living together in London.[8] Sure enough, Elise is described as George's sister-in-law; she, too, is training to become a doctor. According to their descendants, it is possible that neither George nor Elise ever realized that Frances was the girl's real mother. One can only imagine what a burden this secret must have been for Frances to carry. The Hoggans had no other children. One of the many campaigns Frances took up was for equal educational opportunities for schoolgirls and universal co-education; perhaps then, she may well have thought, pupils would be less naïve than she was when sent as a teenager to Paris. She was also a supporter of Aberdare Hall, a hall of residence for female students in Cardiff. Other causes close to her heart included the training of women doctors in India; opposition to racial segregation; support for prostitutes victimized by the Contagious Diseases Acts; and women's suffrage. She and George were both anti-vivisectionists and evangelistic cyclists, vegetarians and campaigners against the wearing of corsets.

We are conditioned to think that women who achieve surprising things must be formidable. Any vision of Frances Hoggan as off-puttingly intimidating is dispelled by a snippet in a Welsh newspaper published in 1886:

> The friends and supporters of every movement having for its object the emancipation of women will be pleased to hear that a presentation is about to be made to Dr Frances Hoggan, as a token of sympathy with her in the anxiety caused by her husband's illness, which obliges her to leave England for the winter, and for the present interrupts her professional career.[9]

She was obviously much loved, and much admired.

George died in 1891, after which Frances retired from medicine, though not from activism, at the age of forty-eight. She died in a Brighton nursing home some thirty-six years later. She enjoyed a career at a time when women doctors were uncommon; she commanded respect and affection despite having been that most despised of creatures, an unmarried mother; she shared her time and her success with those she thought needed it most, and was never strident. Being strident holds you back, she counselled. Don't shout about it, don't make a fuss; just *get it done*.

That is a motto many of the pioneers who populate this book must have shared. Having recently researched the women's suffrage movement in some depth, I tend to find my imagination still happily inhabited by women holding banners and marching for a cause. They are good company: not necessarily militants, just inspiringly committed to natural justice and determined to lead by example. Every campaign has its flagbearers; though the struggle for women to be taken seriously in the professions was necessarily an élite campaign, its principles of non-discrimination and equal opportunity were applicable across British society at the time – and remain so. There are always outsiders in our midst.

Maybe this familiarity with activism explains a fanciful image I have of Frances. In my mind's eye she strides in the vanguard of professional women, carrying aloft a big green banner decorated with the rod of Asclepius and some Welsh dragons (or are they fire-breathing stalwarts of the medical Establishment?). Across the top, embroidered in golden thread – probably stitched by herself – is *Get It Done*. I picture her with Gwyneth Bebb Thomson, their children in their arms, leading all the pioneers in this history of pride and prejudice into an uncertain but exciting new world.

Shoulder to shoulder with Frances, the doctor, and Gwyneth, the lawyer, are representatives of the remaining four professions. Engineer Margaret Partridge was a highly practical person. She was a Devon girl, educated at Bedford College in the University of London where, as part of her maths degree, she studied mechanics. Applied maths, in other words. She loved it. London granted degrees to women from 1881 onwards, yet when Margaret graduated in 1914 those with her qualifications were rare

Three pioneers of the Women's Engineering Society: left to right, Laura Willson, Caroline Haslett and Margaret Partridge.

indeed. 'Is the attempt to teach women mathematicians a waste of time and money?' asked a journalist some years later.

> After exhaustive researches, the professors of the Department of Psychology at the University of Jena [in Germany] tell us that women cannot calculate, and that when confronted with abstract mathematical problems the female intellect breaks down completely.[10]

Margaret Partridge could not have cared less what the psychologists said. She applied to teach maths at a girls' school, but soon realized that the classroom was not her natural home and in 1917 joined a firm of consulting engineers that specialized in heating and ventilation. She was initially employed to work in the office; but, feeling no more comfortable or less confined there than in the classroom, before long she was out on the shop floor as a supervisor and tester at an electrical factory making searchlights and X-ray machines. She moved on to designing small electric engines, and might have stayed at the factory had the gates not been effectively closed to women when surviving servicemen returned from the Great War to reclaim their jobs.

Rather than retreat to the office, the classroom or, worse still, the front parlour, Margaret went home to Devon and advertised herself in the local papers as a 'Country-House Lighting Engineer', no doubt inspired by the celebrated mathematician, inventor and arc-light engineer Hertha Ayrton (1854–1923). 'Install a Paraffin-Electric set in your house,' advised Margaret with a flourish 'You can use it for lighting, ironing, pumping, sawing, sweeping or boiling.'[11] She offered consultations by appointment, and by 1927 had won the distinction (somewhat niche, it's true) of being 'the first woman to wire an English village for electric light'.[12]

Working with hard-won financial backers, and eventually employing several members of staff and training her own female apprentices, Margaret brought electricity to entire villages in Devon, and to the town of Beccles in Suffolk. She built power plants, connecting houses and businesses to them so efficiently that everyone in the community who had signed up to her scheme had merely to flick a switch and – lo and behold, the electricity was on its way. Miraculously, it only took an hour to trickle – leap – fly – whatever it did – from the plant to their homes.

Before lighting people's houses, Margaret illuminated the roads outside. In Bampton, when she first turned on the street lamps in 1926 (always a dramatic moment), villagers ran from their homes to gasp in astonishment. One man decided to sit under a lamp-post to read his newspaper of an evening. Once Margaret turned her attention inside, children were so terrified by the glare in their newly lit bedrooms that for several nights they screamed and refused to be left alone with the light on. Meetings were held to complain about this weird woman and her miles of cable – until she proved what magical things she and the cables could do.

Margaret was tickled by her clients' ignorance and amazement. How can I reach to turn the bulb on when it's right up there hanging from the ceiling? asked one worried and rather short housewife (incapable, naturally, of climbing a ladder). And where does the electricity *go*, once it's turned off? Just as a child imagines the voices in the radio stop talking when they are not listening – I used to try to switch mine off just after they had taken a breath, so they wouldn't die while waiting for me to return – so those new to the wonders of electricity imagined it lurking menacingly round the corner all day until summoned into use again.

As a woman in charge of her own enterprise – the first member of the Women's Engineering Society (the WES, founded in 1919) to be so – Margaret encountered plenty of male employees and clients in the course of her business. Naturally shy, and well aware of the old argument that it was unseemly for a woman to give a man orders, she quickly worked out that 'a judicious administration of praise, and appealing to a man's pride in his job and capabilities . . . will do far more towards getting the best out of anyone than all the vigilant strictness of the most powerful martinet'.[13] Salesmen, jostling to supply components for her machinery, were the worst to deal with, thinking they could get the better of her. 'As a rule, a salesman is not fit to do business with till he has been properly squashed.'[14]

Margaret was an inspiration to her peers in the WES, becoming its president in 1943. When she retired to Willand in Devon, and was told the village hall needed a new lighting system, she summoned members of the Women's Institute, who used the hall most often, and taught them how to wire it themselves.

Twenty years earlier, in 1922, she had published her recipe for success as a woman entrepreneur who by her own admission had 'crawled' into the profession 'through a crack'. It includes some interesting ingredients: the impudence of a small monkey; the epidermis of a hippopotamus; the patience of an elephant; the energy of an ant; a modicum of knowledge of the job – and as much capital as possible.[15]

In some professions, capital was not an issue. Maude Royden must have been busy on the night of the House of Commons dinner, otherwise she would surely have been present, as an old friend of Ray Strachey and Millicent Fawcett, and a staunch supporter of equal opportunities for women in every field. Maude was a famous preacher; a speaker who changed people's minds, softened their hearts, reconfigured their spiritual landscape. Everyone seems to have agreed that she was full of grace and goodness,

Maude Royden.

whether or not they were in sympathy with her startling liberalism. Once met, once heard, this small, physically disabled woman was not forgotten.

She grew up in a numerous family near Liverpool, where her father was a ship-owner and local dignitary. Maude was a bright child, but hampered by her disability (she was born with dislocated hips) and by the fact that as the youngest of eight children, who were all under the age of ten when she arrived, she barely remembered encountering her parents during childhood. She had an uneasy relationship with her mother Alice. 'It is not fair – is it? – to keep women boxed up, and then complain that they are foolish,' she once remarked, with her mother in mind.[16] Yet she still found herself complaining bitterly of Alice's stolid ignorance. Maude could never come to terms with her mother's assertion that God had made her lame, instinctively taking God's side.

Maude read history at Oxford; and though she did not particularly enjoy the matriarchal atmosphere of her college, Lady Margaret Hall, run on Anglican lines by a bishop's daughter, she loved its social life, making passionate friendships and even joining the drama and debating societies. Ironically, given her later career, her hands shook with nerves so violently during her first public speech that she could hardly read her notes. After Oxford she spent a period as a welfare worker in the East End of London and in Liverpool, while struggling to find a spiritual and physical home away from Alice. Religion was always important to Maude, but she was suspicious of accepting received wisdom and could not help asking questions. Should she become a Roman Catholic? Was it weak to be so easily seduced by the beauty of Church ritual? Why were women excluded from so many Christian privileges? Why couldn't women be priests? And (deep breath) why was the enjoyment of sex – which she supposed to be God-given and therefore sacred – so shameful?

The vicar with whom she discussed her spiritual confusion was George Hudson Shaw, an Oxford graduate seventeen years her senior whose wife, afflicted by some unnamed mental fragility, was unable to fulfil her clerical and conjugal duties. In time, Maude went to live with them as Shaw's parish assistant; and eventually, when George was widowed in 1944, she married him. They had been in love, she records, since their first meeting in 1901. It was at his suggestion that Maude embarked on a career first as an adult education lecturer and then, seasoned by years as a speaker on women's suffrage and with a firm belief that the fight for the vote was a Christian mission, as a preacher.

Decades before the Church of England ordained its first woman priest, Maude came as close to that position as it was possible to get. Clergymen appointed her to deliver sermons in their churches; the press reported them; congregations flocked to hear her; celebrities of the day asked her to marry them and baptize their children. Maude's weddings and christenings were not all they seemed, as she was forbidden to administer the sacraments; they were more like services of blessing. Most of them took place in nonconformist churches, which did not worry her unduly, though she remained an Anglican. She was never keen on labels, denominational or otherwise, and quite unafraid of addressing taboo subjects if that's what her conscience directed her to do.

Strangely for a would-be clergywoman, Maude's lack of piousness was one of her greatest attractions. What she said about sex – that it should be joyful, and that young people should be encouraged to celebrate within marriage the ordinary beauty of the divine human form – would have been considered obscene were she not such a genuine soul. Privately she called Hudson Shaw her lover; but she sincerely loved his wife too, and the affection was mutual. Theirs was somehow a reasonably functional *ménage à trois*. Maude admitted her desire for Shaw but understandably considered their decision whether or not to consummate it out of wedlock an intensely private one. She was held in such high esteem that few questions were asked of her moral probity.

There were other aspects to Maude's unlikely flamboyance. She was a dedicated smoker, and on a lecture tour to America in 1928 she made international news when the elders of a church in Chicago banned her from preaching on hearing of her unladylike fondness for tobacco. She retained her love of theatre all her life, appearing in the pulpit in a soft cap looking suspiciously like a biretta, and once considering going to a party dressed as the Bishop of London. She was, as one of her friends put it, 'a king-fisher amongst moorhens'.[17]

Maude used to think she might have been happier at Somer-ville, a non-denominational and more progressive women's college at Oxford, than at LMH. Somerville is where academic Enid Starkie spent most of her working life. Enid was another kingfisher, though her plumage was perhaps a little more garish than Maude Royden's.

Every women's college or hall of residence has its famous eccen-trics. Miss Tuke, Margaret Partridge's Principal at Bedford College, solemnly wore silver slippers to dinner every evening with appro-priately blue stockings. A tutor elsewhere put Maude Royden's fancy into action and really did dress up like a bishop – all the time, not just for parties – with what looked like an episcopal black silk apron covering her surplice-like black dress.[18] This was Annie Rogers, a don at St Hugh's in Gwyneth Bebb Thomson's time – and she looked thoroughly unwholesome in the outfit, which she wore every day, with clumsy boots. It grew increasingly grubby as the term progressed; the obvious message was that she was far too busy being intellectual to worry about the niceties of personal hygiene.

Enid Starkie was up there with the best. She would turn up to tutorials dressed as a Breton matelot, in a beret with a red pom-pom, a stripy top, a navy-blue reefer jacket and wide blue trousers, her face made up with white powder and a gash of scarlet lipstick, smoking a cigarette (I imagine a Gauloise). She was not remotely

Dr Enid Starkie.

French. But she was a great linguist, with an international reputation for scholarship. She was the first person – not just the first woman – to be awarded a DLitt, a sort of super-doctorate, in the faculty of Modern Languages at Oxford; and in 1946 she was made a Chevalier de la Légion d'Honneur for her services to French literature. It is hard to imagine her as anything other than a flamboyant and somewhat distrait academic, and yet she denied having ever had the slightest desire to teach anyone anything.[19]

Enid spoke French with a heavy Irish accent, adding to the bemusement of her students. Like Maude Royden's, her childhood was less than ideal. She grew up near Dublin with a formidable father and a mother who seemed to Enid to be devoid of personality and who insisted on dressing up her tomboy daughter like a doll. The principal people in charge of Enid's upbringing were a grim-faced nanny and a French governess, Mademoiselle Cora, who shared an intense dislike for one another. Nanny taught Enid the dismal lesson that 'cruelty was the aim of existence, its highest and most treasured attribute, and I wondered whether I should ever be cruel enough to be fully grown-up myself'.[20] Mademoiselle taught her French, but little else.

Enid found joy in reading French literature, and in music. Her ambition while she was a schoolgirl in Dublin was to become a concert pianist. There was no doubt that she would need to earn her own living; an unspecified financial catastrophe during her second term as an undergraduate at Somerville in 1917 left her father facing ruin and Enid having to survive on a meagre budget of £2 10s a month (about a quarter of the starting salary for a female academic – which itself would be much lower than that for a male).[21] To try to raise funds she hired a piano and a room at Oxford Town Hall (both expensive), put up posters, extravagantly bought a new dress, and gave a recital. People came, but nerves got the better of Enid – or perhaps the Chopin and Debussy she chose were just too challenging. She stumbled embarrassingly more than once.

It was fashionable for students at the time to claim a picturesque state of poverty as they sat on brightly patterned rugs in their college rooms at 'cocoa parties', perhaps sipping sherry and drawing languidly on a Sobranie the while. Enid really was living on the breadline. She shunned cocoa parties because she couldn't afford to return invitations. She barely possessed a change of clothes, and was once seen poking about in the snow in her nightdress, hunting for a precious hairpin dropped on the way from the bath to her distant bedroom. But she had style. Her programme for the concert was illustrated on the front with a large cameo photograph of her face, in profile, looking romantically into the middle distance. As an undergraduate she once released a red balloon at a formal dinner (it is unclear whether it was safely tied and floated gracefully to the vaulted ceiling of Somerville's Hall, or whether she left it loose to skim flatulently over people's heads; I like to think the latter). On another occasion she smuggled two men in drag into Hall. Her peers were in awe of her showmanship. They called her 'the wild Irishwoman', an image enhanced by a slight squint and a fondness for wearing a chrysanthemum in her scribbly hair.

Rapturously in love with Gide, Rimbaud and Baudelaire, Enid managed to scrape together enough funds after finals to take her to the Sorbonne in Paris, where she won a place to study for a research degree. Her doctoral thesis on a Belgian poet was awarded a prize in 1927, which led to her appointment as a lecturer in French Literature back at Somerville. She had first arrived in Paris in 1921; the only way she could fund six years' work there – subsidized by a scholarship – was to dash home from time to time and teach, first at a girls' boarding school where she was deemed too chaotic to keep on, then as a private tutor to a sickeningly rich American family, and finally as an assistant lecturer at the college in Devon which later became Exeter University. No wonder her first doctorate took so long. During those years she suffered from malnutrition and was involved in a series of intense but doomed love affairs (with men in these cases, though later she was involved with several women); getting the post at Somerville must have felt like entering a safe haven after a lifetime on stormy seas.

Enid did not do calm, however. Although expected to live in, like the other spinster tutors, she demanded to be allowed to lodge outside the college, and the college, unable to withstand the force of her personality, gave in. Once she could afford it, her rented flat in Oxford was done up like a high-class oriental brothel, all red and gold with curlicued furniture and a permanent haze of cigarette smoke. When not dressed as a sailor she would wear a Chinese trouser-suit looking a little like an extravagant pair of silk pyjamas. Her fingers clanked softly with rings, and her tutorial students were as likely to be asked about their carnal knowledge as about the nuances of French expression. She courted academic controversy and was rarely conciliatory. Yet many students remembered her with fondness, and her forget-me-not-blue eyes and subtly wicked smile still greet Somervillians as they trudge up the library stairs towards her portrait. She remains resplendent, in scarlet.

So much for the traditional image of the frumpy virgin academic supposed to have occupied the few positions available to highly qualified women in universities before the Second World War. Like her sister graduates Frances Hoggan, Margaret Partridge and Maude Royden, Dr Starkie was a most surprising person.

To qualify as a medical doctor before the passing of the SDRA in 1919, women were forced to go abroad to sit the necessary exams; to gain a licence to practise from the Society of Apothecaries – until they slammed the door on this route in the 1860s; or to enrol at one of the few medical colleges open to them. The London School of Medicine for Women (LSMW) was founded in 1874 to accommodate female students, but it took time for the long-established teaching hospitals to appoint its graduates to clinical positions to complete their qualifications. That is why the growing number of hospitals and nursing homes set up *by* women (like Elizabeth Garrett Anderson) *for* women, staff as well as patients, was crucial. As far as medicine was concerned, the point of the 1919 Act was not to create professional women, but to allow them to access the bodies responsible for regulating their careers and therefore to set them on the same professional footing as their male peers. It was supposed to acknowledge that they had as much right to exercise a vocation as men did. How well this worked is a question for later. Meanwhile, armed with the successes of medical women on the Western Front, female surgeons and physicians who survived the war and the subsequent influenza epidemic worked together to offer as much clinical experience as they could to their recently qualified sisters. They were anxious to pass their expertise to new generations of women doctors.

Dr Annie McCall (1859–1949) graduated from the LSMW in 1884. She then studied in Switzerland, like Frances Hoggan, before returning to work in London at clinics for poor women and children. In 1887 she opened the Clapham Maternity Hospital – renamed the Annie McCall Hospital in 1936 – which not only treated needy patients, but gave equally needy practitioners a chance to prove themselves. Dr McCall's name crops up time and again in the history of medical women in Britain – and

Dr Annie McCall.

not just medical women. Mutual support across the divisions between disciplines is a hallmark of the entire movement for women to be taken seriously in the professional workplace. That sense of solidarity so fundamental to the success of the fight for the vote readily transferred itself to the fight for a career. Campaign groups engaged women as honorary legal advisers; preachers like Maude Royden (and there were others) sermonized about equal rights; engineers worked on machines designed to make a woman's domestic life run more smoothly, thus freeing her to turn her attention to something else.

At a time when her hospital was expanding in the 1930s, Dr McCall – now in her seventies – commissioned an architect to design and build a new outpatients' department. That architect was Gertrude Leverkus. When she was seventeen, Gertrude had been the first woman officially to enrol at the University of London's Bartlett School of Architecture. The prestigious Architectural Association's school might have suited her better, but that did not admit women until 1917 – and then only grudgingly, driven by economic necessity.

Gertrude's gender was not her only handicap. This was not a good time to have German parents (Gertrude had been born in Oldenburg, though brought up in south London) – and she was seriously myopic. Her mother wept at the thought that her daughter would never marry; who would want a wife barely able to see her hand in front of her face without wearing an ugly pair of glasses? Fortunately, Gertrude was not vain. Her world changed the moment she fixed the wiry arms of her first spectacles behind her ears and clearly saw a robin. She was entranced. 'What did the lack of a husband matter to me!'[22]

The recalcitrant father is a familiar figure in the history of ambitious women. He appears (often unfairly) as a sort of pantomime villain, virtually locking up his Cinderella daughter to while away the inconvenient period between her allotted roles as schoolgirl and bride. 'I wanted to be a doctor, but Papa wouldn't let me.' 'I longed to follow my brothers to university, but Daddy said I must stay at home. I'd only marry anyway, so what was the point of wasting his money?'[23] Mr Otto Leverkus was different. It was he who persuaded Gertrude to become an architect – even though he had not realized himself that women could do such things until reading an article about them in the paper. Gertrude did not remember exactly what the article said; it was possibly a jaunty piece in the *Pall Mall Gazette* of 8 May 1914, about new courses available at university and the exciting prospect of qualified women designing their own kitchens. Gertrude was talented at drawing, having won a national prize at the age of eleven.[24] Besides, her father had always fancied being an architect himself. It all made sense.

The luckiest thing that ever happened to her, according to Gertrude, was being taken on as a pupil in 1919 by Horace Field, a highly respected neo-classical architect working in London. By then she had a degree under her belt; experience in draughtsmanship gained through a holiday job illustrating a book on classical design; and a genuine love of the career her father had chosen for her. She became one of the first women members of RIBA to practise her profession (maintaining that the two who pre-dated her never earned their livings through architecture). Gertrude's ambitions went far beyond designing kitchens. She produced a few 'smallish country houses' for friends and family; Lady Rhondda commissioned her to carry out an elaborate drainage scheme and some internal alterations to her place in Kent. After the Second World War she worked on pre-fabricated homes for the East End (she had a Town Planning certificate) and designed and built the majestic Finchley Road shopping parade in north London, with retail units below and flats above. She refused to be pigeon-holed.

Gertrude Leverkus considered one of her most valuable contributions to the profession – and to society – to be the work she did as architect to the Women's Pioneer Housing Company, converting rambling, empty town houses in London into self-contained accommodation for single women. She lived in a Pioneer Housing bedsit herself after finally leaving home at the age of thirty, and did not move again until she retired at sixty-two (her mother was right: she never married). By that time, she was an associate partner in a large practice based in Portland Place, just by the BBC, with over a hundred staff. Gertrude never had a problem climbing ladders.

When she looked back on her career, she found it difficult to recall any serious episode of prejudice. It was a shame she couldn't be a Fellow rather than just an associate member of RIBA at the beginning of her career: that distinction was not conferred on a woman until 1931. She was certainly well enough qualified, and it might have boosted her credibility. And she could have done with a few more women for company on her university course. Otherwise, life had been good to her. She had no complaints. Clients and colleagues were sometimes a little baffled by her gender when she first turned up on site. One gentleman whisked off his overcoat as she stooped to examine some earthworks, spreading it like Sir Walter Raleigh on the soil for her to kneel on. But that was on her first visit; subsequently he treated her as one of the boys. Another avuncular soul offered her a glass of milk instead of the ale he gave the men, and it was only when she was present, apparently, that the team got chocolate biscuits with their tea, daintily arranged on a plate. There might even have been a doily.

Ironically, one of Gertrude's most difficult clients was Dr Annie McCall at the Clapham Maternity Hospital. She looked alarming, wearing a collar and tie, a Victorian mob cap for work over her hair (which was cut in a mannish short back and sides) and elasticated boots. She sounded alarming too, regularly barking orders for pesky husbands to be banished from the wards. She was a survivor from a different age, according to Gertrude, but wonderfully good at her job. The infant and maternal mortality rates at Clapham were notably low. Gertrude was proud to be associated with her.

If only Gwyneth Bebb Thomson had been one of Dr McCall's patients when her second daughter Marion was born in August 1921. Gwyneth had kept her head down after the House of Commons dinner the previous year, working hard to pass the first round of exams at Lincoln's Inn. She sailed through: no mean feat with a toddler and another baby on the way. Her name cropped up in public from time to time, familiar from that newsworthy episode in 1913 when she was lead plaintiff in a case against the Law Society to contest its refusal to admit women to professional training and examinations. She had represented three other women on that occasion: Mrs Maud Crofts, *née* Ingram, a barrister's daughter who had read history and law at Girton College,

Clapham Maternity Hospital's Christmas Party, 1922.

Cambridge; Nancy Nettlefold, who at the time was still at Newnham College; and Karin Costelloe, Ray Strachey's younger sister,
who later went on to study medicine.

The argument used by Gwyneth's counsel against the Law
Society's exclusion (based on lack of precedent) focused on a
generic clause in previous Solicitors' Acts stating that any references to the male gender, or to a 'person', should automatically
apply to women. This carried no weight with the judge: nowhere
did the law state *explicitly* that women were eligible to hold public
office, he said, and being a lawyer was unarguably a public office.
'I come to the conclusion that there is not enough in the statutes
to shew that the Legislators intended, by their provisions, to open
this profession to women.'[25] Case dismissed.

Gwyneth's legal team appealed against the judgement. Surely
a woman was a person? That was by the by; she still couldn't be a
proper lawyer. Their lordships explained why they refused the
appeal, referring to a precedent from the Elizabethan age:

> The fact that no women had ever been an attorney or solicitor
> during the several centuries since the profession had been rec-
> ognised, was evidence that . . . women were under a disability,
> by reason of their sex, to become attorneys or solicitors, and
> this was confirmed by the opinion of Lord Coke, stated 300
> years ago.[26]

The ruling made headlines, and fuelled reformers' determination
to frame an Act addressing this absurdity. What eventually
resulted was the SDRA – still something of a compromise –
finally allowing Gwyneth to train as a lawyer so that she could
argue cases like hers for the downtrodden plaintiffs of the future.

Who knows how successful this quietly dedicated woman might
have been? At the beginning of July 1921 Gwyneth was admitted to
a nursing home for bed rest in advance of her second confinement.

There were fears the baby might be premature: she confessed to her sister that in the course of her work she had been 'leaping about the country in the most awful heat we have ever had, and [baby] did not like it, apparently'.[27] Gwyneth suffered from placenta praevia and haemorrhaged during labour; Marion died two days after she was born, and Gwyneth two months later. To those who thought her attempt to become a barrister ridiculous, her fate was sad, but hardly surprising (and a waste of a damn good training). The rest of us can only admire her: she almost had it all.

2

England is a Gentlemen's Club

WOMEN IN THE PROFESSIONS BEFORE 1919

These learned maidens might do well to remember
that plants under cultivation lose their natural uses.[1]

In golden days of long ago, it was a common plan
For every girl to be a girl, and every man a man.
The female of our species never wished to change her sex,
And men who aped the woman were all classified as wrecks.
　　　A woman who could cook a meal
　　　Was thought by men to be ideal.
　　　A man who did not look the part
　　　Could never win a woman's heart.
　　　In fact (I think I've made it plain)
　　　In bygone days the world was sane.[2]

THIS LITTLE DITTY by 'A Mere Man' appears in a poetry collection published by Birmingham University's Medical Society between the wars. There are several more stanzas about how women have mutated from dutiful domestic daughters into unclassifiable creatures who are neither male (not having the necessary pedigree) nor female (lacking all the requisite charms). Proof of their eccentricity is a misguided insistence on being allowed to study mainstream medicine. The poem is depressingly reminiscent of an opinion piece in an 1873 issue of the esteemed medical journal *The Lancet*: 'Women's sphere of usefulness in the healing art should certainly be limited to the carrying out of the desires and implicitly obeying the dictates of . . . medical men.'[3] In other words, women might possibly be nurses – people described elsewhere as occupying 'the sere of virginal decay'[4] – but could *never* be doctors. Attitudes to women in medicine, in some quarters at least, clearly hadn't changed in half a century.

When the SDRA was passed in 1919, a number of women were already inhabiting the territory of the traditional professions like squatters – and the majority of them were doctors. In common with most squatters, they were generally regarded by the Establishment as interlopers with no right to be there, though some were tolerated as mavericks or inconsequential freaks. Women first infested the faculty of medicine at Birmingham in 1900 but were staunchly refused membership of the official Medical Society until 1944. This embargo was achieved through a mixture of opposition and denial: we do not want them here, and if we try not to notice those who do slink in, they will probably go away. What that blinkered Med. Soc. poet failed to realize was that by 1930, when he wrote his verses about the golden days of long ago, it was far too late for complaint.

Centuries before the proscriptive Medical Act of 1858 established a register of qualified practitioners and regulated the bodies allowed to examine them, women operated without censure as 'surgeonesses', physicians, midwives and apothecaries. Perhaps the first in Europe was Trotula of Salerno (died *c*.1097), who wrote a famous treatise on gynaecology. Because of the unfortunate location of 'the organs involved in the work of nature', she acknowledged, 'women on account of modesty and the fragility and delicacy of the state of these parts dare not reveal the difficulties of their sicknesses to a male doctor'.[5] That is why Trotula

had studied medicine: so she could offer help, thereby sparing her
patients' blushes and, perhaps, their lives. It was the same impulse
followed by the so-called pioneers some eight hundred years later.
The Guild of Barber-Surgeons in England admitted women after
1572, and every community valued its female healers qualified by
years – perhaps generations – of experience, if not by formal
examination.

One of Britain's best-known Victorian female medics was
Margaret Ann Bulkley (c.1789–1865), who lived and worked as
Dr James Barry. She circumvented the ban on women doctors in
the most pragmatic way possible, by concealing her gender altogether. After training at Edinburgh University, she served as a
military surgeon, mostly overseas. Some thirty years later, Elizabeth Blackwell trained in New York; she was probably unaware
of Dr Barry at this stage, though she would certainly learn her
predecessor's strange story when all was revealed by the press,
with salacious gusto, after Barry's death.

Dr Blackwell managed to slip on to the medical register in
1858 through a loophole, because although she was a graduate of
a foreign medical school (and these were generally excluded), she
satisfied enough of the other terms of the Act to qualify. Specifically, she happened to be at home in England at the time it was
passed; had glowing testimonials from enlightened British medical men with whom she had worked; and was no longer a trainee,
having graduated in 1849. At this point it is important to acknowledge those professional men who played a vital part in encouraging
and endorsing the ambitions of would-be professional women;
without their support, progress would have been even slower.
Elizabeth Blackwell's referees recognized her ability as a doctor
before considering her disability as a woman. They risked their
reputations in recommending her, which in a pre-NHS world
meant risking their livelihoods. We should salute them.

One of Dr Blackwell's students at a medical college she set up for women in New York was a young Englishwoman, Sophia Jex-Blake. Miss Jex-Blake was described as a rather excitable person in her mid-twenties; she had trained to be a teacher in defiance of her parents, who were aghast at the thought of their daughter earning a living, and travelled to America in 1865 to research a book on women's education. Were I not aware of the true derivation of the word 'feisty', so often associated with strong-minded women, that is exactly how I would describe Sophia.[6] During her visit she was offered accommodation at the New England Hospital for Women in Boston, at which an acquaintance, Dr Lucy Sewall, was a resident physician. In return, Sophia was asked to help out with a few minor administrative and nursing duties there. This simple quid pro quo was responsible for changing Sophia's life; from now onwards she never considered doing anything but medicine.

Dr Elizabeth Blackwell instructs her students in New York.

In New York, Sophia was introduced to Dr Sewall's friend and colleague Dr Blackwell, with whom she discussed this new and urgent ambition to abandon the classroom and the writing-desk for the hospital ward. Sophia knew the now-famous Dr Elizabeth Garrett (Anderson), having helped her a few years earlier with a doomed application to medical school in Edinburgh, where Sophia had been living while attending a series of lectures there. She hoped the acquaintanceship might help her own cause now, and enrolled at Dr Blackwell's college in 1868 to study for a medical diploma. Her intention was to return to Edinburgh armed with this fairly rudimentary qualification, and to succeed in storming the Scottish citadel of professional medicine where Dr Garrett had initially failed.

Dr Blackwell wished her well, but was not entirely confident of her success. She had not found the headstrong Sophia particularly impressive. 'I'm afraid she won't be very amenable to discipline,' reported Elizabeth of her erstwhile pupil; 'very certainly she must work harder than I have yet known her to do if she is to gain our diploma.'[7] Sophia did work hard, and when she applied to Edinburgh the following year she was armed not only with the diploma (which was virtually ignored) but with the moral support of many of Edinburgh's most influential women, professors' wives, social reformers and high-profile philanthropists among them.

The story of the next five years is confusing. It certainly confused Sophia. In 1869, Dr Elizabeth Garrett's close friend Emily Davies founded Girton College in Cambridge for the first women undergraduates in the country. The suffrage movement was up and running, kick-started by a petition to Parliament in 1866 presented to MP John Stuart Mill by Garrett and Davies. Florence Nightingale's ultra-respectable School of Nursing had been open at St Thomas' Hospital for nearly a decade. Surely this was an auspicious time for respectable women to attempt to join the vocational and fundamentally caring profession of medicine? Indeed, Edinburgh's

Faculty of Medicine accepted Sophia's application – but the wider university authorities swiftly rescinded the decision, ostensibly on the grounds that it would be too expensive and inconvenient to accommodate one solitary female student.

What followed was like a monstrously slow-motion and increasingly bad-tempered game of tennis. Sophia returned the ball by suggesting a way to overcome those problems: she would recruit more women, who could pay to be taught separately from their male peers. This last point acknowledged a common argument against women entering medicine: that their moral constitutions were unlikely to be strong enough to face (for example) the anatomy of the reproductive system or the whiff of putrefaction. It

Sophia Jex-Blake.

would be disastrously embarrassing for lecturers and male students alike to have to address sexual subjects while ladies were in the room. So what about nurses, ran the counter-argument? They cope; are they not female? Ah, but nurses are most likely *women* (Miss Nightingale being a notable exception), whereas those wanting to become doctors are decidedly *ladies* . . .

There were many other points of contention. It is up to medical schools to protect the reputation of the fairer sex by preventing them from being doctors; chivalry demands no less. A lady should not expect or be expected to handle men's bodies; only nurses (for whom a gentleman suspends disbelief) and prostitutes do that. Even ministering exclusively to women and children is dangerous: think of the money 'real' doctors will lose if female patients develop a preference for female doctors. And anyway, everyone knows women are not as clever as men – their brains are smaller: *quod est demonstrandum*. It therefore follows that the value of a medical degree will be cheapened if simplified enough for ladies to comprehend.

The Lancet published one of the more unusual defences against female medics by referring darkly to the dehumanizing herd mentality of their sex. They might not be too challenging to handle one by one, but have you ever come across them en masse? They are poisonous. 'Women hate one another, often at first sight, with a rancour of which men can form only a faint conception.'[8] When more than a handful of them are gathered together, it seems, they are likely to turn on each other, spitting and tearing at one another's hair in a most arousing manner.

Sophia Jex-Blake tried to ignore the invective. She placed an advertisement in the press:

Sir – Will you allow me to state that the Medical Faculty, Senatus and University Court of the University of Edinburgh, having approved the admission of women to the preliminary examination in Arts and their subsequent matriculation as medical students, it is hoped that separate classes will be opened for their instruction during the ensuing winter Session?

It would be well if any ladies intending to join these classes would at once communicate with me on the subject.[9]

Four women responded: midwife Isabel Thorne; another student of obstetrics, Matilda Chaplin; governess Edith Pechey; and Irishwoman Helen Evans, a widow in her mid-thirties. Had the timing been right, young mother Frances Hoggan might well have answered Sophia's call – but she was away in Zurich, trying to qualify there. The five pioneers were later joined by Mary Anderson Marshall (Dr Elizabeth Garrett's future sister in law) and a former maths tutor at Queen's College in London, Emily Bovell. Sophia dubbed the group the *septem contra Edinam*, or the Edinburgh Seven.

Now the ball was back in academia's court. Grudgingly the women were allowed to matriculate, and to attend lectures, provided they lodged a joint deposit of 100 guineas to guarantee their payment of lecture fees, and a further 4 guineas each (equivalent to about £300 today) for every class they took. The original five complied, and were all awarded prizes. Helen Evans did so well that she came top of her year in chemistry and should

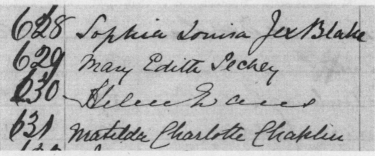

The matriculation record of some of the 'Edinburgh Seven', 1869.

therefore have been given the prestigious Hope Scholarship, which went instead to the highest-achieving man. That was a nasty shot, parried by a refusal on the part of the women to give up. They somehow met their fees, higher than any male medical students were charged, and even arranged their own external lectures when university staff refused to teach them.

Before 18 November 1870 few champions inside the medical school or the wider university were prepared to offer these women public support. However, what happened that day changed minds. When the Edinburgh Seven took themselves to Surgeons' Hall on Nicolson Street – an intimidating neo-classical edifice – to sit the regular Friday exam in anatomy, they were unexpectedly met by a mob of students hurling clods of mud and obscenities at them. The fracas was chaotic enough to halt the traffic in central Edinburgh for an hour. When they attempted to dash into the examination room to escape, the towering doors were literally slammed in their faces. A sympathizer inside heaved them open again, and the women slipped inside. The bullying continued from their whisky-sodden student peers during the exam. At one stage, someone bundled a live sheep into the hall, where it scudded, terrified, along the rows of desks. The hapless invigilator shouted over the din that perhaps the sheep should stay. 'It has more sense than those who sent it here.'[10] With that, the mood began to change.

When the exam – conducted in less than ideal conditions – was over and it was time for everyone to leave, the invigilator suggested that the women escape by the back door to save trouble. They refused, whereupon a group of ashamed male students formed an impromptu bodyguard to protect them. And over the next few days, the tone of press reports shifted. Journalists were now suggesting that the university should show some respect to these brave pioneers. Even some of the students were contrite, one of them explaining in a letter to *The Scotsman* that it was not medics who had caused the trouble at all, but a bunch of unruly chemists.[11]

The pace of the match picked up. Petitions were volleyed from one side to the other. Sophia took the authorities to court; in return the authorities refused to allow the women to graduate officially, or even to give them certificates to prove their attendance at classes. This whole sorry performance, claimed the university Senate, had only ever been an experiment. That experiment had patently failed. The women were expelled: game over.

Edinburgh declined to admit women again as medical students until 1892. By then Sophia and Edith Pechey had qualified at the University of Bern in Switzerland and been granted a licence to practise – like Frances Hoggan – by the comparatively progressive King and Queen's College of Physicians in Ireland. Dr Pechey went on to work in India, while Dr Jex-Blake helped to found the LSMW, which opened with fourteen students in 1874. Three years later the school was recognized as competent to submit candidates for examination in Ireland, and its graduates were allowed on to the wards of the Royal Free Hospital for clinical training. In 1878 the University of London admitted women to matriculate in most subjects, including medicine, and the Royal Colleges of Physicians and of Surgeons in Edinburgh and Glasgow opened formal exams to them. Slowly, over the forty-odd years preceding the First World War, more and more women doctors began to feed into the medical workplace, most of them investing their own training in teaching the next generation (like Annie McCall in Clapham), as well as in the health and welfare of their patients. Some were famous, like the redoubtable surgeon Louisa Aldrich-Blake, whom we shall meet in due course, or Professor Winifred Cullis, appointed to the Chair of Physiology at the University of London in 1919. However, when the SDRA became law that same year, only four women were Fellows of the Royal College of Surgeons in London, and the Royal College of Physicians did not elect its first female Fellow until 1934, another fifteen years later.

OUR PRETTY DOCTOR.

Dr. Arabella. "WELL, MY GOOD FRIENDS, WHAT CAN I DO FOR YOU?"
Bill. "WELL, MISS, IT'S ALL ALONG O' ME AND MY MATES BEIN' OUT O' WORK, YER SEE, AND WANTIN' TO TURN AN HONEST PENNY HANYWAYS WE CAN; SO, 'AVIN' 'EARD TELL AS *YOU* WAS A RISIN' YOUNG MEDICAL PRACTITIONER, WE THOUGHT AS P'RAPS YOU WOULDN'T MIND JUST A RECOMMENDIN' OF *HUS* AS NURSES."

An 1870 cartoon in Punch *reckons pretty lady doctors as fanciful as burly male nurses.*

The headline-making pioneers tend to obscure the assortment of 'ordinary women', gradually increasing in number, who
peopled the medical profession at a more mundane level, going
about their work with a mixture of excitement, exasperation and
exhaustion – much as doctors do today. Dr Anandi Gopal Joshi is an
example. She was born in Pune in 1865, married at nine, had a
child at fourteen and graduated in medicine from a college in
Pennsylvania, with the full support of her far-away family, at the
age of twenty-one. Her baby had died owing to lack of medical
care at ten days old; she vowed to give other mothers a better
chance of avoiding this tragically familiar Indian story and
specialized – like Trotula of Salerno – in obstetrics. In Dr Joshi's

case 'ordinary' is a relative term; few were as emotionally invested in their vocation, and naturally as brilliant, as she was. Like Gwyneth Bebb Thomson, she died far too young, succumbing to tuberculosis shortly before her twenty-second birthday.

These women's reminiscences, where we are fortunate enough to have them, give us glimpses of busy lives led not by self-promoting trail-blazers, but by individuals simply pursuing a career of highs and lows. Louisa Martindale is a cheerful figure, scuttling to a tea-and-ice-cream party in the 1890s to celebrate someone's exam success in company with booming 'Bobs', a sturdy Russian countess who is a close relation of the Tsar and has human bones sticking out of her coat pocket, absent-mindedly swept up from the dissecting room. Tiny Isabel Hutton from Scotland can't afford a skeleton of her own from which to revise, so Sandy the grave-digger from home has dug up a skull for her to use. She is inordinately proud of it.

Gladys Wauchope's mother will only let her practise as a doctor if she continues to live at home. Gladys agrees, resignedly screwing a plaque to the wall outside the family's front door and getting a handyman to connect the bell-push to an alarm by the bed she has occupied since childhood for night calls. To allay maternal fears about her going out to see patients after dark, she loads her medical bag with enough heavy objects to brain any would-be attacker. General practitioner Mary Murdoch insists on driving herself to house calls in Hull but is quite happy to admit that she is possibly the world's worst motorist. After a few day-light attempts, those teaching her to drive resorted to taking her out by the light of the moon, to minimize the risk of terror and carnage in the local community. She once slid backwards down a Yorkshire hill because she had blithely selected the wrong gear, overturned the car and crashed spectacularly into a shop window. When inevitably taken to court for dangerous driving she reduced her London counsel to white-knuckled silence after collecting him from the station in her shiny new vehicle. Her patients love her, but know to keep well out of her way when she takes to four wheels.

Slowly, but relatively surely, the concept of medicine as a career for women who could afford the training began to take hold. By the end of the nineteenth century most universities (except Oxford and Cambridge) were admitting them as medical students, and a growing number of teaching hospitals accepted them as juniors, though clinical appointments were far more difficult to secure in competition with male peers, unless they involved specific low-level or undesirable work relating to the supervision of female health: as a medical officer attending to women in factories, perhaps, or in an asylum. As the world skipped largely unconcerned towards war, medicine was the most progressive of the traditional professions, despite the sort of institutional prejudice that now makes us squirm to contemplate. But that still begged a question, posed by another university poet in 1902.

> *Though all the world's a stage and we are acting,*
> *Yet still I think your part is not dissecting.*
> *To me the art of making apple tarts*
> *Would suit you better than those 'horrid parts' . . .*
> *Your knowledge – of the frog should only be*
> *How they are cooked in France – or making tea!*
> *And as for learning Chemistry and that,*
> *'Twould be a nicer thing to trim a hat.*
> *I know your aims in medicine are true*
> *But tell me, is there any* need *of you?*[12]

In 1881, a compendious publication entitled the *English-woman's Year Book* appeared for the first time, listing 'all institutions existing for the benefit of women and children'. It is a fascinating document of the social history of Britain's emerging middle classes, being at once a directory of voluntary organizations to which ladies might contribute time and bounty, and a catalogue of opportunities for – whisper it – *paid work*. After a slightly alarming advertisement for Oldridge's Balm of Columbia, match-less for restoring Hair, Whiskers and Moustaches, and another (more comforting) for Brown and Polson's glossy Blancmange, a bold editorial claims that remuneration for women's work need be neither vulgar nor demeaning, as long as that work is carried out in the Victorian tradition with a sacred sense of duty towards humanity; in 'obedience' and 'pervaded by the spirit of love'.[13] Duty, obedience and love transmute even the basest metal into something 'noble and beautiful'.

Having thus paid lip-service to polite society's norms, the *Year Book*'s editor and publisher, the social reformer and Anglican deaconess Louisa Hubbard, develops her radical theme, quoting the latest population statistics proving that there are now more than half a million more women in Britain than men. That number is likely to increase as more officers and gentlemen are dispatched to run the Empire, or lose their lives on foreign battle-fields. Then women will have to fend for themselves.

> The prospect is not at first sight a pleasing one, for it destroys the time-honoured assumption by which every woman becomes in due course a wife and mother, and lives supported by the labour and cherished by the protection of her husband, until, at his death, her sons rise up and call her blessed, and she dies peace-fully in a green old age. This, thank God, is the history of many a happy life now, but by no means all, and the exceptions to this fortunate lot are becoming so many as to form a new rule of their own, and require provision accordingly.[14]

She offers some suggestions for how this 'superfluity' of women might profitably spend their lives, in a dizzying list of jobs already being done by their enterprising sisters, extrapolated from the lat-est census return. They include 204 photographers, 157 surgical instrument makers, 143 prison officers, 30 farmers, 23 undertakers and one anchor-chain manufacturer.

If these pursuits do not appeal, Miss Hubbard recommends a variety of occupations suitable for those seeking some degree of responsibility, and quotes the salaries they might command. A matron in one of the country's 730 workhouses or 66 lunatic asylums can earn up to £100 a year (£1 in 1880 is equivalent to about £66 today in terms of purchasing power). A first-class milliner can command £125; a book-keeper £80; and a nursery governess £30 all found. An artificial-limb manufacturer, meanwhile, earns just £9, the same as a collier-woman and slightly less than a military-ornament maker. But if an artificial-limb manufacturer, or a collier-woman, is what you yearn to be, do not let a false sense of decorum deter you. There is an inherent dignity in earning one's own living, as long as it's not by way of the oldest profession of all.

This is a brave sentiment, especially in the light of a popular argument against women entering the professional Establishment: that in so doing, they will compromise its own essential dignity. The only true profession Miss Hubbard is able to advocate for women is medicine, for which she does not venture to quote a salary, only the cost to women of training at the LSMW – some £125 (£8,250 now), excluding living costs and extra fees for courses in vaccination, practical pharmacology and midwifery. The closest job she can find to being an architect is a plan-tracer (5d an hour). An aspiring engineer might become a gas-fitter (9s a week), a would-be lawyer a copyist in a solicitor's office (2d per folio or page), and a churchwoman a non-ordained, low-paid deaconess like her (ministering pastorally to parish women), or a lay worker with no salary at all.

And, of course, there's always teaching.

The *Englishwoman's Year Book* was published annually until 1916. By then it was a far more authoritative volume. There are still advertisements in my cherished 1915 edition – for Atora suet and Ronuk furniture polish – but they are joined by appeals for donations to the Building Fund of the Chelsea Hospital for Women; a notice about the School of Mining and Metallurgy at the University of Birmingham; exhortations to join various societies in support of women's suffrage and – no doubt in the interests of impartiality – for the National League for Opposing Woman Suffrage (objects: 'To resist the proposal to admit women to the Parliamentary Franchise, and to Parliament, whilst at the same time maintaining the principle of the representation of women on municipal and other bodies concerned with the domestic and social affairs of the community').[15]

This time the section on medicine is much expanded. When the first edition was published, there were only twenty-six women on the register of the General Medical Council; now there are nearly five hundred. There's a war on, of course, which has changed things. Oxford and Cambridge universities remain out of bounds to female medical students, but almost every other medical school is now open to them. Many hospitals admit them to the wards, and some even have women on their boards of management. About twelve hospitals have 'ladies' committees' to supervise the needs of female members of staff. Eighteen women doctors – just eighteen – who *teach* medicine are listed as role models, with a brief list of available scholarships and a directory of respectable boarding houses and hostels where students and young professionals may lodge while they study. There are twenty hospitals exclusively for women patients in London alone; inevitably they attract the highest number of female trainees.

It might not be clear from the tone of the handbook, which judiciously keeps a stiff upper lip at all times, but other sources suggest that medicine was not always a serious business. Male students famously had their sports, rituals (including the baiting of women undergraduates) and exclusive social clubs to defuse the stress of the day job and affirm their solidarity; women appear to have relied on camaraderie and good humour. In 1915 some of them compiled an obstetric ABC for medical staff at Dr Annie McCall's Clapham Maternity Hospital.

> *A is for Annie, our Medical Light,*
> *B is for Babies, addicted to night,*
> *C is for Chorion, plenty we hope,*
> *D is for District; take masses of soap.*
> *E's exploration when hunting for C.*
> *F is for Forceps by Janet M.D.,*
> *G is for Glycerine – can't get no more,*
> *H is for Haemorrhage, rather a bore.*
> *I is for Icterus, mild or malig.*
> *Jaundice it's called, if you aren't talking big.*
> *K is the Knot that we hope is a reef,*
> *L is for Laudanum, bringing relief.*
> *M is Mistura, Alb, white, Rubra red.*
> *N is for Notes that we write on the bed.*
> *O is Ophthalmia, otherwise Eyes,*
> *P is the Pelvis, one long-drawn surprise.*
> *Q is Quin. Sulph. which we barely afford,*
> *R is for Rules of the wretched old Board.*
> *S for the Stages we time by the clock;*
> *T for undiagnosed Triplets, some shock!*
> *U is the Uterus; where is it found?*
> *V is a Version, or turning around.*
> *W's Whiteleg, a serious case,*
> *X is Excitement on getting a Face.*
> *Y is the Yawns when our slumbers we miss.*
> *Z is the Zinc for the babes' tails – and this.*[16]

For non-medics, the chorion is part of the placenta; mistura and quinine sulphate are drugs; and whiteleg is associated with deep vein thrombosis. Glycerine was in short supply because of the war

(it was used in explosives). I don't know who Janet M.D. was –
but it doesn't matter. What does matter is the sense of fun and
community evident in the Alphabet.

By now, architecture and engineering have appeared on
the list of 'Employments and Professions', but the new editor –
novelist Geraldine Mitton – is not convinced of their suitability
for women. Despite popular opinion, it is not enough to be good
at drawing for the former; 'good health and strength are essential,
and also [given the likely prejudice encountered] a strong character,
with tenacity of purpose'.[17] Engineering 'has not many attractions
to most women . . . The period of training is almost impossible
to state definitely, as for our sex the various objective employments differ so materially from men's, that different duration of
training would be necessary.'[18] Perhaps she hasn't heard of Sarah
Guppy (1770–1852), a businesswoman, writer, mother of six and
prolific inventor from Bristol. Mrs Guppy was an engineer in all
but name, said to have influenced Thomas Telford and her friend
Isambard Kingdom Brunel on the construction of the Menai
Bridge and the iconic Clifton Suspension Bridge respectively. In
1811, before either Telford's or Brunel's bridge was opened, she
took out a patent for 'a new mode of constructing and erecting
bridges and rail-roads without arches . . . whereby the danger of
their being washed away by floods is avoided'. What's that, if not
a suspension bridge?

The section on the law summarizes Gwyneth Bebb Thomson's 1913 test case and subsequent appeal, and mentions that it is
already possible in France for women to act as 'Avocat', as it is in
Sweden, Finland, Denmark, Canada and Egypt. Miss Mitton
might have mentioned suffragist Eliza Orme (1848–1937) at this
juncture. Eliza read Law at the University of London – the first
woman to do so – graduating at the age of forty. Before that she
attended public lectures at the university (then still closed to
women undergraduates) and attracted considerable attention for

her sophisticated and therefore unfeminine understanding of legal history and processes. The MP John Stuart Mill suggested she work in the chambers of a barrister friend in Lincoln's Inn, which she did from 1873 to 1875. She was encouraged to apply to read for the Bar, Mill's stepdaughter Helen Taylor even offering to pay the necessary £75 application fee; but, perhaps realizing the futility of the exercise and having no wish to act as a political figurehead, Miss Orme opened an office with a female partner in Chancery Lane instead. They offered an expert service drafting conveyancing and other legal documents; while working there, Eliza completed her degree. A confident woman – so much so that she sometimes smoked a cigar in the company of gentlemen clients – prosperous Miss Orme is said to have inspired the character of Vivie Warren, the daughter in George Bernard Shaw's play *Mrs Warren's Profession*. 'People are always blaming circumstances for what they are,' says Vivie briskly in Act II. 'I don't believe in circumstances. The people who get on in this world are the people who get up and look for the circumstances they want, and, if they can't find them, make them.'

Miss Mitton doesn't mention the ridiculously ambitious Bertha Cave either. The first woman to apply to one of London's Inns of Court, Bertha approached Gray's Inn in 1903 at the age of twenty-two, asking to be allowed to read for the Bar. Bertha's father was a butler; where she found the financial wherewithal to study the law is unclear, but she must have had at least moral support from her family. A barrister was persuaded to tutor her, and to bolster her self-confidence. Women lawyers already worked in Europe and the United States, so why not here? And though there were no regulations providing for their admittance to training, there were none forbidding them either. Predictably, her application was flatly rejected, at which point she immediately appealed to the House of Lords on the grounds that her gender was not enough, in law, to disqualify her.

The Lord Chancellor asked if she had anything to say at the appeal. She repeated the arguments put to Gray's Inn, adding that she really wouldn't mind having to wear a wig and gown or eat her dinners in Hall, if that's what they were worried about.

The Lord Chancellor appeared to be much amused at the frank admission. Lord Alverstone and the other Justices were also unable to preserve a severely judicial countenance. They did not hesitate, however, over their decision.[19]

The entire hearing was over in a matter of minutes. The press were broadly sympathetic with Miss Cave at this second rejection, but couldn't help spending more column inches on her appearance than on her cause:

Her lithe, slight form was habited in a short blue walking skirt, with an open coat of the same material, showing a light blue blouse underneath.

Perched on her raven-locked head was the smartest of hats trimmed with black and white pompoms. The only touch of legal authority in her costume was a stand-up masculine collar.

Below her skirt appeared a dainty pair of very high-heeled boots. A fresh blush suffused her pretty face as she tripped along and her dark eyes flashed determination.[20]

Miss Mitton evidently thinks it unwise to steer her readers towards the sort of unregulated eccentricity enjoyed by Eliza Orme, or risk subjecting them to the lascivious attention endured by Bertha Cave. Instead, the ambitious are invited to consider becoming factory inspectors, rent collectors, secretaries or hospital almoners. These are skilled positions commanding respect; the implication is that they will prepare women well for the time ahead when, at last, they will be on an equal footing with men.

This measure of confidence had little to do with presentiment. It was not that the editors of the *Englishwoman's Year Book* and other such publications (of which there were several) divined that the law was going to change in a few years' time to give them a vote in Parliament and invite them into the élite professions. They were reporters, not sibyls. It was, rather, a sign of the times. Over one million men had joined up since the declaration of war in August 1914; the government was in the process of framing the Military Service Act (passed in January 1916) conscripting single men between the ages of eighteen and forty-one; four months later, a second Act included married men. Women were encouraged to deputize for working men on the home front, as an act of war service.

They poured into factories, as munitions workers, mechanics and machinists; they worked in public transport in just about every role imaginable except as engine-drivers. The iconic image of the lady 'clippie' or bus-conductor with her pragmatically short skirt and cheery smile was very much based on reality. Women's patrols employed uniformed ladies to keep the peace near factory gates and hostels – looking out more for wayward women than for misbehaving men – and these ladies evolved into women police officers. There were female firefighters, bank clerks, even Civil Service administrators. The one thing they all had in common was that they were paid less for the work they were doing than the men whose places they filled. This led to problems with the trade unions, who feared that when the war was over, employers would prefer to keep on cheaper, female labour rather than to reinstate returning servicemen on higher wages.

The Sheffield branch of ASLEF, the Associated Society of Locomotive Engineers and Firemen, passed a resolution in 1916:

That in view of the fact that women have been introduced on the railways as shunters and are also learning signalman's [*sic*] duties and rumours being current that they are to be placed on the foot plate, the branch request the General Secretary in the event of any attempt being made to introduce female labour on the footplate to immediately call the [committee] together to take whatever steps may be necessary to protect us and if necessary call a stoppage of the footplate staff.[21]

The war lent women of every class permission to work for a living, and one should never underestimate the value of precedent. Because they were doing these jobs now, in a period of national emergency, they would stand a better chance of doing them again in peacetime. But the greatest legacy of the war in terms of women's entry into the traditional professions was the opportunity for doing so by stealth: for entering the Establishment by . . . not even the back door, but that half-hidden gate a little way down the road at the rear of the building.

In 1917, an article was published in a national journal under the title 'The Future of the Bar'. There had recently been a fresh proposal that women be admitted, to boost numbers (and therefore income) at the Inns of Court. 'Naturally this foolish motion was rejected by a majority of about nine to one . . . If there is one calling in the world for which women are conspicuously unfitted it is the Law,' scoffed the author. 'Women have no idea of relevance, or analogy, or evidence.'[22]

Gwyneth Bebb Thomson, with the greatest of respect, would disagree. Her position as 'Assistant Commissioner, Midland Division' at the Ministry of Food gave her responsibility for the enforcement of wartime regulations to do with food production and consumption. It was her job to prosecute black-market offenders. She was, in other words, a paralegal – and was one of the first women to be recognized with an OBE for her efforts. Carrie Morrison was a Girton alumna with a first in Medieval and Modern Languages. She worked for the Military Permit

Office during the war, and then with Intelligence attached to the Army of the Black Sea in Constantinople (now Istanbul). It is never stated explicitly, but one can reasonably assume she was a spy. Her war service gave her exemption from part of her law training after the passing of the SDRA, as did the fact that she had earned a degree, which is why she leapfrogged others in November 1922 to become the first woman in England to qualify as a solicitor, closely followed by Maud Crofts, Mary Pickup and Mary Sykes.

Solicitors' daughters sometimes worked in their fathers' practices – particularly in the provinces – while their brothers, destined to inherit the businesses, were away fighting. If the brother was killed, it was likely that his sister would take his place – but only as her father's unofficial and unpaid articled clerk. Occasionally she would inherit the practice on his death. The same pattern emerged in architecture, though to a lesser degree. By 1915 women were allowed to study the discipline at the universities of London, Liverpool and Manchester; to train at a number of schools of art elsewhere (notably Glasgow); or to qualify through being articled to an established practice. The Architectural Association's school opened its doors to women two years later, simply because it needed the money. A more oblique wartime route into architecture was via the agencies tasked with inspecting buildings for safety after bomb attacks – sometimes a woman's job – or through planning housing and post-war reconstruction schemes. Just as female doctors were assumed to be interested solely in paediatrics and in matters 'down below' (obstetrics and gynaecology), so female architects were automatically linked to domestic interior design. However, if that was their ticket into the profession, most would take it.

Women in engineering workshops during the war were too frantically busy getting things made to worry overmuch about professional status. That came later, when the pioneers emerged in peacetime in their oil-stained overalls with practical expertise and managerial experience, ready for independent careers. Teaching, in schools and universities alike, was a reserved occupation for men from 1916 to 1918, so opportunities were perhaps not as plentiful for women's advancement in further education. There were fewer university students anyway, despite the recruitment of more women undergraduates.

Most of the Church's parish workers were women, and they were run off their feet during the dark times of the war, with clergymen leaving to serve as chaplains to the forces and so many people and communities relying on the Church for comfort and guidance. Very few of them would have contemplated taking the same path as the radical Constance Coltman, who was ordained as a preacher in the Congregational Church in 1917 and later appointed minister at the King's Weigh House Chapel in Mayfair, where Maude Royden was a familiar speaker. But they gained invaluable experience; and, as Mrs Coltman said herself, women had always been society's best unofficial counsellors and confessors. That did not mean that the Anglican Communion was any closer to recognizing a vocation in women to join the professional clergy on the same terms as men; that was a blasphemous notion.

A few inspirational oddities, like Eliza Orme, took advantage of the war to prosper and to create a precedent for women entrepreneurs. One of these was Beatrice Gordon Holmes, usually known as plain Gordon Holmes. When she published her autobiography *In Love with Life* in 1944 she proudly claimed that since the age of twenty she had never possessed an unearned sixpence. One of four children born in the East End of London into what she called 'poverty', she was a rampant tomboy who hardly went to school. In fact, the supposed poverty was relative: her father was a doctor and – perhaps because of his demeanour: he claimed to hate his profession and perversely thought medics did more harm than good – there never seemed to be enough money to go round. The education of girls was not his priority.

Gordon did not get on well with her grumpy father or her overbearing mother, who mortifyingly insisted on making all her daughter's clothes to her own design until Gordon was thirty. This frumpy wardrobe, Gordon believed, had a lot to do with her lack of friends during childhood and youth. By the age of fourteen she had finished with school, having endured a couple of short stints at the cheapest establishments her father could find. One of her fleeting teachers had spotted Gordon's potential and suggested she apply to become a pupil–teacher at the prestigious North London Collegiate School under its headmistress Dr Sophie Bryant. That would have cost her father nothing. But Gordon hated the thought of teaching; she preferred to learn – she just didn't want to do it at school.

After a few years at home, during which the only money she had at her disposal was 9d a week from her brothers for darning their socks, Gordon persuaded her father to lend her four guineas (about £300 now) to pay for a shorthand typing course. Armed with this solitary qualification she got her first job, earning £1 a week. She paid her ailing mother a quarter of her salary so that Mrs Holmes could have her shopping delivered to the house; this she declined to do, spending the money instead – according to an aggrieved Gordon – on 'extra pots of jam' for the brothers.

In about 1908 (Gordon is a little sketchy on dates), a Canadian uncle-in-law arrived on the scene and agreed to teach her science and maths. For two years she described herself as in 'mental ecstasy' until he disappeared back across the Atlantic. This was a low point. Then she was dismissed from her job for incompetence – but soon found a better one with a company improbably importing Danish eggs. The next step up was even better: in 1912 she joined a firm of financiers in the City, excelled, and made a fortune as a stockbroker selling war loans from 1914 to 1918. Her principal at the firm was habitually away for months at a time, which meant she was in charge, interviewing clients – increasingly often women – and handling bigger and bigger deals. Come the Armistice, Gordon Holmes was rich.

She put her success down to personality, an ability to recognize and maximize opportunity, and political engagement, especially with the suffrage campaign.

> [The] suffragette movement helped to make the women of my generation. It gave us pride of sex, helped to stop the everlasting apology within us for being women, taught us to value ourselves and our abilities, and taught us to fight for those valuations in terms of pay and responsibility, public and private.[23]

She never broke free of her mother, though. In her fourth decade she was permitted to shop for her own clothes, but otherwise remained in what she called 'emotional bondage' until Mrs Holmes's death when Gordon was well into middle age.

Gordon Holmes was not alone in appreciating her experience as a suffragette. Ideologically, the struggle for a voice in Parliament was closely linked to the struggle to be taken seriously in the professional workplace, but there was more to it than that. Before they came together as campaigners, most women had no experience of sisterhood outside the family; of organized networks, the offering and acceptance of practical and moral support from people one did not necessarily know but with whom one shared a purpose. It was like belonging to a regiment or the old boys' club of a public school. Members of the suffrage movement had their rituals – as did the judiciary, for instance – involving uniforms, processions and regalia. They sang rousing anthems written just for them, and were bound together by loyalty and the implicit promise of mutual benefit and protection.

Crucially, the suffrage movement was a breeding ground for role models, sorely lacked by would-be high-achieving women in a man's world. Think of the people at that Westminster dinner in 1920. Millicent Fawcett's sister Agnes and cousin Rhoda Garrett were both apprenticed to an architect, who was commissioned to design Millicent and Agnes' other sister Elizabeth's New Hospital for Women in London. They specialized in interior decoration, setting up their own successful business in 1875. Christabel Pankhurst, daughter of suffragette leader Mrs Emmeline Pankhurst, read law at Manchester University, the lone woman among her law-student peers, graduating in 1906 with a first. Her ambition was to become a practising and fully accredited lawyer as her father had been – but at that time, she could not.

Like Christabel Pankhurst, suffragist Emily Phipps stood for Parliament as soon as she was legally able to do so, in December 1918. She was 'only' a teacher, but as inspirational as any figurehead could be, agitating during the war not for women's votes – because suffrage societies had agreed to desist for the duration – but for equal pay for women teachers with the same workload as men. She was elected president of the National Union of Women Teachers (NUWT), and never missed the chance to alert Parliament and the public to the crass injustice of what we now call the gender pay gap. And 'only' a teacher? That is unfair; her father was a dockyard coppersmith in Devonport with numerous children, yet Emily found her way to the University of London, where she took a first; then to training college in Cambridge (financed by working as a pupil–teacher); and then to the headship of a highly regarded girls' secondary school in Wales. She was an infectiously cheerful person, energetic, witty, an accomplished musician and embroiderer; full of zest for life. Her pupils probably left school in a far more robust and aspirational frame of mind than when they entered, familiar with one of her favourite mottoes: 'If you make yourself a doormat, do not be surprised if people tread on you!'[24] To her there was no such thing as 'only' a teacher, man or woman.

If anyone's story embodies the situation of professional women before the passing of the SDRA, and demonstrates the wide embrace of the suffrage 'family', it must be Louisa Martindale's. All her life, Louisa lived among extraordinary people. Her mother – a committed suffragist also called Louisa – was left a widow when our Louisa was four. It is difficult to imagine a more traumatic time: when Mrs Martindale lost her husband, she was pregnant with Louisa's sister Hilda; and the very same week, Louisa's two infant siblings also died. Perhaps understandably, Mrs Martindale shut up house in London, where her husband had worked as a businessman and she had devoted herself to political activism and philanthropy, and with her surviving children left the country.

After a few years in Germany and Switzerland, the Martindales returned to England, settling first in Lewes in East Sussex and then, from 1880, just up the road in Brighton. Mrs Martindale focused closely – almost obsessively – on the girls' education, developing a progressive but eccentric philosophy. She built a gymnasium and hired a teacher to drill them; during breaks from callisthenics they learned to ride horses (astride, not side-saddle like piffling young ladies) and to master that new-fangled feminist apparatus, the bicycle. When they were old enough to attend Brighton High School, Mrs Martindale had a governess take and meet them every day, not so much to protect them as to extend their lessons beyond the school gates.

It was her mother who decided that Louisa should be a doctor. She sent her first to Royal Holloway College for two years and then, in 1892, to the London School of Medicine for Women. Louisa gamely did as she was told, much enjoying the company of her sister students at the LSMW. When they were taught dissection in a fascinating, chill, zinc-floored chamber, a curtain was

The London School of Medicine for Women.

put up so that for the first few weeks they would not have to look at the cadavers. Louisa was thrilled when the curtain shifted in the breeze, revealing a tantalizing smorgasbord of body parts awaiting the attention of her scalpel. She remembered her peers with affection, particularly another Louisa, the young Miss Aldrich-Blake, formidably focused even then. Her student hall of residence was run by Miss Eleanor Grove (sister of the famous musicologist George), who had a horror of wedlock. 'If an unfortunate student came back from her holiday saying she was engaged to be married, Miss Grove sent for her, and when the student emerged from the interview she was pale and shattered.'[25] The hall's residents were not all studying medicine: there was a Dutch baroness, learning to be an artist even though she could only paint horses, and a glamorous friend of Louisa Aldrich-Blake, who once came back to her room after being presented at Court still dressed in her feathers and train. These young women were not, by definition, 'girls of slender means'; but their energetic community spirit seems very similar to that described beguilingly by Muriel Spark in her novel of that name published some seventy years later.

Louisa Martindale qualified in 1899 and moved home to Brighton before being head-hunted by Dr Mary Murdoch, the GP who drove so appallingly, in Hull. She worked with Dr Murdoch as a locum assistant, and though she was barely paid for her services and toiled day and night for five weeks, she counted the experience one of the most valuable of her career. After a year's travel and private research into medical treatments abroad, Louisa joined Dr Murdoch in a permanent capacity for five years. Later, when Dr Murdoch fell ill, she chose Louisa as her own doctor, travelling all the way down to the south coast to be cared for. I like to think that Louisa looked after Dr Frances Hoggan, too, when she retired to Brighton: it's quite probable. I imagine the widowed Frances finally spilling the secret of Elise, and Louisa nodding kindly, understanding.

It was important to Dr Martindale to ensure, before opening a private practice, that she would not be treading on anyone's toes professionally. She was not worried about rival male doctors: they could look after themselves. But she was anxious not to steal patients from any other women who might already be trying to establish themselves in Brighton. She duly checked: there were two lady doctors in that area of Sussex, but both happened to be working in neighbouring Hove, which left her home town free for Louisa. She soon joined the staff of the Brighton Dispensary for Women, with surgeon Louisa Aldrich-Blake and Dr Helen Boyle – the latter a great friend, incidentally, of stockbroker Gordon Holmes (and so the network grows). The Dispensary later developed into a fully staffed hospital, the New Sussex Hospital for Women and Children, with funds raised by Louisa's mother, Gordon Holmes and Lady Rhondda: an old girls' network of considerable force.

Dr Louisa Martindale.

Mrs Martindale died in 1914. Louisa was devastated. A bracing holiday with Dr Murdoch helped restore her spirits and energize her enough to leave her practice from time to time. She travelled during the war, joining the staff at the Scottish Women's Hospital at Royaumont in northern France, where she developed a particular interest in radiology.

This brings us to a further legacy of the First World War. For the first time, significant numbers of women were able to work abroad in roles for which they were uniquely qualified. The Women's Auxiliary Army Corps, later named the Queen Mary Army Auxiliary Force, was founded in 1917 to recruit women into the forces in administrative and other non-combative roles, thus freeing soldiers for the front line. By the end of the war, 57,000 'WAACs' were serving at home and in Europe as mechanics, drivers, cooks, clerks and similar. They wore uniforms, were subject to military discipline, played hockey and cricket to keep fit, and even took part in morris dancing (which suggests that regular soldiers did too: there's a thought). WAACs were deputy soldiers, placeholders employed merely for the duration.

WAACs were not the only women to enlist. The Voluntary Aid Detachment (VAD) was established in 1909 to provide care to injured servicemen at home and abroad. Its members were civilian volunteers, the vast majority of whom were women. Professional nurses also operated in the field, joined from November 1914 onwards by qualified female doctors. That is when the Scottish Women's Hospitals were established, funded and staffed by members of the non-militant suffragist societies. They ran establishments in France, Salonika, Serbia, Russia, Romania, Corsica and Malta, at which everyone from surgeon to kitchen orderly, chief medical officer to ambulance driver, anaesthetist to launderer, was a woman – except for the odd cook. These hospitals not only provided precious experience for doctors and surgeons at the highest level; they generated important research, notably into the effects and treatment of gas gangrene. Dr Louisa Martindale's hospital at Royaumont had a conspicuously low mortality rate.

Dr Martindale was forty-seven when the SDRA was passed, hugely experienced but with her most pioneering work still ahead of her. She was influential, well respected, and popular with colleagues and patients alike, who were fond of this petite, chic and smiling person. She was happy in love, never marrying (Miss Grove would have been proud) but living with Miss Ismay Fitzgerald, an aristocratic Catholic acquaintance whom Louisa invited to stay for a fortnight in 1911 and who never left. But was she accepted in her chosen profession on her own merits, as a doctor rather than a woman, or did the medical Establishment fall silent – with a few exceptions – and stare at her open-mouthed when she entered the room, as it were, like a trespasser in a gentlemen's club? She was too polite to say, but remembering that riddle about the surgeon and her son in the car accident, one might hazard a pretty good guess.

3

Working Girls

As a child I wanted to be Prime Minister,
a great writer – and the mother of at least twelve children.[1]

IT CAN BE no surprise that gentlemen were aghast at the thought
of women invading sacred ground. During the fight for the vote
it was argued that wives and daughters, spinsters and widows, had
no claim to a voice in Parliament, since British democracy had
been fashioned, maintained, policed and protected entirely by
men for more generations than anyone could remember. Power
was a man's birthright. Who were women – untutored, temperamentally unfit, inexperienced and over-emotional – to trespass
now? A woman's voice was by turns pretty and shrill, seductive
and petulant, not comfortably gruff like any statesman's. Men
shared a code that even – in extremis – transcended class, with
which they expressed and understood each others' intentions
without having to resort to the spoken word. It was rooted in a
common bond of decency, honour and an inherent appreciation
of the fitness of things. The default mode of women – however
well educated – was silliness.

For Parliament, read the professional workplace; any workplace,
in fact, traditionally associated with men. Women campaigning

against this patriarchal attitude were well aware of how ridiculous they must appear to the Establishment. The quotation above, about wanting to be Prime Minister, is taken from the autobiography of Lady Rhondda, who has appeared more than once already in this history. Looking back, she thought herself laughably over-ambitious – though in truth it was the 'twelve children' part that she reckoned was beyond her, not the rest.

Margaret Thomas was the only child of the first Viscount Rhondda, a Welsh politician and industrialist who expected his daughter to do as other debutantes did: marry someone suitably rich and bring up the next generation of the ruling class. Margaret was scantily educated by governesses at home until 1896, when

Margaret Haig Thomas, Viscountess Rhondda.

she was thirteen; then, after a few years at Notting Hill High School for Girls and the bracing St Leonard's boarding school in Scotland, she drifted home to be presented at Court and launched into the marriage market. As her first London season progressed, Margaret's heart (and her mother's) began to sink: no one eligible had taken an interest in her. At the end of her third season, still husbandless, Margaret chose to spend her time studying history at Somerville College, Oxford, instead. It was less embarrassing.

Unfortunately, university life did not suit Margaret; she thought her younger contemporaries petty, her tutors stuffy and Oxford lacklustre. She left after a year and returned to Wales, eventually marrying a local landowner, Humphrey Mackworth, in 1908. It was not a happy match, ending in divorce after fifteen years. During this period Margaret worked for her father as his secretarial assistant-cum-managing director (the Thomas portfolio included several publishing houses and a number of collieries) at a fantastic salary of £1,000 per annum. She was returning from America on a business trip on the *Lusitania* when it was torpedoed in 1915; as one of the 763 of 1,960 passengers who survived, she resolved never again to be frightened of *anything*.

Margaret was an enthusiastic suffragette, catching the habit from Florence Haig, a cousin of her mother, and counting as one of her proudest achievements her imprisonment for arson in 1913 (she set fire to a pillar-box). The passion and commitment she brought to the fight for the vote, and to her career as a business-woman, were later directed into the campaign for women's equality in the workplace and elsewhere. Whenever there was a protest to be made, a celebration to be enjoyed or an injustice to be exposed, as the keenest of activists Margaret was there.

In 1920 she founded the long-running feminist journal *Time and Tide*. She was canny enough to make it palatable to the general reader, even comic at times: there was political mileage in making sex discrimination laughable. Aping the women's magazines that were becoming so popular at the time, she introduced 'Our Men's Page', for example, edited by that fictitious stalwart of good taste, Sir Duffer D'Amboring, who addresses the pressing questions of the day.

These pressing questions are largely, of course, about fashion. 'Should men Shingle?' In other words, should they grow their hair long enough to cut it in the latest fashion for modern women, cropped and tapered at the back but longer at the sides to cover the ears? Is it dangerous to talk about . . . *certain garments*? Sir Duffer invites reader participation in a poll about public decency:

> Dear Gentleman Readers, So many of you have called my attention to the indelicacy of the phrase – Trouser Press – used in a letter from Mr ★★★ire last week that I append the following Coupon, and ask you to choose between the two little elegancies – 'Inexpressibles' and 'Indispensibles' – which one you prefer that TIME AND TIDE henceforth employ instead of T★★★★★★. The word Press, of course, is not objectionable.[2]

There is a piece on 'Equal Rights for Men', dealing not with politics (far too taxing) but with the suggestion that functionaries at public ceremonies in the City of London be allowed to dispense with the below-the-knee garters they use to keep up their white ceremonial hose and wear what modern women do,

> namely, the type of suspender that fastens about the waist under the clothing, and from each side of which depend elastic strips which, fastened to the sock or stocking, unobtrusively, but efficiently and painlessly, keep said sock, or stocking, from sinking to the ground.

And, as in all the best magazines, there is a correspondence section. This letter from a Mr Obadiah Jones is headed 'How to Allure':

Dear Sir Duffer, I am going to spend a weekend with my wife
next April, and should be so glad if you could give me some
advice about what suits would be most suitable, because I
lately overheard a very catty uncle say that I was becoming 'fat
and dowdy'. Also I no longer attract my wife as I once did.
She is losing interest in me, and no longer finds me as fascinating as she should. How can I regain her affection? Do you
advise corsets? I have just £234 to spend on clothes for this
wonderful week-end, and will faithfully follow any advice
you are kind enough to give me.

Going shopping with £234 in your pocket in 1920 would be like
having £10,000 to spend today: poor Obadiah. Sir Duffer replies
that he sympathizes, having occasionally noticed an inexplicable
lack of interest in *him* on the part of his own wife; he definitely
recommends a corset 'to give you that straight effect that is so
alluring these days', a reassuringly expensive subscription to his
Correspondence School of Clothes Culture, and a novelty waist-
coat made of dog skin with exploding buttons. Those are sure to
do the trick and 'force a smile' to the lips of Mrs Jones. With
deadly precision, Lady Rhondda not only ridiculed men's attitude
to women by reflecting it in this crazy mirror; she also satirized
the scope and appeal of trashy women's magazines. *Time and Tide*
was a brilliant publication, owned and run entirely by women.

Unlike Sir Duffer D'Amboring, the male workforce was not
generally so mutton-headed that it did not realize what was going
on in this brave new post-war world. At one end of the scale,
'threatened' men contemplated industrial action, as the ASLEF
members had during the war, while at the other they convened
what were politely called 'indignation meetings' to protest; but it
was obvious that things were beginning to change, not just
because of legislation like the SDRA but through *force majeure*.
There had been more single women than men *before* 1914; now
there were many, many more, and huge numbers of these had lost

access to male financial support and were themselves having to support other family members – widowed mothers, fatherless children, incapacitated husbands. The state could not afford to keep them all.

Widows' and disability pensions helped, with a scattergun assortment of benefits, but these were fairly rudimentary during and immediately after the war, and women routinely received less than men. We have just been admitted into 'the larger world', Lady Rhondda told her female readers in her first *Time and Tide* editorial, and we need work to do. Seasoned by four years' labour on the home front and abroad, armed with a vote (some of them) and given a fanfare by the SDRA, women were poised at the brink of this new decade to enter the stage and start playing their parts as responsible wage-earning citizens. 'A person shall not be disqualified by sex or marriage from the exercise of any public function,' runs the wording of the Act, 'or from being appointed to or holding any civil or judicial office or post, or vocation, or for admission to any incorporated society (whether incorporated by Royal Charter or otherwise).' Welcome to our world, ladies, it seems to say. Welcome, and come along in.

When I explain to people the subject of this book – pioneering women in the traditional professions – there is a predictable response. It is usually accompanied by a wink, actual or implied. Ah yes. Professional women. We all know what *that* means: after all, what's the oldest profession in the world? And it is true; women have been sex workers for ever. I have tried describing it as a book about working girls instead, but that doesn't help. Even today, the term 'working girl' is a euphemism for prostitute. Other jobs have traditionally been associated with women. Domestic service is one of them. According to the 1901 census, slightly less than a third of females in England and Wales from the age of ten were in paid employment. Of those, 40.5 per cent were in domestic service, as menials, highly responsible chatelaines and everything in between. By 1921, the proportion in service had fallen to 33 per cent. Then, in descending order of popularity, came the textile industries (12 per cent); seamstresses and tailors (11 per cent); shopkeepers and assistants (9 per cent); clerks (8 per cent); and teachers (4 per cent), with the remaining 23 per cent shared out sparsely among a variety of other often localized trades or businesses, including the manufacture of silk buttons in Cheshire, of pins in Gloucester, and of lace in Nottinghamshire and parts of Buckinghamshire; acting, nursing, architecture, engineering and medicine.[3]

In 1920, the political profile of women in the textile industry, and in other factory environments, was growing. The Women's Industrial Council was founded in 1894, a year after Clara Collet was appointed the Board of Trade's first women's labour correspondent. Miss Collet was an economist, a close friend of the Marx family who first trained as a teacher and then – after taking a master's degree in Mental and Moral Science at University College, London – emerged as a social and educational reformer and one of the Civil Service's first women of influence. Among the Industrial Council's investigators were Karl Marx's daughter Eleanor and Dr Louisa Martindale's younger sister Hilda. They worked with the women's trade unions to bring to politicians' attention the inequalities and inhumane conditions of life for working women in the industries, and to lobby for legislative reform, long before they had a voice in Parliament.

There were several other organizations designed, if not to change the world for working women, at least to keep them as safe as possible in the world as it was. The Women's Protective and Provident League was a late Victorian umbrella organization encouraging the formation of trade unions for women in a range of different occupations; 'friendly' and 'sick' societies were cooperative savings banks-cum-insurance companies, while organizations like the Women's Co-operative Guild and the various suffrage associations demonstrated the power of mutual support and solidarity. Most were founded and/or run by women, and played a supportive role in episodes like the dispute at London's Royal Army Clothing Depot in 1879, when 1,500 women were made redundant and then invited to re-apply for their old jobs at a lower wage, and the famous Bryant and May matchgirls' strike ten years later.

The first female factory inspectors were appointed in 1893 – all two of them. It was their job to visit firms around the country to make sure that the machinery was not unnecessarily dangerous for women; that the shop floor and any accommodation provided were not overcrowded; that women were not asked to clean or repair equipment while it was still in motion (risking stray hair or clothing being caught up, with potentially fatal consequences) or expected to work unreasonable hours. Workers could appeal to them if they thought they had a case against their employers, but only on health grounds – not, for example, on the grounds of decency: it couldn't be helped if there was no ladies' lavatory, or if a woman had to ask the male foreman for a key every time she needed to use it, or even if there was no door on the cubicle, which was not unusual. If your employer neglected to inform you of your right to speak to an inspector, you were voiceless, unless the inspector happened to have the time to make a visit and explicitly invite comment.

Inspector Isabella Ford from Leeds was appalled by the lack of welfare provision in the industrial sector, and encouraged women workers to join together to protest. She recognized that they were often the last to complain, whether through natural reticence, fear of retribution for making a fuss, or a sense of despair. She supported the appointment of qualified women medical officers, not only to check the general health of females when they were first employed – often still children – but to keep on checking. Miss Ford lobbied for these medicals to be carried out in a separate room from the men's, and for intimate examinations to be conducted by women, in private.

It is ironic that while people like Clara Collet, Hilda Martindale and Isabella Ford were campaigning for the dignity of working-class women, they were themselves, as pioneering professionals, subject to the sort of bigotry that beggars belief. In 1918 there was a debate about the possibility of women being admitted to the higher grades of the Civil Service – itself described as the ultimate gentlemen's club[4] – via the same application process as men. The Civil Service Commissioner at the time was splenetic.

> Do you think that merely because a woman is equal to a man in competitive examinations, therefore she is his equal or vice versa? . . . It is like comparing Chinamen with Englishmen, or Hindus with Englishmen, or Hindus with Chinamen.[5]

As the 1920s progressed, women's trade unions tended to be amalgamated with men's, but organizations like the National Union of Societies for Equal Citizenship (NUSEC) – formed as a successor to the National Union of Women's Suffrage Societies by Millicent Fawcett in 1919 – continued to press for equality of opportunity in the workplace (including the Civil Service) and for closure of the gender pay gap: still work in progress a century later.

There was a special clause about the Civil Service – 'the State made flesh'[6] – on the very first page of the SDRA. To please the mandarins and stave off the revolution, it was stipulated that this bureaucratic leviathan should be exempt from the terms of the Act in respect of the conditions on which women were admitted, and those on which women already appointed were to continue in employment. They should not be paid the same as men, even if occupying a similar position or grade; nor should they expect to serve overseas in the Foreign Office. Some posts could be reserved exclusively for men. It was not until after the Second

World War that women emerged as diplomats. Before then, they were not considered the 'right type' of person to represent Great Britain (Queens Elizabeth I and Victoria notwithstanding). A woman wasn't really 'one of us'.

It might come as a surprise, therefore, to learn that in 1920 more than half the entire staff of the Civil Service was female. The Post Office had been employing women clerks and telegraph or telephone operators since the 1870s; more recently, typists had swarmed into just about every branch of the Home Office. They were a success: 'The girls are not only more teachable, more attentive, and quicker-eyed than the men clerks formerly employed, but . . . more trustworthy, more easily managed, and . . . sooner satisfied with lower wages.'[7] Most of them were assumed to come from lower-middle-class or middle-class 'fish-fork' families (so called because they aspired to own sets of those completely useless utensils, dreamed up and marketed by cutlers, in order to appear refined; the upper classes never used fish forks). They were required to be single on appointment and to remain single while in post. There were opportunities for advancement, but not at the same salary or the same speed as their male counterparts; women were not eligible for promotion until between six months and eight years later than men at the same stage of their careers. This was definitely a case of gentlemen before ladies.

Being a clerk in the Civil Service could be tedious, but that was no problem: women were said to have a much higher boredom threshold than men. They had less going on in their lives; less going on in their heads. 'It is always the man who sits at the big desk with the telephone and the woman who sits at the little desk with the typewriter,' noted the feminist writer Winifred Holtby.[8] Still, at least the typist had a job, and money to spend at one of those glamorous new department stores, a café or a dancehall or the cinema – if she had time, after her long working day.

A handful of women did manage to appropriate the big desk.

After 1922 females were allowed to sit the entrance exam for the higher administrative grades alongside males; but even before that, a few brave individuals worked for the Board of Trade, the Treasury and elsewhere. Some of them found their way in under wartime conditions; but others, such as Gwyneth Bebb Thomson, Hilda Martindale, Maria Smith and Adelaide Anderson, were all appointed before 1914. We already know about Hilda's childhood as Louisa's sister; Hilda was also sent to Royal Holloway College by her mother, but with no vocation in mind. She trained herself afterwards to work with and on behalf of children in care, attending public lectures on hygiene and sanitation, designing herself an extensive reading list and amassing work experience in children's homes, including Dr Barnardo's, and with charities.

Hilda met Adelaide Anderson, one of the Home Office's first women factory inspectors, at a lecture Hilda gave about social services abroad on returning from her round-the-world tour with Louisa and their mother. Miss Anderson head-hunted Hilda, who remained with the Civil Service until retirement in 1937, by which time she was in charge of more than 80,000 women across the entire organization. Conveniently, she never married – which meant she could keep her job. She wrote a book in 1938, *Women Servants of the State*, generously dedicated to those men who had encouraged her and other women to follow the career of their choice. It was an honourable gesture: sometimes it is too easy to forget that this battle to win professional recognition, like the battle for the vote, was not drawn up strictly on gender lines. Some women deplored the idea of females in the professions; and male allies were invaluable.

Adelaide Anderson – later Dame Adelaide – was one of Hilda's heroines. She was tiny and looked impossibly frail, yet navigated herself to the top of her profession from Melbourne, Australia (where she was born), by way of Girton College, Cambridge, becoming a private tutor, lecturing to members of the Women's

Hilda Martindale.

Co-operative Guild at the suggestion of her friend Isabella Ford and progressing through the ranks of the Civil Service to become Her Majesty's Chief Inspector of Factories in 1897. Her colleague Maria Smith – as tall as Adelaide was short – was already a Superintendent of Women in the Post Office Savings Bank at the age of twenty-two. Millicent Fawcett's husband Henry, who was Postmaster General at the time, considered Miss Smith 'one of the ablest officials in the postal service'.[9] She was somewhat stern, disinclined to suffer fools gladly and frighteningly incisive.

Certain photographs of Hilda Martindale suggest a serene and even ethereal personality. In reality these 'biggish women'[10] must have had at their disposal a powerful arsenal of confidence, tact, ambition and integrity. There were so many grounds for criticism: too manly (usually implied by someone like Maria Smith being described as 'statuesque' and 'reserved'); too girly

('Miss Fluffy Femininity'[11]); too clever ('women were such beastly swotters'[12]); too stupid ('temperamentally suited to routine work'[13]) – or just too womanly, posing 'grievous moral dangers'[14] to the rest of the staff. Thanks to them, those who joined the Civil Service in the 1920s did at least have a selection of role models, even though the restrictions stipulated by the SDRA suggested that the career trajectory for ambitious women in the Home Office might not be quite as steep in the years to come as it had been in the past.

The Civil Service was not the only employer of secretarial staff in these years. Offices everywhere were slowly filling up with flappers, or what the writer Arnold Bennett sneeringly called 'salary-earning girls' whose only interest (according to him) was in making and spending money. 'The typists were not the girls one married,'[15] he remarked, probably failing to appreciate that this might have been as much to do with their fear of redundancy as with any perceived lack of charm. There were very few salaried occupations for women around 1920 that were not confined in some way – officially or customarily – to spinsters or widows. We shall explore the impact of the 'marriage bar' later: it was huge. Medicine could be an exception, especially when husbands and wives went into practice together, as Drs Frances and George Hoggan did. But nursing, for example, relied on single women who were often required to be resident at their places of work, unless they ventured into the community as district nurses or midwives.

Florence Nightingale's career as a nurse was rooted in the time she spent at Kaiserwerth in Germany, where an order of celibate Protestant deaconesses cared for the sick. For the rest of her life and well beyond, nursing assumed a vocational, almost spiritual aura. It is no coincidence that nurses were called 'sisters', like nuns. The quasi-religious ethos attracted thousands of women to this most feminine of professions, while deterring others who considered themselves too worldly for such a special calling. In fact, her influence could be considered unhelpful to others trying to find a place in the working world. It was the opinion of a high-ranking teacher that 'the over-zeal of Miss Florence Nightingale affected all the pioneer women of the time in other professions and many young teachers were called upon for, and responded to, efforts far beyond their strength and suffered accordingly.'[16]

The war changed society's attitude to nursing, transforming it from a sacred duty into a supremely practical means of improving, even saving, people's lives. For many years nursing was one of the three alternatives – maybe four – girls were habitually offered on leaving school as a stop-gap before marriage: secretary, nurse, teacher – and hairdresser. That is the exclusive quartet I was offered by my careers adviser in the late 1970s. I instinctively took against all four choices, desperate to be different, and so failed to realize how fulfilling they might be. Of course, added the adviser, I might want to go to university if my parents could spare me; but a degree was no guarantee of job satisfaction, or even a job. Why bother?

For many, teaching was the best bet, despite the depressing fact that, because of the marriage bar, the average working life of a woman teacher was shockingly brief. At least it was respectable and influential; there were plenty of places available, and if one remained single it could be a job for life. All these were attractive propositions not just for young women looking for a career in the early 1920s, but for their fathers, faced with having to support them at home.

Lesley Thornbird, a young woman from Croydon, became a teacher at just this time.

> It wasn't my choice, you know, not really. At 14 my father said to me, 'You're growing older and you must make up your mind what you're going to do.' And his attitude was that . . . it was your duty to leave the world a little bit better than you

found it, so you should be doing something towards the bet-
terment of the world . . . I was sitting playing the piano when
he had this serious talk to me, and I turned round to face him
and got cramp in my thigh. And my father was one of those
people you couldn't let on, you know, I was hanging on to my
thigh and trying to answer his question. Anyway, he said I'd
got to make up my mind . . . So I went to mother and I said,
'What can I do?' I'd no idea what I wanted to be. 'Well,' she
said, 'make a list of all the things you can think of.' So I made
my famous list, my famous list was teaching, nursing or office
work. Now I don't think that there were any other openings
at the time, were there? So I couldn't face being an office stool
and that came out; I couldn't – I really didn't fancy nursing,
so that came out; so I said I wanted to be a teacher but, you
know, it wasn't really true.[17]

Lesley put down on the application form for training that she
would like to teach girls, rather than infants. When questioned
about this decision, she artlessly replied, 'My father said any fool
can teach infants.' This meant that on student-teacher placements
in schools she found herself in charge of a class of fourteen-year-
old girls, despite being only sixteen herself. She put her hair up
and tried very hard to look old.

There were several well-worn paths into the teaching profession at the beginning of the twentieth century. Under the
pupil–teacher scheme (think Jane Eyre) established in 1846, girls
officially left school at thirteen and were then apprenticed to the
same school or another for five years. After that they could apply
for one of the popular Queen's (later King's) scholarships which
financed a course at teacher-training college on condition they
remained in the profession for five years after qualification. After
1902, Local Education Authorities (LEAs) were set up to provide
and supervise more training colleges, and organize the allocation
of teaching posts in their region. There were still plenty of

unqualified teachers about, however, working in elementary or private schools. Perhaps they had degrees; perhaps just a burning (or vague) desire to equip young people to lead useful lives. Whichever it might be, if you had no qualifications as a woman in teaching, it was pretty certain that you needed money instead, either to set up your own school or to supplement your income as a low-grade employee.

You were unlikely to earn a high salary as a teacher in 1920, unless you were a headmistress, which was extremely unlikely in any LEA secondary school before the Second World War because men traditionally appropriated the top posts. The NUWT was set up in 1909 to lobby for equal pay and encourage its members not to roll over quietly in the presence of their assertive male colleagues but to fight to prove their worth. Teaching was always heavily politicized, thanks to the leadership of suffragists like Emily Phipps and the reforms of those anxious to feed more young women into universities at both undergraduate and postgraduate levels. Even private governesses had their own union in 1912, benefiting as self-employed people from the shared experience of their members.

A Yorkshirewoman called Daisy never forgot the abject poverty of her early career. Unlike Lesley, she *had* fancied being a nurse, but suffered from rheumatism which meant (she supposed) that she would have to settle for something else. Teaching appeared the only alternative. After training college she was offered a job in London, but she and her family could not afford the high living costs of the capital city. She had a younger brother who was due to go to college after her. If she accepted the London job he would be denied his chance: it was one or the other. So she stayed in Sheffield instead.

I can't remember what the annual pay was but I remember receiving my first salary. The man came with a Gladstone bag and you all went in . . . I was bottom on the list . . . And I remember feeling very sad and almost weeping because I couldn't afford to buy myself an umbrella.[18]

It rains a lot in Sheffield.

Another young schoolmistress, Amy Barlow, could hardly tell the difference between being a pupil and being a teacher. At the boarding school where she first worked, staff were allowed two baths a week; she shared a bedroom with two others; there was only porridge for breakfast and hard-boiled eggs for lunch every day; and nowhere was warm enough to dry her washing except the kitchens, which meant everything she wore smelt of cabbage and onions, however clean. And she was expected to tidy the school once a week. 'Teach?' scoffed a friend when Amy began her training. 'I'd rather sweep a crossing.'[19]

If teaching appealed to (some) young women and their parents, it was not always a popular vocation with suitors. If you became involved with a young teacher, the stakes were high. When things got serious, she was going to have to choose between you and her job, at least until she had worked off her scholarship. In an era when it was traditional for married women to stay at home, this might not have appeared too much of a problem. But in 1920, traditions were crumbling everywhere one looked: ask the old-school surgeons, or those Masters at the Inns of Court. Expectations were changing. There is no record of whether the educationalist Lilian Faithfull, who nurtured the minds of generations of young women before 1921, ever had to make that choice. In many ways she was the archetypal Victorian pedagogue. *Punch* published a cartoon in the 1880s of a desiccated-looking schoolmistress (inexplicably wearing dark glasses) admonishing a pupil. 'I wonder what your mother would say if she knew how backward you are in Geography?' she asks. 'Oh, my mother says she never learnt Jogfry and she's married, and Aunt Sally says *she* never learnt Jogfry and *she's* married; and you did and you ain't.' This was the popular image of someone like Lilian Faithfull, wedded to her job because no man would have her.

The reality was different. Miss Faithfull was unimpeachable; a pillar of society who became a Justice of the Peace and Fellow of King's College London and who lived for her work. Yet she was modern, engaged, attractive and much loved. Her academic career began in 1883 when she went up to Oxford to read English. One of eight children, she was taught by her uncle who ran a boys' prep school at which Lilian was the only girl pupil. At the time Oxford did not award women degrees; if they had, Lilian – like Gwyneth Bebb Thomson – would have left with a first. Normally the knowledge that one had taken the appropriate exams and achieved a particular result was enough – it had to be – but some 'graduates' understandably wanted more formal recognition. Lilian was one of them. She sailed to Dublin as a 'steamboat lady', taking advantage of Trinity College's offer to give degrees *ad eundem* to any Oxbridge woman who had earned one.

She taught for a while at Oxford High School, and then in 1889 was appointed a lecturer in English Literature at Royal Holloway College, where she briefly overlapped with Hilda Martindale. Next came a highly successful stint as Vice-Principal of King's College (Ladies' Department) in London. When she arrived, King's was little more than a venue for lectures; thirteen years later it had become an academically progressive university college with its own hall of residence, a flourishing extra-mural programme (Lilian was a gifted hockey player herself) and a speciality in teacher training.

In 1906 Lilian was persuaded to apply for the terrifying post of headmistress at Cheltenham Ladies' College, as successor to Miss Dorothea Beale. Allowed to visit the best-known girls' school in the country incognita before committing herself, she was quickly beguiled by the air of 'busy leisure and leisurely business',[20] where no bells rang and the girls were expected to take responsibility for themselves, and took the job. At Cheltenham Lilian was held in great affection, 'very nearly' learning all her pupils' names, making herself accessible to them and to her staff, always looking discreetly fashionable, and caring for the well-being of the whole school with kindness. She remembered having to tell a heartbreaking number of pupils during the war years that their fathers or brothers had been lost in action: it was one of the hardest parts of her job. But her pupils recalled those difficult times with gratitude; she was so gentle and wise, with a soothing voice and obvious compassion.

Lilian, who described herself as 'one of the first generation of professional women', was well aware of the pitfalls of being a high-profile female leader. Married male teachers had it much easier: they had wives at home to feed them and to worry about domestic and family cares. Men also, she considered, possessed greater stamina to deal with the rigours of a long, unbroken day. Lilian was nothing if not pragmatic, however. Instead of a wife she found a really good maid: 'one of the best gifts that Providence can send to any professional woman'. And she unfailingly took a nap every day after lunch.

It was in Lilian's nature to be generous. She was keen to share the fruits of her experience as a career woman. Choose an inscrutable, unemotional secretary who does not take things personally, she advised. 'We all have our moods,' and the last thing you need, when you're in one, is an oversensitive right-hand woman dabbing her eyes at you reproachfully. Make sure your work is as varied as it can be, otherwise you'll lose enthusiasm (which is infectious) and become a 'dull dog'. Do something completely different in the holidays. That is when you can catch up with your precious family and indulge a hobby – hers was antique collecting. 'Probably the most priceless possession in life generally, and in professional life in particular, is a strong sense of humour, with which is allied a sense of proportion. It changes the whole aspect of the day.'

Her sense of humour does not seem to have deserted her during her working life; it was only when she retired that the darkness set in. She did not express this in so many words, but it is implicit in her reminiscences that to her, the hardest thing about having a career was *not* having a career any more. She thought it a duty to pass on 'posts which are prizes in the profession' and let someone else have the experience she enjoyed. Therefore she retired in her late fifties. But no work meant no holidays; every day was the same. She wasn't needed any more. She imagined this was what a mother must feel like when her children had left home. It was so quiet, all of a sudden. 'The silence is something like the silence of death.'

Lilian wrote that last sentence in 1924, only a couple of years into her retirement – which lasted some thirty years and, after this short, dispiriting lull, was full of action and achievement. And hardly silent: she developed an interest in fast cars and motoring, and founded an 'Under-Forty Club' to involve young professional women in practical philanthropy and social work. So here was another inspirational role model to add to the pack.

Careers advice, like sex education, was almost non-existent in girls' schools before the Second World War. Vague exhortations to make your parents proud or help people, mirroring oblique advice not to disgrace yourself or let a boy go 'too far', were of little use. Being told that it was your duty 'to make the best use of the talents – taking talents in the widest sense – which nature has given'[21] did not help clarify what you were to do with your life. Between the 1890s and the 1930s a plethora of books about Careers for Girls appeared, all spotlighting a corps of traditional professions discussed with varying degrees of optimism, and then introducing a supporting cast of increasingly unlikely extras. It is as though the editors of these books were in tacit competition to lure young women into the most recherché job imaginable. A series of interviews for *The Queen*, a women's journal, was published in 1895. The editor, Margaret Bateson, is heavily prejudiced against clerical jobs. Who wants to 'waste the glamour of life's June in a musty study or a fusty office'? Instead she suggests becoming a homoeopath or a stockbroker, or trying journalism (like her) – which she describes as 'vulgar to the vulgar, sordid to the sordid, prosy to the prosaic, entertaining to the humorous and beautiful to them that love beauty'.[22] She has no patience with anyone who discourages young women from having careers on the grounds of a corresponding dereliction of domestic duty. 'All roads lead to the altar,' she complains. 'The professional woman who, I frankly concede, is often in no hurry to reach the bourne, has my sympathies when she chooses the longer way in order to enjoy the journey as she goes.'[23]

Emily Forster was more expansive in her *ABC of Careers for Girls* (1922). After rattling through architecture (expensive), medicine (even more expensive), law (where you are 'bound to have a pretty hard time'), and engineering (a great idea), she moves on to careers one hardly knew existed. Why not train as a scent blender? An historical dress designer? A film censor, perhaps? Elsewhere readers are informed that 'Girls Make Good Dog Doctors'[24] and are also quite acceptable at horticulture, administering patents, arranging window displays – and hairdressing.

Writing books about how to earn a living was all very well, but they did not materially help to place women in employment. In August 1919 – some ten years after the first labour exchanges were established for men – the Ministry of Labour had a more constructive idea: to set up a register of professional women in need of jobs and attempt to match them with vacancies. Now that the demobilization process was complete, it was possible to see clearly how many people were genuinely unemployed, and who they were. Thirty thousand educated women were currently working in temporary posts or not at all, most of them having previously done war work full-time. One solution to the economic problem they posed was to send them abroad. From the seventeenth century to the twentieth, government-sponsored emigration has repeatedly figured as one way of dealing with a surplus or problematic population, whether a glut of distressed gentlewomen in the 1850s, for instance, or too many illegitimate children: all could conveniently be dispatched to Australia or Canada as cheap labour.

The professional women's register did offer advice on resettlement abroad, but warned its clients that they might not be able to travel straight away, as shipping was still needed for more urgent business in the aftermath of war. They should not trust anyone who promised them a large salary, and should be prepared to do domestic work, as that was just about all that was available at present. However, the register's organizers concentrated their energies on finding work – and candidates to do it – in Great Britain.

At the end of January 1920 an internal report was produced on the registry's progress during the first six months of its existence. It listed the vacancies of which it had been notified – all rather specialized and none very lucrative. Here is a selection of what was on offer, with the annual salaries approximated to today's values:

Resident Assistant Matron with Domestic Science Diploma
for Orphanage £2,400

Resident Superintendent of Hostel for English Girls on the
Stage in Paris £4,500

Editor of a Missionary Journal £6,000

Graduate at the National Physical Laboratory £7,500

Resident Private Secretary to a Composer £4,500

The final two – of some forty-five situations in all – lacked any information about pay:

> Research worker in Archaeology with knowledge of French and German and experience of reading in British Museum.
>
> Governess to a Cabinet Minister's daughter.[25]

Except for Margaret Bateson's *The Queen*, most of the popular magazines on the market in 1920 agreed that the highest vocation of all for a woman continued to be motherhood, which naturally meant acquiring a husband to support you. The Victorian ideal of a feminine domestic sphere had dissipated somewhat during the war, but there were still those who thought that encouraging women to work outside the home was unpatriotic and unnatural. It had been a desperate remedy for desperate times; now more than ever, when families needed making whole again, spinsters were expected to marry if they possibly could and produce 'A1' children, plentiful and strong enough to protect the nation in the future.

In many ways it was too late for that. However strenuously reactionaries tried to hustle VADs or surgeons, munitions workers or ambulance drivers, spies or strategists back behind their front doors, feminism had taken root. It was growing steadily, nurtured by the campaign for women's suffrage and by the harsh and energizing realities of the war. Pandora's Box was open.

I saw a book at an antiques fair recently which I thought might illustrate nicely the status quo for 'ordinary' middle-class women at the beginning of the 1920s. It was a diary for housewives, published for the following year by Charles Letts and Company in 1920, claiming to contain 'a mass of useful information to all Housekeepers . . . a perfect system of Household Accounts, and [slightly alarmingly] an Insurance against accidents for £1000'. It attracted me as a document of social history, because it revealed what society thought important for women to know at the time. I leafed my way through the advertisements for Ideal Milk ('whole Milk and nothing but Milk'), for Morton's furniture and pianos, Dr J. Collis Browne's Chlorodyne ('Cuts short attacks of Spasms, Hysteria, Palpitation') and Polivit silver polish. Then came a series of post-war appeals for the Salvation Army, the Royal Merchant Seamen's Orphanage, the Friends' Emergency and War Victims' Relief Committee and Battersea Dogs' Home. The 'mass of useful information' included features on baby care, descriptions of new gadgets for the kitchen, a glossary of French names for food (with which to dazzle the boss and his wife when they come to dinner, presumably) and advice on poultry and rabbit-keeping: rationing had only recently come to an end, and some foods were still comparatively scarce.

There were copious numerical tables explaining how family doctors arranged their fees (amputation of a leg, arm, foot or hand cost £5); how to calculate the due date of a baby; which lessons should be read at church for every Sunday of the year; and postal collection times. First aid hints followed, with a list of abstruse antidotes to various poisons, and recipes for such delicacies as French Soup (made from, among other things, dripping, turnip, lettuce and a lump of sugar) and Mock Scallops (bits of boiled Jerusalem artichoke covered in anchovy-flavoured white sauce and baked with breadcrumbs on top; you could use your fish knives to enhance the illusion).

If the housewife had any time for leisure, she could consult seating plans for every London theatre or a map of the Zoo. She could decide when to go to the theatre or the Zoo by consulting the information on term dates for public, private and council schools (very broad-minded) and a list of public holidays. And she could work out whether she could afford such treats by referring to the advice on how to keep accounts and when it is necessary to repay war loans. A 'Household Ready Reckoner' gave her an ingenious way of working out butchers' bills – if meat was 3d per pound, for example, she could rapidly find out how much 7lb 5oz would cost (one shilling and tenpence-farthing, for the record).

Just as important as everything else was a section on 'Useful Toilet Hints' imparting the secrets of banishing freckles – you simply bleached them away – and getting rid of greasy skin. That was a little more complicated, involving rubbing the face with porridge in the morning and then wiping it with cucumber skins two or three times a day. 'To avoid wrinkles a cheerful disposition should be cultivated and worry over trifles avoided.'

This sort of thing is just what I love to furnish the background of my books. But this diary offered a bonus: it had been used, by a woman called Adèle Mager from Purley in Surrey. Social history was instantly transformed into a personal story. I learned how much Adèle spent on food, beer and wine, children's clothes and a haircut. Intimate details of her budget were carefully laid out: an expensive new hat cost eight shillings (and a hairnet elevenpence); stockings were another eight shillings; a window cleaner cost two shillings a month and her library fine in March was twopence; she paid two shillings to take part (unsuccessfully) in a Grand National sweepstake; one shilling and fourpence for face cream; half a crown for a bottle of whisky; and three shillings and sixpence for a Golliwog Book.

I know how much she paid for a cab into town and what she and her husband Len went to see when they got there: a play called *Sunday* put on by the Barclay's Bank Amateurs. Adèle and Len had two children, a baby and an older boy; she noted when the baby first spoke, and when the toddler got a new pair of boots. She was able to afford resident child care – nurses (or nannies) came and went – and a maid. The family went on holiday to Bognor in the summer, not for a fortnight but for three whole months. Both the children and the adults seemed constantly to be

fighting colds, croup or 'Flue'. In fact their first-born infant did
not survive; Adèle took flowers to the grave on the anniversary of
'dear little Baby''s death on 3 March.

Aunts and uncles visited regularly; there was a cryptic note
tucked between the pages from one who had not managed to get
to Purley for a while. Reading it is like eavesdropping:

> My dear Adèle, Your letter this morning was a real pleasure.
> I am often thinking about you all. Dear little Peter I should
> love to see. I hope to see you all again if I live a little longer.
> Sometimes I think my life will soon be over, the cold I feel it
> to almost finish me. I cannot tell you how very much we
> regret we cannot say come on Friday. I am feeling very tired
> you must excuse more. I am leaving it to Gertie to tell you our
> great trouble that we cannot say . . . With more love than I
> can express for you all, Your Old Aunt, Edith Lill.

Adèle and Len often went out with friends or as a couple for
picnics and cycle rides in the country, while Nurse looked after
the children. The sight of the first skylark was carefully recorded,
and the sound of the first cuckoo. Spring cleaning took everyone more than a week. There was a shortage of coal during a
chilly May because of the miners' strike. The comment 'went to
see Lord Richard in the pantry' flummoxed me for a while,
until I realized that this was a play by Sidney Blow, written in
1918.

The more I read, the more I wanted to know about Adèle's
life. I bought the diary, of course; it is open in front of me as I
write, at the page where the toddler goes to the dentist for the
first time and has to have two fillings. He is awfully well behaved.
I have since discovered that Adèle (*née* Schnetzler) came from
Sheffield; that her husband Leonard was a solicitor; that their dead
baby was called Joan; and that one of the 'darling' sons she writes
about in the diary later went on to do well at Malvern College

school, worked as an insurance broker at Lloyd's of London, married – and was killed during the Second World War in 1944.

Most modern women ('modern' being a euphemism for feminist) saw their entry into the professional workplace as part of an evolution; something they could demonstrate would lead to the progress of civilization, given time. But it is important to remember that not all women in 1920 were modern women. Some were housewives like Adèle, doing their best to pick the embers out of post-war life and get on with being wives and mothers. Perhaps the greatest gift of the SDRA was the remote possibility it offered to women of making a choice about how they spent their lives and earned their money.

4

Biggish Women

THE PIONEERS

To dream and not make dreams the master, or yet lose sight of them in everyday life, is very hard indeed. That's the problem of being a pioneer.[1]

THERE IS A danger, when studying the lives of women in the past, of assuming that masculinity automatically conferred a silver spoon at birth, and that gender was as much an advantage to men as it was a disadvantage to women. The fight for the vote was all about giving women a voice, we say, forgetting that before 1918 millions of men were also silenced by disenfranchisement. Female undergraduates might not have been allowed into British universities before 1869, but that was only a few years after Jewish men were admitted to Oxbridge, and before Roman Catholics and nonconformists could take up fellowships there. It was difficult for men without means and influence to become doctors, lawyers, architects and the like at the beginning of the twentieth century; that is not in doubt. But women, who shared men's handicaps, had one more: their gender. This is not a history of 'them' and 'us'; it is about natural justice.

The point of the SDRA was to place women who aspired to be members of chartered professional associations on an equal footing with those of the male élite who already were. The job was only half done in 1919. As we have seen, the Civil Service was specifically exempted and the Act was framed in such a way that academics at Cambridge, for example, were able to resist both the spirit and the letter of the law for another thirty years. It was designed to foil a more radical Private Member's Bill, the Women's Emancipation Bill, introduced earlier that year by the Labour MP Benjamin Spoor, which would have granted women the franchise on equal terms with men and the right to sit in the House of Lords as well as eligibility for civil and judicial appointments. In combination with separate Bills enabling women to become lawyers and Justices of the Peace, which were progressing nicely through the House of Lords at the time, Spoor's legislation would have made it considerably easier for most of the women in this book to feel like valid members of society.

David Lloyd George and his Tory-dominated coalition quashed all three Bills with the introduction of the more circumspect SDRA, which though ground-breaking – notably in its provision for women to sit as jurors and magistrates for the first time – still delivered less than it promised. 'Into every avenue of life into which women have advanced they have had to force the gates; they have never been opened from within,'[2] declared Lord Buckmaster, counsel for Gwyneth Bebb Thomson in her action against the Law Society in 1913. One could argue that the SDRA at least unlocked those gates, and maybe even oiled the hinges a little; but they remained heavy and forbidding.

Silver spoon or no, the route to a professional career for young men was clear-cut. There were four core requirements. First came *encouragement* from family and friends, bolstered by a classical *education* (and an education in Classics); this led to a formal period of *training*, followed finally by *qualification*. Then out into the world they went, with a network of useful contacts supporting them like a guiding hand in the small of the back (with a family signet-ring on the left little finger). There they would

LADY JURORS AT BATH QUARTER SESSIONS.

The Bath Chronicle *reports the city's first women jurors, October 1920.*

make their way, marry well, and expect the next generation of sons to do exactly the same as they had done. On such comfortable continuity are empires built.

How easy was it for women pioneers to follow the same path, once the 'no entry' signs had been removed? Some of them had a fortunate inheritance, too. Had engineer Rachel Parsons been her father Charles's son rather than his daughter, no one would have commented on her career choice. He was one of the most prosperous industrialists of his age, the inventor of the steam turbine engine. Yet eyebrows were raised and questions asked when his daughter followed him into the family business, even though to both parents it seemed the natural thing for her to do. They supported Rachel wholeheartedly.

Similarly, surgeon (and later Dame) Louisa Aldrich-Blake was brought up by her clergyman father and heiress mother to think that nothing was impossible for a woman. They taught her Euclid, how to swim, how to break in horses and always (in a nebulous way) to do her duty. Though she didn't go to school until she was sixteen, she never felt disadvantaged – or indeed particularly feminine, which helped. Known as Harry, she was a keen boxer, enjoyed a 'gentlemanly appearance' and in later life was described as 'a tall, massive individual who wore a stiff collar and tie like a man'.[3]

Perhaps she *was* a man? That's how some of her contemporaries – male and female – chose to explain her prodigious success. Privilege alone was not enough to propel a woman to the top of her chosen profession.

These two had both money and family support behind them. Others had one or the other. Octavia Wilberforce (1888–1963), the granddaughter of the Bishop of Oxford and great-granddaughter of abolitionist William Wilberforce, was enviably well connected. Yet when, at the age of twenty-three, she announced to the family her intention to enter medicine – worse still, to be a doctor, rather than a nurse – her mother had to call for the smelling-salts. What was Octavia thinking? Becoming a doctor would 'unsex' her; she wasn't robust enough to withstand the training; she was too old to begin a course at medical school (while too young to live away from home); this would waste the best years of her life; everyone else she came into contact with would be *middle-class*; and she would never have the satisfaction – palling rapidly for Mrs Wilberforce at the moment – of becoming a mother. Conversely, engineer Caroline Haslett's father was a railway signal-fitter with little money to spare and a determination not to let that compromise his daughter's education or ambition. This determination he shared with Hannah Billig's father, a Jewish cigarette-roller. Three of his children, including Hannah, became doctors.

It is fascinating to glance through admissions registers at the Inns of Court for the few years following the passing of the SDRA. Each registration form is printed, with spaces for the candidate's name, his father's name and occupation, and a signed declaration by referees that they 'believe him to be a gentleman of respectability'. 'Him' and 'gentleman' were usually crossed out in the case of female applicants – but not always. A random survey across the four Inns of Court from 1919 to 1925 reveals applications from daughters of a sugar manufacturer from Guyana; of several merchants; of many barristers and solicitors; and of a wool-broker, someone who made wallpaper, a rabbi, and a dead piano-builder. Solicitor Catherine Tietjen's father was a hotel waiter in London – she came first in the 1924 Law Society finals; Mary Pickup's was an engine-fitter, born in an East End slum.[4] It would be intriguing to know who financed these and other relatively impoverished women. Scholarships were still few and far between for women at any stage of their education, and it would take an extremely progressive philanthropist to favour an outstanding female candidate over a reasonably capable male one. Personal sponsorship was one possibility, though hard to find; working and studying part-time was another.

For some of the most successful women pioneers, self-motivation overrode family circumstances. Cornelia Sorabji was inspired by a community of voiceless women in India, where she grew up: upper-caste Hindus in purdah, not allowed to speak to men outside the close family and therefore unable to protect their own property or petition for basic rights. Cornelia would be their voice, their public face, their champion. Her barrister colleague Helena Normanton was another people's champion. She had had a difficult childhood; her father's body – he was the dead piano-builder – had been found on an underground railway line in 1886, his bag neatly stowed inside the carriage from which – it was surmised – he had jumped. Helena vowed to learn the law at the age of twelve after witnessing her widowed mother's confusion on visiting a solicitor. Mrs Normanton was obviously befuddled by his use of jargon and patronizing manner, but he noticed that Helena appeared to be following what he said. Perhaps the little girl could help you understand, he suggested to Mrs Normanton. Helena proceeded to explain the situation perfectly. My goodness, said the solicitor; quite the little lawyer, aren't you, dearie? She was indeed. Her extraordinary career offered her an escape from the ignorance and vulnerability of her mother's existence (and from their penury); explaining the law to other women was her payment for the privilege.

Helena Normanton.

Debutante Octavia Wilberforce's mission had its origin not in the insecurities of poverty but in boredom. A housemaid had a persistent cough. The family doctor decided it was just one of those things and would probably go away in time. The implication was that it wouldn't really matter if it didn't. Octavia was convinced there was something more serious wrong. She insisted on the maid having an X-ray – an expensive, new-fangled procedure in 1911 – and, with the help of her friend and neighbour Dr Louisa Martindale, diagnosed tuberculosis. Octavia organized a fund-raising concert for Louisa's Brighton hospital in gratitude, and meanwhile fell in love with medicine – at which point she had to face her horrified mother, the sal volatile to hand.

So much for encouragement. While a supportive family was obviously helpful for an ambitious woman, it was not sufficient on its own, and nor was money. A good education was crucial. Octavia was forced to acquire hers by stealth. As the eighth child of the family (the clue is in the name), she described her woeful schooling as 'second-hand'. Frustratingly, she lived near one of the best girls' schools in the country, Roedean, which pioneered the teaching of science to young women. She could easily have gone there had her parents chosen to send her. The opportunity was missed; after a couple of years elsewhere between the ages of sixteen and eighteen, Octavia went home to sit out that awkward period the *Girl's Own Paper* described as the '*mauvais quart d'heure*' between childhood and motherhood. 'When I was eighteen I would have married anything that might have asked me,'[5] she remembered – although the alliance would not have been much fun, as she was firmly of the opinion that love was a load of 'silly rot'. No one did ask her, and to fill the endless weeks of her 'tepid existence' Octavia bravely went to meet the headmistress of Roedean to ask for private coaching. Keeping this secret from her family, she decided after the episode of the housemaid's cough to sit for the matriculation exam at the London School of Medicine for Women. She failed the maths paper first time – and second time, and then again. Eventually she was allowed in anyway, as long as she passed the blessed thing before the end of her course. She got it on the sixth attempt, when she was twenty-eight.

Perhaps sensing defeat, her parents allowed her to remain at the LSMW, though they kept up a constant barrage of correspondence trying to persuade her to give up medicine and come home where she belonged, especially when her father died just after the third attempt at the maths exam. But Octavia was enjoy-ing the comparative freedom of her student life too much to surrender it. Everything about it was intoxicating. She spent her own money in the canteen, choosing what she wanted to eat – which is not something women of her class were used to doing: if at home, mother set the menus with Cook; if eating out, the men ordered for you. Hot lamb was a favourite at fourpence; potatoes, bread, butter and cheese all cost a penny, as did cheese-cake for dessert. Invariably, 'the cheesecake was a mistake'.[6] When a lesbian tried to seduce her she was staggered: she never knew such people existed. How thrilling. And she was making friends with the most inspiring people, among them Louisa Aldrich-Blake, whom Octavia described as good-natured and serene; someone who thought the surgeon's life the happiest in the world.

Louisa herself had barely had any more in the way of formal education than Octavia. She, too, was 'taught' at home (about Euclid and horses, you remember) until being sent to a local school at sixteen and thence to Switzerland to be 'finished'. She had no intention of finishing, however, and arranged for herself to attend Cheltenham Ladies' College (before Lilian Faithfull's time) and prepare for matriculation at the LSMW. She chose medicine because it was interesting and useful and she felt she could do it well, not as a particular vocation or to earn large amounts of money.

Eminent ophthalmologist Ida Mann had a somewhat more conventional education than Octavia and Louisa, though she didn't enjoy it much. Her mother, anxious about her daughter's health (for no discernible reason), terrorized the teachers – and, it seems, Ida herself: 'I wore a woolly body belt, and if I forgot to put it on Mother would run down the road waving it at me. Shame!'[7] Ida considered herself a free spirit, stuffing the mortifying corset and brassière Mother said she must wear at the back of a drawer in her bedroom. 'I hated underclothes,' she wrote cheerfully at the end of her life, 'and still do.'[8] Ida's father encouraged her obvious intelligence up to a point – he paid her for achieving good marks – but withdrew her from school at sixteen as a matter of principle, consigning her instead to a commercial college where she was expected to prepare for a career in the Post Office Savings Bank. She did as she was told and got the job, but hated it. Hundreds of clerks like her were expected to sit in rows in a vast hall doing the same dismal work day after day. It was almost Dickensian. She once witnessed a young woman 'go mad at her desk' before being carted off, never to be seen again. This was depressing, and the naturally buoyant Ida was often unwontedly ill.

One night, she had a dream. She could remember it only vaguely; it was something to do with summoning up the courage to open an unknown door to let the sunshine in. Soon afterwards she was invited to visit the London Hospital, after supporting a fund-raising event. Ida was excited by the prospect; she had always been keen on dolls as a child – not dressing them up in frilly frocks and having pretend tea-parties, but plonking them down in disarray on makeshift beds and dosing them with potions and a sadistic glint in her eye. Not the best attitude for a doctor to her patients, perhaps; but Ida's visit to the hospital convinced her that a career in medicine was what that dream was all about. She made herself an appointment to see those in charge of student admissions at the LSMW – for which she donned a business-like suit of brown gabardine, sensible shoes and an unlikely hat embellished with long pheasant tail-feathers – and got herself a place, passing the matriculation exam in the first division. She was ecstatic; and her parents, while surely dazed by her proactivity, paid what they could to help her on her way.

There seems to be a pattern developing here of pioneering women seeking out their own education – which is hardly surprising, given that systems for the rigorous teaching of girls were still in their infancy. Edith Morley became the first woman in England to hold a university chair, but the achievement isn't something one would have predicted for her. Her parents – a dental surgeon and his wife – had planned to engage a governess for their daughter, but Edith pleaded to be sent to school instead, where her favourite subject was natural history and her least favourite anything girly like needlework or dancing. At fourteen, as was usual for a young lady of her class, she was dispatched to a finishing school for three years − hers was in Germany − and was then expected to sit still until a suitable husband materialized from behind a chair in the drawing-room. Every afternoon she was required to accompany her mother and grandmother on a stultifying two-and-a-half-hour carriage ride. She passed the time doggedly trying to persuade them to let her study for a degree. Her first choice was Bedford College in London; that was vetoed because it would have meant Edith having to use public transport to get there and thus mix with the vulgar. King's College, then situated in Kensington Square, was more suitable: decorously chaperoned, she could walk there. She studied for the King's College matriculation exam by correspondence course, which her father sanctioned as long as she agreed to take cookery classes too.

Girls' education was handicapped until well beyond the First World War by a lack of opportunity to gain the working knowledge of science, maths and Classics that was necessary for studying almost *anything* at university. Only those with an 'unnatural' aptitude for the subjects, or the means to acquire coaching outside the usual channels, were able to tackle them. There had been some improvement in the 1870s, when standardized, nationwide co-educational exams were introduced, roughly equivalent to today's GCSEs and A-levels, but it took a few generations of university-trained women teachers to feed down into their schools an ethos of high achievement and capability in the core subjects of a previously male curriculum. And even when that happened, the education on offer had to be bought.

In many ways, Elizabeth Bryson (1880–1969) was lucky. Though she grew up in poverty, she did live close to St Andrews University in Scotland, which offered competitive bursaries to local students. However, only boys at her school were prepared for university entrance; girls were not thought worth teaching the necessary maths or Latin. When she was just ten years old, Elizabeth agitated for this to change. She sat a scholarship exam to Harris Academy, given in memory of his schoolboy son by a local benefactor. When she won it she was summoned to the town hall in Dundee for a congratulatory interview. What did she want to be when she grew up, Elizabeth was asked? A teacher, perhaps? No, replied Elizabeth firmly, a doctor. 'A doctor? Nonsense! Not a nice little girl like you!'[9]

Elizabeth tore through her school career with almost frightening precocity, winning a bursary to enter St Andrews at sixteen. No one there was allowed to study medicine until they were nineteen, so Elizabeth whiled away the interim by taking a first-class degree in English Literature.

It was not always necessary to possess a university degree in order to study medicine, as long as a medical school agreed to admit you. Ella Pringle, a secretary working at Edinburgh University typing up medics' MD theses, was so fascinated by the students' research that she decided to take up medicine herself. Her only qualifications beyond a basic education were enthusiasm, wide reading and determination. In time, she became the first female Fellow of the Royal College of Physicians in Edinburgh. It was the same with law. Of the first one hundred women to qualify as solicitors after 1920, only twenty-six were graduates.[10] The others served a five-year apprenticeship as articled clerks, often in the practices of family or friends. Architects followed a similar pattern – like the Charles sisters, Bessie and Ethel. They were both privately educated in India, where they were born, and in Europe; both went up to Somerville College, Oxford, together to read modern languages; and both left, restless (just like Lady Rhondda), after a year. Their real education began when they outlandishly chose to train as architects in 1892 and joined the high-profile practice of Sir Ernest George and Harold Peto in London.

Which brings us to training. The Charles sisters were the first women to be admitted as associate members of the Royal Institute of British Architects, Ethel in 1898 and Bessie in 1900, after fierce opposition from within. Their training had been necessarily unconventional. Though it helped that they were taken on by George and Peto, they were denied the other compulsory elements of an apprentice's training, including attendance at evening classes run by the Architectural Association. When they attended lectures at London University's Bartlett School (where Gertrude Leverkus was the first official female student a few years later) they could study architecture only as an art, not a science: that is, they learned about its history, appreciated its aesthetics and discussed its abstract principles, but were taught nothing about its practical application. In other words, they studied architecture, but not how to become architects. That was something they were left to glean from the stubble after their male peers had reaped the harvest of a full and specialized education.

Not only did the Charles sisters miss out on formal training, they never experienced the camaraderie of exploring a new subject in the company of others. Arguably medical students had the best of that experience among female professionals, as their numbers were greater. In 1920, immediately after the passing of the SDRA, most universities and hospital medical schools admitted women. St George's in London was an exception; it had closed its doors to them in 1919, implying that now the war was over, it didn't need them any more – and nor did the medical profession as a whole. There was no reason at the time to suspect that this was anything but an unfortunate one-off. Women surgeons and physicians had acquitted themselves with honour, courage and great skill during the war; many had then established private practices or secured hospital appointments and were eager to support the next cohorts of female students. The Medical Women's Federation (MWF), founded in 1879, was well supported and active in campaigning for the rights of its members in terms of equal opportunity and pay, and even the Royal Colleges were grudgingly beginning to accept a few women as members (though women Fellows remained few and far between).

However in 1921, the London Hospital also barred women students; St Mary's admitted no more after 1925; Charing Cross, Westminster and King's College Hospitals followed suit in 1928; and University College Hospital limited its intake of women to a meagre dozen each year. Thus the number of places available to women nationwide was slashed by half within a decade. The justification for trying to strangle women doctors at birth seemed perfectly acceptable to many male doctors at the time. Returning servicemen deserved every opportunity the country could afford them, and those who chose to enrol or to continue interrupted studies at medical school should not be hindered in any way. So far, so unarguable; but surely women might be accommodated as well as men? There was room for medical schools to grow, and an appetite among women practitioners and patients for more female doctors. And what about the SDRA? Ah, the Act's about lawyers, and anyway, it doesn't say we have to admit women; only that we can if we like. We know that while 100 per cent of men remain in the profession, only 50 per cent of women do. The other 50 per cent get married, so that's a waste of a good training. The MWF disputed this on the grounds that according to their statistics, collated after a survey of members, only 16 per cent of women medical students married, and of those, 6 per cent carried on working – which was a perfectly reasonable and even advantageous thing for a married doctor of either sex to do.[11]

Well, what about the quality of life for medical students, then? More women at medical school means fewer men from which to choose the rugby team, and every fool knows a school's reputation stands or falls on its prowess on the rugby field . . . Out came the old chestnuts, unearthed from their wartime burial, about men being embarrassed by women in the room while discussing 'delicate' body parts and conditions, or women indulging in mass vapours when confronted with a grisly medical scenario. The MWF wondered how men were going to cope in that case with female patients or in the company of nurses, and whether women doctors' heroic experiences on the battlefield had counted for nothing.

Despite lobbying, most of the medical schools mentioned above did not open their doors to women again until the end of the Second World War. Until then, female trainees had to make do with the LSMW, which became the Royal Free, or to study outside London. That's why most of the student reminiscences we have by medical women of the inter-war period describe life at the LSMW. Elizabeth Bryson was an exception: as we have seen, she studied in St Andrews – and then at Dundee, where male undergraduates used the impressive portal and entrance hall to a brand new students' union building, while females were required to slip in discreetly by the back door. Elizabeth didn't particularly mind; she was just glad to be there at all.

Had Ida Mann been at Dundee, one suspects she would have ignored the rules and made straight for the front door. As it was, in London she relished life as a trainee. She observed in a detached sort of way that she was not particularly popular; perhaps it was because of her consistently high marks, or the fact that she looked disturbingly eccentric. Ida devised herself a uniform (unlike poor Elizabeth Bryson, whose sole tweed skirt endured the whole of her student career, gradually getting shorter and shinier). It comprised a Norfolk jacket with lots of pockets for various bits and bobs of medical equipment, and a stout skirt. 'My suit was designed to last for years,' she remembered proudly, 'and was varied by different shirts and violently coloured stockings of emerald green, purple . . . or scarlet.'[12] She had her own skeleton, probably dug, as most were

at that time, from the battlefields of the Napoleonic wars. Her
teachers were exceedingly strong characters. Mr Clayton Green
was nicknamed 'Satan'. He was a brilliant surgeon,

> tall, hawk-faced, sardonic and ruthless, who spoke little and
> hated students . . . I well remember Duncan C. L. Fitzwil-
> liams, a dashing and drastic surgeon who had acquired the
> most artistic and extensive tattoos I have ever seen. The red,
> green and blue dragons encircling his muscular arms writhed
> and rippled as he moved . . . Sir Arbuthnot Lane had it in for
> the colon.[13]

On visits to St Mary's Hospital she was taught by Sir Almroth
Wright – a notorious misogynist, a virulent anti-suffragist and
altogether terrifying. Ida was unfazed. She dubbed him 'Sir
Almost Right' and was amused rather than offended that he managed never to speak directly to a female medical student – ever.

Sir Almroth Wright, like Sir Henry Maudsley (an eminent
psychiatrist and commentator on higher education for women),
was one of those old-school physicians who considered females
physiologically and emotionally incapable of meaningful intellectual activity. Maudsley's famous argument was that women
had a finite amount of life-force in their bodies, and that if they
spent it all on thinking, their wombs were likely to atrophy. By
the time people like Elizabeth Bryson and Ida Mann were studying
medicine, however, no concessions were made to their supposed
frailty. Ida appears to have had the constitution of an ox; but even
she got exhausted occasionally. During her training in domicil-
iary midwifery, when she was 'on call' for home confinements,
the lack of sleep was almost overwhelming. 'One ghastly morning I was pedalling along, with a splitting headache, the leg of my
pyjama pants hanging below my skirt, and a dead baby in a brown
paper parcel on the carrier, when the back wheel caught in a

tramline, and I fell in the mud.'[14] The parcel with its grim contents was catapulted into the road, and just as Ida was picking herself up and about to retrieve it, a policeman arrived.

Most of Peggy Kenyon's training took place before she even got to King's College Medical School. The First World War had just come to an end; she had spent it nursing wounded soldiers invalided to a 'Cripples' Home' in Baschurch, Shropshire. Peggy (1894–1979) was a volunteer who hoped one day to train as a nurse – but without much confidence. She could cope with the horror of it all – maggoty wounds; quiet sobbing at night – and responded well to her patients on a personal level. But she was notoriously absent-minded, constantly forgetting things. She was supposed to wear a blue overall on duty, buttoning at the back and open from the waist down; on one occasion she forgot to put a skirt on underneath. 'Our knickers were long and modest, but I felt very draughty.'[15] She was teased by one of her favourite patients, a self-educated miner from south Wales called Albert Bolton.

> He told me I was a dreamer and ignorant . . . and once made me very cross by saying all I had to do, at my exams, was to smile at the examiners. 'Your blue eyes will get you through.' 'You must take me seriously; I mean to train as a nurse, when the war is over.' He startled me by his reply: 'No – you must be a Doctor.' How I laughed.[16]

But her ward sister and her father persuaded Peggy to take Albert's advice; she secured a job as a physiotherapist and took a correspondence course to prepare her for matriculation while housekeeping for her (widowed) father in London.

Like Octavia Wilberforce, Peggy was challenged by the requirements of the entrance exam. 'I did wonder why a doctor should have to know so many irregular French verbs. Mathematics remained a hideous mystery.'[17] Nevertheless, she passed, and was immediately swept up in the excitement of being a student. She was tempted to join no fewer than thirteen societies in her first term, including the Wireless Society where one could learn Morse code – until she realized it was for men only. She went to a lecture given by Einstein and another by the exotic Bloomsbury artist Roger Fry; once she was asked by a fellow student to go to a PM with him at lunchtime and, imagining this to be a post-mortem, eagerly agreed; it turned out to be a prayer meeting.

If the social side of life was wonderful, more wonderful still was the work. She was entranced by dissecting an earthworm with its five pairs of tiny hearts and a crayfish whose liver looked like a yellow chrysanthemum. Exams were a necessary evil; if one tried not to panic (an ambition helped by smoking very many Wills Gold Label cigarettes) things usually worked out in the end. But this wasn't the case for everyone: there was an attrition rate in most of the professional training establishments attended by women, higher than that among men, perhaps, but only because women were more frequently recalled by their families to perform domestic duties at home, or if the family money looked as though it was running out. A daughter's aspirations were usually sacrificed in favour of her brother's.

Medicine and law had the most heavily structured training programmes of all the professions. When Gwyneth Bebb Thomson was accepted by Lincoln's Inn the day after the passing of the SDRA – and the day after her daughter's birth – her first obligation was to attend the Inn to present a £100 bond guaranteeing her good character and the monies due for her training. Gwyneth's bond was signed by Lord Buckmaster. She was required to explain why she would be unable to deliver it on 7 January, the date on which she had been invited to do so. 'I was admitted to a nursing-home as a patient on Monday last,' she wrote obliquely on 27 December (when the baby was four days old).[18] In those days new mothers who could afford it were confined for more than a fortnight after giving birth; Gwyneth reckoned she would not be free to visit Lincoln's Inn until at least 15 January. This delay meant that she was not the first woman to be admitted to training for the Bar; that honour went to Helena Normanton on 30 December 1919 at Middle Temple.

The next stage in a barrister's training was to 'keep term' by dining in Hall at one's Inn on a certain number of days in each of four terms, normally for three years. Helena found these dinners daunting. In some Halls, women were required to sit on a separate table, where – though set apart – they were keenly observed. Theodora Llewellyn Davies, an early student at Inner Temple, took her sister with her as far as the doors of the Hall for moral support when she went to her first dinner, and was much relieved when someone escorted her to the far end of the table to sit down, so that she wouldn't have to negotiate clambering over the middle of a long bench in her ankle-length skirt, with scores of spectators. Pioneers like her were minor celebrities, photographed in the papers with endless comments about being modern-day Portias. The *Daily Mirror* reported in January 1920 that Helena Normanton had suffered a mishap. 'Portia Breaks Rules At Dinner in Temple', gasps the headline. 'Nearly Fined a Bottle of Wine for Talking'. The text goes on to describe a howling faux pas at her first statutory dinner: she forgot the etiquette of the mess and actually attempted to speak to her neighbour. Shocking. But she was forgiven. After all, 'Miss Normanton is a charming young woman,' noted the *Daily Mirror*, 'very attached to her work.'

All would-be barristers were required to attend lectures and sit a series of exams on Roman and constitutional law; legal history; contract and tort; and property, company, common and criminal law, with papers on evidence and general legal procedure. If Helena had not had an acute coughing fit during one of her papers (thus failing it) she would have been the first woman to be called to the Bar. As it was, she was beaten by a 42-year-old academic, Dr Ivy Williams. Dr Williams was called in May 1922; unlike Helena, she never practised as a barrister, becoming a tutor and lecturer in Law at her old college, the Society of Home Students in Oxford, later known as St Anne's.

Robina Stevens was seventeen when she joined Gray's Inn from school in October 1920. There were only three other women there when she arrived, though she hoped there would be a few more by the time she was called to the Bar (if all went well) when she was twenty-one. Robina was a startlingly able trainee, running neck-and-neck in terms of exam results with her peer Hartley Shawcross, who later became Attorney General. Yet she was never complacent, which endeared her to her contemporaries, male and female. She kept a diary of her time at Gray's Inn in which she describes returning from the summer vacation in 1921 to prepare for her next exam. She's worried about revision. 'I have not done as much as I should have these hols. I have put the idea of a first out of my mind. Hope to goodness I get through.'

> *Oct. 4th*. So glad when the day for the exam at last arrived. I got up to Gray's Inn where the exam was to be held at 9.30 and while I was waiting outside talking to another lady from Middle Temple, [an usher] came up and said we could go into the cloakroom and he would knock on the door just before he let the others in.[19]

In other words, the women were offered sanctuary from male candidates and possibly the press, and the chance to occupy their (isolated) seats in advance.

> To my surprise, Mrs [Mary Selina] Jones came in. She had tried for the Constitutional Law [exam] the day before but came out without having done anything. But as she had only worked for both for three weeks I am not surprised. I quite liked the paper. The first question on Lunacy was so nice . . . After I finished

the paper I went to the common room for lunch with Mrs
Jones. Shawcross was there but he didn't seem to have liked the
paper much. He had made various bad mistakes.[20]

It would only be human nature, surely, for Robina to feel a little
smug at this stage. She got a first – but then she got a first in all
the papers she ever took.

Pioneers are not necessarily pioneers because they want to
stand alone. Robina Stevens enjoyed the company of her peers;
and, as a student at one of the Inns of Court, she had more chance
to do so than a pupil in a solicitor's office. The Solicitors' Act of
1922 stipulated for the first time that articled clerks should attend
lectures approved by the Law Society for a year in order to qualify, unless they already possessed a law degree. Here was a chance
to get together with others like oneself; but that sense of living
and learning in a crowd was otherwise largely absent from a
solicitor's training. It is something barrister Cornelia Sorabji particularly enjoyed at Oxford, where she was the first woman to
pass the BCL (Bachelor of Civil Law) examination, and later at
Lincoln's Inn. Helena Normanton remembered Cornelia looking
radiant in a bright red sari, always enthusiastic and keen to contribute to debates – though by then she was in her mid-fifties and
well beyond the ardency of youth.

The 1921 census lists 24,218 medical practitioners in the UK, not
counting nurses. Of those, 1,253 are women. It confusingly lists
20 female barristers (trainees must have jumped the gun by claiming the profession before they had qualified); 17 female solicitors
(for whom the same must apply); 49 architects; and – perhaps
surprisingly – 147 nonconformist ministers. The census also lists 49
female consulting engineers. It seems to me that engineers were
the most mutually supportive profession of all, not across the gender divide (with notable exceptions) but within the ranks of female

Cornelia Sorabji.

apprentices and practitioners. This had much to do with uniting in adversity. During the war, women answered the government's call and flooded into munitions factories, shipyards, aircraft hangars; they maintained searchlights, ran furnaces, repaired road and railway engines and manufactured all manner of tools and machinery. Everyone, including the men's trade unions, acknowledged that we couldn't have done without women engineers.

Yet when peace came, and a massive reconstruction programme was developed, those same women engineers were frozen out.

Many of them had been workshop supervisors; skilled mechanical, naval or electrical engineers in their own right, with ambitions
to qualify formally once the emergency was over, and perhaps to
expand their talents into that real no-woman's-land of civil engineering. They were soon disillusioned by employers' ubiquitous
refusal to train and recruit women if men were available, as
though there were only a finite number of jobs to go round. A
member of the Women's Engineering Society (WES) described
this as the barometer argument: professional women were like the
lady in those traditional little weather houses. She only came out
when the gentleman went in; when he came out again, she disappeared indoors.

In early 1920 the government passed the Pre-War Practices
Act, which promised ex-servicemen the same opportunities for
work as they had enjoyed before the war. It backfired somewhat
when men in engineering workshops were laid off soon after
returning because they were incapable of working as efficiently as
the women they replaced. The preferred solution to this problem
was not to re-employ the women, but simply to moan about the
scarcity of skilled labour, meaning *male* labour.

Later that year another piece of legislation came under debate:
the Women, Young Persons and Children's Bill, banning these
three populations from working wherever a two-part night-shift
(a wartime measure) remained in place. It was considered undesirable that they should be wandering to and from work in the
dead of night, absent from their families and possibly alone. That
was the official line, at any rate; the hope that this piece of legislation would result in women resigning or being made redundant
was unarticulated. The ban probably made sense for children
and *young* young persons, but for women? Women who had kept
the country afloat by working all the hours they could? Women
who needed all the experience and training available, in order
to qualify formally as engineers? Whose responsibilities at work

required them to supervise others round the clock? This was nonsense.

Engineering is a practical profession. It is not surprising, therefore, that women engineers tackled obstacles pragmatically. They had formed the WES in 1919 as a lobby group and professional organization to promote members' interests, support one another and offer opportunities for training. At its head was Rachel Parsons, who was furious at this institutional discrimination. It is difficult not to descend into cheap journalese when describing Rachel, distinguished as she was not only by a heavy-lidded, flame-haired and insolent-looking beauty but gentle birth, intelligence and fearlessness. Her father Charles Parsons was at the top of his profession when war broke out; the son of an earl, educated at Trinity College Dublin and Cambridge, he had worked his way up from an apprenticeship in Armstrong's engineering works in Newcastle to the head of his own company manufacturing the compound steam turbine he had invented. His wife Katharine, Rachel's mother, involved herself in every aspect of the company, and, as we have already seen, encouraged their gifted daughter to do the same. Rachel was the first woman to read Mechanical Engineering at Cambridge – she went there in 1910 – and when war broke out it seemed obvious that she should take the place in the family business of her brother, who was away fighting.

Rachel thrived, and particularly delighted in training other women at the family's plant on the River Tyne. She knew at first hand how enthusiastic and capable they could be, and was perfectly placed to judge their potential as professionals, with the right level of support. She was herself one of the first women to be admitted to the Institute of Naval Architects in 1920. As founding president of the WES, she piloted the profession of engineering from its chauvinistic history towards a more inclusive future. A writer in *The Woman Engineer*, the society's journal, pictured this progress as a series of tableaux.[21] 'The Past' shows a young woman sitting with her mother and sisters in the parlour. She's using a sewing-machine, but enjoys mending it when it goes wrong more than she likes making clothes. 'The Present' shows a group of women in a workshop, glad to be there but wishing they could have turned up earlier so they wouldn't be playing catch-up all the time. 'The Future' shows an interview for the position of assistant manager at the A & Z Gas and Oil Engine Company. The applicant is a young woman – and she gets the job. (What would be today's scenario, I wonder? Maybe the interviewer would be a woman, and the position would be for company chair.)

To bring this dream to life, WES members established businesses of their own, like Margaret Partridge's domestic lighting company in Devon, if they could raise the capital to do so. Rachel and Katharine Parsons were always generous supporters, morally and financially. An 'instructional factory' was set up in Loughborough during the war to train munitions workers; it rapidly developed into a centre of engineering excellence where many of the students were women, living in hostels, carrying out research in state-of-the-art laboratories and instructed by women (and men) with an enviable range of expertise. Students learned turning, tool-setting, milling, grinding, fitting, smithing, oxy-acetylene and electric welding, aircraft woodwork, drawing and tracing, aero-engine testing and more.

Loughborough Technical College – which blossomed into the present-day university – was 'successful far beyond our expectations', according to an editorial in The Woman Engineer; yet established engineering firms still declined to take women apprentices seriously. The Engineer – organ of the Society of Engineers – declared in response to the editorial that women should be 'content to call themselves mechanics, machinists, fitters and so on' and not aspire to anything more.[22] An article in the house magazine at an engineering plant near Kirkcudbright, with a largely female workforce manufacturing Galloway motor cars,

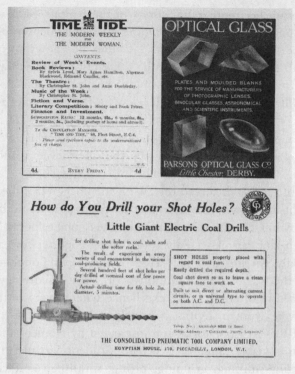

Advertisements in the September 1925 issue of The
Woman Engineer.

wryly suggested that qualified women were not being given proper
work to do, even if they did manage to secure apprenticeships.

> There is a certain factory in Scotland . . . where girls are gen-
> erously allowed to train in all branches of Labouring and
> Scavenging. They are allowed quite openly to clean their
> machines, remove the chips, fill their suds tanks, and to fetch
> and carry the work to and from their machines . . .
>   Pressure has been brought to bear on the local branch of
> the Amalgamated Society of Scavengers, and they have at last

consented to admit women members. But a society for women exclusively is being formed, its object being to further the aims of Women Scavengers, to enable them to get more technical training and for its motto it has adopted one of Shakespeare's gems – 'Men must work and women must sweep.'[23]

Loughborough Technical College had its own magazine, *The Limit*. It is not easy to work out the target readership of its early issues, in which reports of the latest engine-testing results, physics research and sports fixtures on campus appear alongside peculiarly feminine advertisements. One has an Aubrey Beardsley-like drawing of a woman gazing at herself in the mirror in an elegant state of undress. That's for corsets. Another is for a cooking range, showing a lady sitting knitting by the fire with a kitten at her feet while her female friend, with a strangely maniacal smile, slides something into the oven.

Annette Ashberry was one of eight women engineers who came together in 1920 to found Atalanta Ltd. The original Atalanta was a virgin goddess in Greek mythology, suckled by a she-bear; single, fierce and proud. Annette, on the other hand, was the daughter of Jewish immigrants, born in Hackney (her birth name was Hannah Annenberg). She worked in various engineering plants for the duration of the war, in London, Coventry and at that Galloway factory in Kirkcudbright, making shells, inspecting fuses and checking magnetos. Frustrated by the lack of opportunity for further training and a career, she gathered together a group of financial backers and found a site for a new workshop near the Loughborough campus. Things did not look promising; all she and her partners could afford at first was a space with three walls and a mud floor, with a few pigs and chickens still in residence. The eight women built the fourth wall, put down a concrete floor, laid gas pipes, bedded in their lathes, and set to work manufacturing oil burners and 'hand-scraped surface plates'. By 1922 the company had relocated to London and was manufacturing small tools such as adjustable spanners, screwdrivers – 'the blade never slips' – and drilling jigs.

The inventors at Atalanta were nothing if not eclectic. Annette Ashberry patented a vegetable peeler which sold remarkably well, and in 1922 won a prize for designing a prototype dishwasher. Three years later, she became the first woman elected to the Society of Engineers, having finally qualified in a profession she had been practising for over a decade.

The process of qualification for engineers, male and female, was as well defined as for all the traditional professions. Like the law, it could be approached in different ways, either by practical experience and apprenticeship, or more academically via university, culminating in membership of one of the Institutes of Engineers – Naval, Civil, Electrical, Chemical, Structural or Mechanical. Victoria Drummond was a debutante – another one – who veered off course: in her case, by deciding to qualify as a marine engineer. Born in a Scottish castle, she boasted Queen Victoria for a godmother, and was educated genteelly at home by a governess. None of this seems to have influenced her as much as her grandmother, who was an uncommonly fine wood-turner. Victoria was passionate about all things mechanical. During the First World War she worked in a garage in the Scottish city of Perth for two years before being apprenticed to a Dundee shipyard. After another four years she was appointed 'tenth engineer' on a round voyage to Australia for the Blue Funnel Line – this was in 1922 – and passed her second engineer's examination at the third attempt.

Despite this success, she could only find a position as a fifth engineer, because – she maintained – she was a woman. She was determined to get her chief engineer's certificate, and sat the Board of Trade exam *thirty-seven* times. On every occasion, she was failed – again, she said, because she was a woman. She never had any trouble from her crewmates; it was only the bigwigs who misjudged her. Victoria went on to enjoy a stellar career at sea, especially during the Second World War when she won an MBE and a medal for devotion to duty. She did eventually serve as chief engineer on foreign vessels, but never quite reached the summit of her profession in her homeland. The achievements of people like Rachel Parsons, Annette Ashberry and Victoria Drummond were inspirational; but, as another eminent engineer, Verena Holmes, said in 1928, the doors to the engineering profession stood barely ajar. It would take many decades and another world war to push them fully open.

Qualification in medicine was more straightforward. If you passed the necessary exams, you qualified. If you passed some more – as long as you were allowed to sit them – you became a member of the Royal College dealing with your specialism. You might eventually be elected a Fellow of the College, in God's good time. Dr Louisa Aldrich-Blake accomplished all that was asked of her, and more. In 1895 she became the first woman to be awarded a Master of Surgery degree. In 1902 she started work at the Elizabeth Garrett Anderson Hospital, becoming its senior surgeon in 1910. She was the first female anaesthetist at the Royal Free Hospital and developed a pioneering interest in the surgical treatment of cervical and rectal cancers. Meanwhile she worked at the Canning Town Women's Settlement Hospital in London's East End whenever she could – and still managed to maintain a private practice. During the First World War she wrote to every woman on the Medical Register, to enlist their help in staffing field hospitals abroad. When she was appointed dean of the LSMW, she took a course in accountancy, the better to understand her role. She appeared to be utterly inexhaustible, and completely happy in her work. 'Dame Louisa was perhaps something lacking in humour,' noted a member of a women's club to which she belonged, 'with little sparkle, but with great dignity.'[24] There; one can't have everything.

Helena Normanton didn't do badly. She passed her Bar finals on her wedding day, 26 October 1921, and was called with ten other women on 17 November 1922, at the age of thirty-nine. Her gown, made especially for her, along with her hood, her marcasite buckles and her beautiful lace jabot, are preserved in the Women's Library in London, hanging in a basement room as though waiting for their absent owner to return for one more case. Helena was the first woman to appear as defence counsel in a criminal county court trial: her client, in 1924, was Charles Eyles, charged with false pretences. He was found not guilty and Helena was complimented by the judge on her performance. She probably found that rather patronizing. By now she had fought and won another battle, to keep her maiden name not just at work but on her passport. This was feminism at its most radical in 1920s Britain — and did not endear her to the Establishment, which did her no favours in return. There was a disciplinary inquiry into her conduct after she was accused of 'self-advertising' when journalists started stalking her and pestering her for interviews and quotes. She had always promised herself that education would be an important part of her professional life, in memory of her mother. Her mission to familiarize ordinary women with the legal processes affecting their lives was important to her. Again, this laudable aim attracted accusations of shamelessly seeking the spotlight and touting for business when she gave talks to women's groups or wrote articles in newspapers and magazines.

In ecclesiastical contexts, formal qualification takes the form of ordination. Maude Royden was certainly a priestly presence, being allowed to preach as an Anglican in the churches of other Christian denominations – notably the King's Weigh House Chapel in London – but not to be ordained, as Constance Coltman was, in her own church. Another preacher-by-invitation was Edith Picton-Turbervill, a trained missionary, whose conversion to the religious life came during an epiphanic moment on a train (the Bridgend Express from London). She campaigned alongside Maude Royden and was invited to preach a mainstream Anglican sermon by the Bishop of London, which was all very well, but didn't address the question of when women would be eligible for ordination because of *who* they were, not *what* they were. 'No priesthood ever made a claim more arrogant than this claim of man to stand between a woman and her God,' wrote the Christian suffragist Hatty Baker of the Church of England, whose clergy were apt to say encouraging things over tea, she noted, which they then denied in the pulpit. According to her, only the Quakers and the Salvation Army were enlightened, considering the sexes perfectly equal – perhaps because neither had a priestly hierarchy.

For the record, the first woman to be appointed a minister in the Unitarian Church in Britain was Prussian-born Gertrude von Petzold in 1904. She trained at Manchester College in Oxford. The first given pastoral charge in the Baptist Church was Edith Gates, who looked after a parish in Oxfordshire from 1918, living in the manse with her sister, who played the organ. It is uncertain whether she was ever officially ordained. The first female Methodist minister in the UK was not consecrated until 1974, and the first female rabbi a year later.

In the 1920s, people were too busy trading biblical quotes about the arguments for and against women priests to achieve anything concrete. Romans 16, 1–2: 'I commend unto you Phoebe our sister, which is a servant of the church . . . that ye assist her in whatsoever business she hath need of you.' 1 Timothy 2, 12: 'But I suffer not a woman to teach, nor to usurp authority over the man, but to keep silence.' Philippians 4, 3: 'And I entreat thee also, true yoke-fellow, help those women who laboured with me in the gospel.' 1 Corinthians 14, 34: 'Let your women keep silence in the churches, for it is not permitted unto them to speak.' Galatians 3, 28: 'There is neither Jew nor Greek, there is neither bond nor free, there is neither male nor female: for ye are all one in Christ Jesus.'

Architect Ethel Charles entered a professional competition in 1905. Architects are always entering professional competitions, but this one was for the best-designed essay rather than building. The title was 'The Development of Architectural Art from Structural Requirements and Nature of Materials'. Ethel's essay won. The judges must have forgotten another piece she had written earlier, published in the professional journal *Builder*. Somewhat easier for the amateur to understand, it was simply called 'A Plea for Women', and is a personal entreaty for people like her to be encouraged to practise architecture.[25] When she says people like her, she means individuals who have the capability and aptitude to succeed; who are artistic and love beauty; who understand the rules of mathematics and have natural authority. Actually, 'plea' is the wrong word, in Ethel's opinion, because it sounds apologetic. People like her have a *right* to be considered for qualification if they are capable enough. They don't have to be physical Atlases: climbing a ladder is no more complicated or strenuous than riding a bicycle. The great Sir Christopher Wren never fancied ladders much: he used to be hoisted up the walls of St Paul's Cathedral in a basket. It never did him any harm. And contrary to popular belief, architects do not have to resort to foul language to keep their workmen in order. We all know how forceful gentleness can be.

People like her, she concludes, should be judged on their own merits as professionals, and not according to the prejudices of others. Their sex should be entirely coincidental.

Dream on, Ethel.

5

Those Charming Impostors

The room is your own, but it is still bare.[1]

ETHEL CHARLES'S HOPES of equal opportunities for women were shared by novelist Virginia Woolf, whose address to a group of Cambridge women students in 1928 has become a keystone of modern feminism. Always fascinated by architecture, in *A Room of One's Own* Woolf pictures a building wherein women might feel safe and inspired to flourish; where the possession of 'a room of one's own' away from the traditional cares and expectations of wives and mothers, sisters and daughters, will free them to live life on their own terms. This space is located far from the kitchen, the bedroom, the nursery and the sewing-room. It is society's utopian gift to half the human race: a space to grow, a sanctuary, the ante-room to personal and public success. I reread *A Room of One's Own* recently. At the time I had just come across Ethel's plans for a group of cottages in Falmouth, Cornwall; they immediately brought to mind Woolf's famous essay, looking elegant in a way that was both Elizabethan and arts-and-craftsy; light, comfortable and stylish. They are supposed to be for labourers but look curiously feminine, just like a series of rooms of one's own. Of course, Woolf's (élite) women were labourers too, intellectually and creatively, so perhaps the connection is not so far-fetched after all.

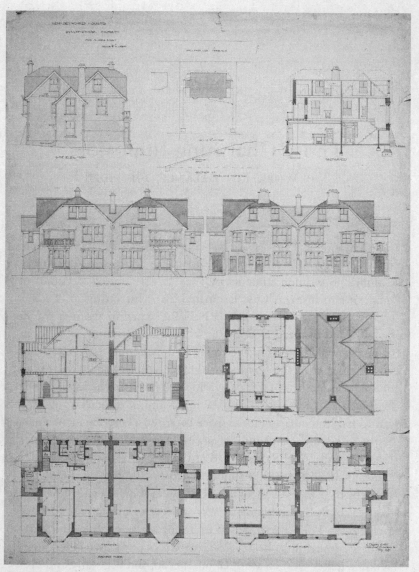

Ethel Charles's designs for semi-detached houses in Falmouth, 1907.

In 1931, a couple of years after her Cambridge lecture, Woolf gave another talk. This one was at a meeting of the National Society for Women's Service, which later became the Fawcett Society. Now she suggests that despite what she calls the 'miracle' of the SDRA, despite universal suffrage (finally granted in July 1928) and despite the fact that women with professional careers are no longer a novelty, 'this freedom is only a beginning – the room is your own, but it is still bare'. She is being a little harsh. By then professional women had been busy trying to furnish their own rooms, metaphorically (and physically) speaking, for years, in order to achieve the sort of work–life balance that would help them feel less like guests in their own careers, and more at home. Inevitably, some were more successful than others in achieving equilibrium.

When Gwyneth Bebb Thomson began working for the Board of Trade before the First World War, she was informed that as a woman with the equivalent of a first-class degree from Oxford her salary would be £150 per annum (about £11,000 now, and – as a matter of policy – less than a similarly qualified man's); she was entitled to thirty-six days' holiday a year; she had no right to a pension, gratuity or allowance on termination of her contract, and although the usual hours were from 10 a.m. to 5 p.m., her 'whole time' was 'to be at the service of the Office if required'.[2] Such terms were normal. Somehow Gwyneth found time to have a life as well: to study independently, meet the man who became her husband, keep up with her family and even enjoy a little social life. She belonged to the University Women's Club (UWC), for example, formally opened in 1897 as 'The University Club for Ladies'.

The writer George Augustus Sala once described a gentlemen's club as 'a weapon used by savages to keep white women at a distance'.[3] The UWC, though built on the traditional model, was different, and not just in the obvious sense. Its members were almost exclusively university or medical-school graduates, or undergraduates of at least a year's standing; the few who had no formal qualifications were heads of houses at women's colleges or prominent social reformers denied a university education simply because they were born too soon.

Things did not go too well in the early days. Committee meetings were frequently non-quorate, and the club was short of both money and members (which essentially amount to the same thing). It was as though women did not quite know what a club was for. They certainly weren't sure how to run one on a budget so tight that the cakes for tea were optimistically sought from the bakery on a sale-or-return basis and there were long discussions about how many glasses one could squeeze out of a bottle of wine while still keeping the customers satisfied.

Gwyneth Bebb Thomson joined in 1912, when the club's headquarters were in George Street, near Hanover Square in the West End of London. By now there were, in addition to a smoking-room, a number of bedrooms to put up members visiting from the country, or disinclined to travel home to the suburbs after a busy day – though only boiled eggs and coffee were available to eat after 7.30 p.m. unless something else had been ordered in advance, and one evening a week there was nothing but cold meat for dinner, so the cook could have a night off.

It is difficult to imagine heated discussions at a gentlemen's club about how much the maid is being paid (not nearly enough, according to several UWC members); where the club curling-tongs and face-powder are stored; whether someone should daringly go to the brewery to collect the screw-top beer or whether they could afford to have it delivered; and where members' bicycles should be kept (in their bedrooms, it's decided, so as not to block the corridors). Dr Louisa Aldrich-Blake – an early member – must have kept people on their toes, but some problems appeared insurmountable. How to chase up members' debts, for instance, without resorting to vulgar chivvying or offending these often trenchant personalities.

In 1921 the club moved to its present premises in South Aud-
ley Street, Mayfair. It changed its name and published a fearsome
pamphlet of thirty-five Rules and Regulations and fourteen Bye-
Laws. At this point there were around a thousand women on the
books, each paying a joining fee and an annual subscription. The
club as a whole felt less like an impostor among the neighbouring
establishments of its male peers, and its members grew in confidence and number through the following decades. They included
several more of the professional sisterhood, including Maude
Royden, Winifred Holtby, Vera Brittain, Ray Strachey and
Nancy Nettlefold. It was designed to be a collective 'room of
one's own'; a place to think, read, talk, enjoy company and, most
importantly, to share the mutual support that only those who
know what you're experiencing can give. It catered to an élite
group, naturally, but it is the same élite group who were attempting to shatter that crystal ceiling on behalf of us all.

There were other social clubs for women in London and
beyond. Liverpool University had a famous 'Tea Club' for female
staff and the wives of male academics, offering social events and
a convivial place to meet. It was like a smaller-scale version of the
Lyceum Club in London – perhaps the closest thing to a traditional gentlemen's club for ladies – which by 1920 was housed in
an impressive residence at 138 Piccadilly. The Lyceum was unfeas-
ibly grand; so much so, in fact, that it ran out of money and
closed down in 1933. Until then it strove to offer ladies 'a sub-
stantial and dignified *milieu*' where they might 'discuss matters as
men did' in surroundings 'that did not suggest poverty'.[4] When
Gwyneth and her companions decided to sue the Law Society in
1913, the Lyceum Club is where that ground-breaking action was
first announced. Members were cultured and well heeled. They
probably considered the presence of the club's art gallery, in-house
hairdressers and seamstresses as essential. There were club 'circles'
for members from – or interested in – America, Belgium, France,

Ireland, Italy, the Orient, Poland, Russia and Scotland; for art lovers, amateur geographers, musicians, photographers, poets, billiards
players, bridge enthusiasts and even psychics. Frequent lectures and
monthly concerts were held on the premises, while overseas
branches were set up in Paris, Berlin, Florence and Rome. Dr
Louisa Martindale was a member, though how often she was able to
attend, being based on the south coast of England, is unclear. But
then Brighton had its own social scene, particularly for the women
medics who seem to have gathered there (as they did on Nottingham Place in London, incidentally, where Louisa Aldrich-Blake
lived at no. 17; her predecessor as dean of the LSMW – with the
resplendent name of Julia Ann Hornblower Cock – at no. 15; other
LSMW graduates at no. 10; and Samuel Garrett, the brother of Dr
Elizabeth Garrett Anderson and Millicent Fawcett, at no. 13).[5]

Slightly less exalted and reputedly 'bluestocking' than the
Lyceum was the Forum Club, set up in 1919 for members of the
Women's Institute and run, in part, by Lady Rhondda. The Pioneer Club and the Minerva Club were for political activists; the
Ladies' Automobile Club was self-explanatory. These were all in
London; there were also several residential clubs in cities around
the country whose main purpose was to offer accommodation
either to ladies visiting from elsewhere or to 'gentlewomen' who
needed somewhere respectable yet affordable to live while
working – a little like the Women's Pioneer Housing Company's
bedsits in London designed and inhabited by Gertrude Leverkus.

Some professions set up in-house organizations and publications, which functioned as physical and/or virtual meeting-places
for members. The Women's Engineering Society ran premises in
Dover Street, London, as well as issuing a quarterly journal. The
NUWT was a highly political organization, constantly lobbying for
equal pay and higher status for women in the classroom. Its journal,
The Woman Teacher, is one of the best publications of its kind; it
served as a virtual club, publishing articles on such live topics as

'The Social Disabilities of Women', new pension schemes or the marriage bar, and publicizing depressing examples of the everyday sexism of the time. 'A lady in a South Wales town, talking to a man about equal pay [in 1920] was told that as an average woman's brain was smaller than an average man's brain, therefore, women were less intelligent than men, and should not have equal pay for equal work.'[6] Where does this leave elephants, wonders the editor innocently?

The Woman Teacher is not all about business. There are classified advertisements for such places as a vegetarian guest house in Bath, for example; a bedsitting-room with partial board and a gas stove in Bloomsbury; and a very superior apartment in Wembley with a kitchenette, electric light, use of drawing room, a piano, a bath, a large garden and another teacher ready installed as a sympathetic flatmate. And lest readers should feel overwhelmed by the injustice of their working conditions and lack of prospects for promotion, there are little pieces dotted about to cheer them up – like this one I can't resist repeating.

> Here is a story of a Bethnal Green six-year-old. It was Friday afternoon and the teacher was reading a story from one of the children's own books. It was about a small boy who had neither father nor mother, so he wandered into the woods. There he found a nice house owned by a kind old sheep, who said the boy might live there if he would make the bed, cook the porridge and comb the sheep's fleece. The little boy agreed, but after a few days he found that the bed was too large, the saucepan too heavy, and that it took him too long to comb out the fleece. So he went into the woods again and found another house and another sheep, who gave him the same tasks. But again he found them too heavy, and he wandered from house to house until he found a dear little house kept by a black lamb. The bed was just the right size, the saucepan was the right weight, and it didn't take him too long to comb the lamb's fleece. 'Coo!' said Teddy, who had been listening enthralled, 'they *all* had fleas!'[7]

The journal of the MWF – founded in Manchester but based in London – was less cheery, but no less political. Its profile was high in these years; in 1926 the British Medical Association passed a resolution from MWF members for equal pay (a campaign they continue to fight under the banner of the gender pay gap nearly a century later). In the decade following the passing of the SDRA, which should have changed the professional climate for females in medicine (but did not), the MWF journal ran a series of articles about role models, including Dr Nesta Wells, appointed a police surgeon in 1927 and determined to make the examination of women and children after alleged sexual assault more humane; Dr Mary Scharlieb, who only started operating in her forties yet quickly became, with her tiny hands and quiet determination, 'one of the six greatest abdominal surgeons in the world';[8] and Flora Murray, who – having memorably organized dog shows for LSMW students' pets – went on to more serious pursuits, tending starving suffragettes (released under the notorious 'Cat-and-Mouse' Act of 1913) and dying soldiers at a military hospital she headed in London during the war.

There are several provocative features on surgical treatment for breast cancer, eugenic birth control, the use of insulin in diabetes, vivisection, sterilization for the 'mentally defective' and research into the effects of the menopause, accompanied by specialist advertisements for such delights as the 'Gastroptosis belt' – a complex variety of truss – and 'a Palatable, Simple, Assimilable and Safe Sedative and Mild Hypnotic, taken as a Soup or Broth'.[9] This is a toothsome cocktail of sodium bromide with added fat.

The classified section in this journal is highly specialized. A doctor in Margate seeks a convalescent as a paying guest (she must have been struggling to make ends meet as a woman practitioner). A qualified lady is wanted 'at once' for an Indian mission hospital. Several women GPs need practice partners and there's a maternity hospital for sale in Gillingham, Kent. Could someone please volunteer to tour around girls' schools talking about menstruation? Pupils and mistresses alike need to realize that it's not an illness. All a girl needs to do during her period is 'take a bath' and she'll feel ready for anything.

In 1926 Dr Ethel Williams wrote a fascinating article on 'Thirty Odd Years in General Practice'. She reckons women make particularly good GPs, and implies it's a good thing Elizabeth Garrett Anderson stuck to surgery. Ethel remembers the great pioneer once confessing that she could never do much to help her 'neurotic' patients – 'I do dislike them so.'[10] Ethel loves her career, being just as happy tinkering with the car she uses to pay visits as examining an obscure pathology slide under the microscope, pondering a tricky diagnosis or reassuring an anxious patient. Developing strong personal relationships is the most important part of her work as a doctor – even if she doesn't always tell the truth. Sometimes lying to a patient is justified, she confides, 'if it helps preserve courage and endurance'.

The Women's Provisional Club, for 'Professional and Businesswomen', was founded in 1924. It was based in a series of London restaurants, which says something about its attitude to socializing. Unpretentious yet effective, it attracted serious working women like architect Gertrude Leverkus, engineer Caroline Haslett, parliamentarian Eleanor Rathbone, Dr Louisa Martindale (again – obviously an eminently clubbable person) – and the ubiquitous Lady Rhondda, its first president. Its aims were similar to those of the all-male Rotary clubs, with which the 'Provisionals' hoped to amalgamate one day (but never did): to 'encourage and foster high ethical standards in business and the professions; [to] encourage and foster the ideal of service as the basis for enterprise'; and to 'quicken an interest in public welfare and to co-operate with others in civic, social and industrial developments'.[11]

A 'who's who' of members in 1938 included representatives of a remarkable range of careers, including Civil Service scientists, an international lawyer, the manager of an advertising agency, a governor of the BBC, lots of barristers and solicitors, accountants and doctors, an industrial psychologist, the Hunterian Professor at the Royal College of Surgeons in London, a silversmith, a dental surgeon, and the statistician in charge of retail and trade figures at the Bank of England. The Provisional Club was not just about networking; it was about looking at society more broadly and, as the modern idiom has it, 'giving back'. Members raised funds for associated causes, notably the conversion of Crosby Hall, a medieval merchant's house in Chelsea, into a hostel for international women students. It was one of the first organizations for women in the professions to reach out from a position of strength, when the instinct of many similar associations was to huddle together for safety and self-protection.

It is becoming clear, as this narrative progresses, that pioneering women in the professions were quick to learn how to network and look out for one another. Clubs and organizations helped; so did the appointment of a female architect, say, by a female doctor building a hospital for women, or the pursuit by a firm of women engineers of a female solicitor for legal guidance (as in the case of the WES, which retained Helena Normanton as a voluntary adviser). They liked to keep things in the family, in other words. Sadly, nowhere have I found evidence of an organized support system for those in personal distress; of women psychiatrists or preachers formally counselling peers who felt overwhelmed. Even if there were such a system, it is unlikely many people would have taken advantage of it. This was an age when 'mad' was still a valid medical diagnosis. One of the most popular arguments against allowing women to invade public life in any capacity was their well-known mental frailty; their incipient hysteria and tendency to break down and sob messily at the most inopportune moments. It would take a brave woman to seek help for just that kind of vulnerability; and when you are feeling fragile, you are rarely feeling brave as well.

The Federation of University Women was formed in Manchester in 1907, principally to raise money for women academics' research projects. Members went on to campaign for equal rights in other spheres, especially the Civil Service, but academia was its original focus. It dealt with policy, however, not with individual cases, so could not help the distinguished Polish anthropologist Maria Czaplicka.

Maria struggled against poverty all her life. Warsaw was under Russian control when she was born there in 1884; as the daughter of a railway stationmaster from a once noble Polish family, she was entitled to only the most basic education – so she went underground, attending lectures at the so-called 'Flying University', run secretly by and for Polish students. She earned money as a tutor, a secretary and a lady's companion before becoming the first woman from her country to win a prestigious travelling scholarship, which brought her to Britain in 1910. The award funded a year's study of anthropology at the London School of Economics (LSE). Desperate to research her subject further, when the year was up Maria applied to Somerville College in Oxford, where Principal Emily Penrose (a member of the UWC) found her another scholarship; this, together with money from a trust fund at Bedford College in London and private subscriptions from the pockets of sister students at Somerville, meant that at the age of twenty-six Maria could begin working for a diploma in Anthropology and on her first book, a résumé of studies on the aboriginal people of Siberia.

In May 1914 Maria embarked on an ambitious field trip which would lead to another, more accessible book, *My Siberian Year*. She was the expedition leader; her companions were an American academic from the LSE, Henry Usher Hall, who was collecting material for the Pennsylvania Museum of Archaeology and Anthropology; an ornithologist, Maud Haviland; and an artist, Dora Curtis. Colleagues may have thought it a little unusual that she was leading the enterprise, given that a perfectly capable man was present, but Maria never doubted her eligibility – and nor, it seems, did her companions.

Maria described the next thirteen months in a series of letters to Emily Penrose and in her travelogue, which mentions nonchalantly the facts that she was so seasick on the way to Siberia that she vomited blood, and so cold when she got there that she adopted 'native' dress, stuffing her feet into a bag made of the winter coat of a reindeer buck, with dog's-hair stockings and two pairs of hairy skin boots on top. The rest of her was similarly clad, everything with 'an indispensable substratum of Jaegers [woollen underwear], occasionally doubled' underneath.[12]

When the other two women went home at the end of summer, just after news of the outbreak of war (and, more materially, when there were no birds left to observe and no light for painting), Maria was left with a slight problem. It would not be healthy for her reputation to continue alone with Henry; so she engaged a Siberian woman to travel with them as her chaperone. The wool-lined tent they all shared had a modest dividing 'wall' made of fabric down the middle. All was well.

When Maria returned to Britain in 1915, she was unable to remain at Somerville, which had been requisitioned as a military hospital. Realizing this, the Principal of Maude Royden's old college, Lady Margaret Hall, offered to accommodate Maria instead. She implied there was a special fund that would cover the cost. In fact there was no such thing; unbeknown to Maria, the Principal paid the necessary fees herself. Her name was Henrietta Jex-Blake, niece of the redoubtable medical pioneer Sophia. Miss Jex-Blake's kindness, together with the money British students raised for Maria, echoed the support she had found in the 'Flying University' at home in Poland. This early form of crowd-funding was an expression of solidarity; a vote of confidence in a flag-bearer, a disadvantaged student with a brilliant future ahead of her.

During the war Maria Czaplicka lectured on her Siberian

journey at venues all over the British Isles; she also raised funds for
Polish refugees – like herself – and for the cause of women's suffrage. A spot of work for British Intelligence and a stint as a land
girl in Devon were followed by her unprecedented appointment as
a lecturer in Ethnology at the University of Oxford in 1916. It was
a post she held until 1919, when the previous male incumbent,
Leonard Dudley Buxton, returned from the war – at which point
Maria was automatically dismissed. She enquired about the possibility of working at an American university, without any luck, but
did manage to secure a lectureship at Bristol. This, together with a
medal awarded by the Royal Geographical Society in recognition
of her Siberian work, should have meant that Maria was set fair to
achieve mainstream academic success. That was all she ever wanted.

But the contract at Bristol was short-term. She had incurred
debts of over £200 in the course of her research (buying essential
scientific equipment) and could not rely on kind friends to subsid-
ize her for ever. She was certain that, had she been a man, given
her credentials, there would have been no question about funding. Putting this to the back of her mind, she applied for a major
travelling scholarship which would have not only wiped out her
debts but put her on a sound financial footing while she finished
her academic report on the Siberian expedition.

Maria was given to understand that all that stood between her
and the scholarship was her nationality; if she became a naturalized
British citizen she was virtually assured of success. This she agreed
to do, informing the administrators that although there would
be an inevitable delay until her papers came through, she was sure
there would be no problem. They did come through – but too late.
On 26 May 1921 the award went to somebody else. Unable to bear
the thought of a future without her work, the following day Maria
drank mercury, and died.

In the following days, the newspapers were full of this 'brilliant
young Pole', this 'lady of intellect and infinite courage' who had

come to Britain to escape prejudice. 'Though a daughter of Poland,' wrote one obituarist, 'she was England's adopted child, and, as such, will be honoured and mourned.'[13] Yet who has heard of her now?

Maria was a poet as well as a scientist. Here is a fragment she wrote called 'The Truth about my Soul'. It's chilling.

> I possess only a woman's body
> but have an abnormal soul:
> what is a gift for both sexes
> I have to stand in myself.
> I have a man's hungry, unsatisfied eagerness,
> and steadfast bravery,
> as well as female vacillation and tenderness
> and permanence of emotions . . .
> I surpass you with my womanhood,
> yet do not cede in manliness –
> and derisively proud of this monstrousness,
> I poison myself with my own laughter.[14]

No one can claim that Maria Czaplicka lost her life because she was a woman in a man's world. Who knows what private battles consumed her? But the hostility of the academic Establishment did her irreparable damage. A functional work–life balance was not possible for Maria: they were the same thing. If one failed, then so must the other.

The pressure on professional women to succeed in the 1920s and 1930s came from various sources – as did the pressure not to succeed. Maria was relentlessly self-motivated. Perhaps she might have fared better had she had family around to support her, but we cannot assume that. Some parents were determined to quash their daughters' inconvenient ambitions by keeping them at home. Business director Gordon Holmes was constantly having to persuade meek but promising young trainees that they did not have to run home to help mother at the drop of a hat, any more than their brothers did. University archives bristle with letters from fathers or brothers recalling female students to domestic duty; the same thing occurred at medical schools and the Inns of Court. What is the story behind Alice Griswold's register at Inner Temple? She was first admitted as a student at the age of twenty-four; left after two and a half years; was re-admitted nearly five years later; withdrew again after eighteen months; returned eight weeks after that; and finally departed after another two years – some eleven years after first enrolling.[15] Is this a tale of failure on her part, or of success?

Conversely, women could be pushed into careers for which they were unsuited by a misplaced sense of duty. Dr Winifred de Kok remembered a sister student at the LSMW whom she first met in the dissection room 'where we shared a part – an arm it was, I remember'. This girl chose medicine

> because the man she was going to marry was killed in the war. She had no real knowledge of what the work meant: I think she probably had a vision of herself as a doctor, going about amongst the suffering and curing them. Gladly sacrificing her life because she now had nothing that made life worth living. It did not take her long to realize her mistake.[16]

Another young woman, Deirdre, studied medicine because her father was a doctor, and expected her to follow him. Perhaps, like so many engineers and solicitors, her brothers – natural heirs to their father's business – were also casualties of war. Deirdre was never reconciled to the life, but, unlike Winifred's colleague, she lacked the confidence to leave. According to a friend, she endured 'years of quarrels with her colleagues who, in her view, were always plotting against her. I think it was a mistake on her part to take up medicine; she once confessed that she hated illness and sick people.'[17]

One doctor-father covered all bases at once, managing to keep his three daughters at home and in the family firm while furnishing them relatively cheaply with careers to suit their tastes and talents: the first was his partner in the practice, the second was his pharmacist and the third his chauffeur.[18]

'Work has been the twentieth century's greatest gift to women,' declared an editorial in Lady Rhondda's *Time and Tide* in 1926. 'It is dignified, which puts her, as far as the chance of happiness is concerned, upon the same level as men.'[19] However, for many women entering the workplace, happiness was – and is – not always the priority. Sometimes it's just about what keeps you going. There was a memorable caretaker at the girls' boarding school Downe House during the 1920s. This individual had a deep voice, wore a monocle, and stomped moodily around the site in a broad-brimmed hat, belted serge overalls and rubber boots – or sometimes a monk's habit with a packet of Woodbines tucked into the front of it, looking (according to a pupil at the time) 'like a sinister priest in a Goya etching'. This was the mysterious Maria Nickel, perhaps Polish, perhaps Russian, who had allegedly studied forestry and medicine before the war, then come to England as a refugee and been given a job at the school by its founding headmistress, Olive Willis. Maria taught geography, science and cookery. She was outstanding at puff pastry and cooked virtuosic steak-and-kidney pies over a Bunsen burner. She also taught woodwork and gave violin lessons in a small chamber over the school's water-tower, like something out of a Grimms' fairy tale. She designed and carved the beautiful linen-fold panels in the school library. But she was not a natural communicator. Some unspecified family tragedy had turned her mind, it was rumoured; she had never been known to smile.

Maria Nickel was happiest in her caretaker's role, spending her days *almost* mending leaky roofs, *nearly* clearing the drains, improvising lively electrical circuits and bodging engines. She drove the school car like Dr Mary Murdoch drove hers in Hull – with terrifying panache. Miss Willis banned her from going faster than 15 mph, but still Maria managed on one occasion to slam the car into the back of a taxi, having failed to make sure her brakes were working properly; the oil in the car's headlamps ignited the taxi, which was reduced to a pungent heap of ashes. The cabman luckily escaped.

At night Maria would retire to Miss Willis's bathroom, muttering under her breath, and lie down to sleep on the floor. In happier times she might have practised as a doctor, or become an academic or an engineer. As it was, the sensitivity of her colleagues allowed her to carry on in the best way she could, using her skills to earn a living.[20]

An increasing number of women were now doing this more conventionally. Despite the aftershocks of the First World War, whose victims included not only the dead and grievously wounded but their families, their lovers, survivors burdened with guilt at actually having a future; despite the ravages of Spanish flu, the Great Depression, the General Strike in 1926 and the recalcitrance of old-school reactionaries in every profession, women were not only gaining ground in the workplace but enjoying themselves there. Was this disloyal to the dead? Were women behaving like nationwide scabs, not just by rushing to drive trams and cart rubbish during the strike but by daring to enter the professional workplace at all when there was so little money to go around? While pundits and politicians wrestled with these questions, the women got on with things as best they could, given the circumstances – as everyone did during the turbulent twenties.

Scottish architect Edith Burnet Hughes was flourishing, having set up her own practice in Glasgow in 1920 after studying at the Sorbonne and at art school in Aberdeen. There was a slight hiccup when she tried to join an established partnership in

London and her application was unimaginatively refused owing to there being no ladies' lavatory, but that did not detain her for long. She specialized in kitchens, and also won competitions to design Glasgow's Mercat Cross and a war memorial in Coatbridge. What is more, she was married, with three children. Her Irish contemporary Eileen Gray spent the 1920s in France, first as an interior designer with a glamorous shop in Paris, then as a practising architect whose modernist 'E-1027' villa in the Alpes Maritimes, built in 1926, is iconic. She influenced Le Corbusier.

WES member Mrs Laura Willson built her first houses in July 1925 – and they're still standing, at Club Lane in Halifax. Laura had been a half-timer at a textile factory at the age of ten; seasoned by her community's trade unionism and the fight for women's suffrage, she educated herself. After her marriage to the owner of a lathe-making factory she took charge of his female workforce and was one of the earliest members of the WES. Since then she had turned to construction engineering and was earning serious money. By September 1926 she had completed seventy-two dwellings, all sold and occupied; a further sixty were 'built to the roof' while a hundred more were in process of construction. Her mission was simply to give ordinary women a good standard of living. Maybe she fitted out her kitchens with some of the gadgets made by engineer and metallurgist Mabel Matthews, who gave a talk at Leeds in 1925 about her innovative work in stainless steel. She supplied tin-openers, bacon-slicers, shiny tea cups, and, for the more adventurous client, small parts for their guns, their typewriters, even their false teeth.

By this time, Congregational minister Constance Coltman had her own London parish, which she ran in joint charge with her husband. The Unitarian Gertrude von Petzold had graduated from her theological training college at Oxford years ago (the first woman to do so) and ministered at churches in Leicester and Birmingham, but owing to a period spent in the United States

WORKMEN'S HOUSES.

Modern.
Attractive.
Durable.

Can be built in quantities of 48.

64 HOUSES

Price £400 each (Freehold).

ENQUIRIES SOLICITED.

LAURA A. WILLSON. M.B.E., Jumples, Halifax.

Mrs Willson's housing estate in Halifax was completed in the mid-1920s.

her application for British naturalization during the war, unlike Maria Czaplicka's, was refused (no doubt the fact that she was Prussian by birth did her no favours). She returned to the UK on visits during the 1920s to preach and to rally support for other women to follow her career path, assuring them that there was no work in the world, except perhaps the slaughtering of other people, which women couldn't do as efficiently as men. They just needed the same training and opportunity. Sadly, both remained in comparatively short supply for would-be clergywomen.

Helena Normanton's fame was growing. She wrote for fashionable new ladies' magazines like *Good Housekeeping*, first published in Britain in 1922, and for those newspapers that didn't delight in making mealy-mouthed fun of her. She enjoyed doing Poor Persons work – a forerunner of the legal aid scheme – and taking random 'dock briefs' directly from prisoners in court, rather than via a solicitor. This was making a virtue of necessity: journalism supplemented her income, and any brief was better than none. Trad-itional briefs were hard to come by for someone like her: someone who was obviously highly intelligent but of working-class heri-tage; someone by whom (through no fault of her own) the press was constantly fascinated; someone who was not only a woman but a feminist. Occasionally she was chosen by prisoners because in her wig and glasses she looked like a man; it could be rather a shock to them to find they had picked a Portia.

When Helena embarked on a lecture tour in America in 1924 there was a problem about her passport. The authorities refused to accept that she could be married and yet still be called, offi-cially, by her maiden name. Her husband offered to change his own name to hers, temporarily, if that would help. After what I suspect was an extremely frank exchange of views between Helena and the passport officials, this was not found necessary.

Any celebrity will tell you that being in the public eye elicits extreme reactions. Helena certainly had her admirers. Her auto-graph book includes some charming entries, including this one: 'The Lord has made you a woman and made a good job of it. You have made yourself a lawyer and followed His example.'[21] A sister barrister, Enid Rosser Locket, was not so sure, on either count, calling Helena a 'war horse from the Old Feminist days, and the terror of her male colleagues': 'She was a comic character, quite without fear, and physically unattractive. She can only be described as large and blowsy but she was an amusing tho' incredibly com-mon, not to say vulgar person in many ways.'[22] Yet Enid finds it impossible to dislike Helena, as she has the gift of learning from her mistakes, and is good-humoured and entirely without malice.

Enid Rosser Locket was adept at balancing her work and pri-vate life. One gets the impression that her default mode was delight, which always helps. She was born of middle-class parents in Swansea, who brought her up to value social responsibility, good humour and enthusiasm. At St Hugh's College, Oxford, she was not quite the model of a demure lady student, going for long walks with a man she had met at a lecture (chaperoned by the gooseberry junior librarian) and attending cocoa parties at which she daringly drank not cocoa, but the altogether more sophisticated beverage, coffee. She enjoyed sports, learning to swim at Parson's Pleasure, a pool on the River Cherwell in Oxford where dons notoriously bathed naked.

During the war Enid did a stint as a VAD; after the peace, her parents envisaged for her a career in the Civil Service. Maybe that was what Mr Rosser had had in mind for her brother Arthur, killed at the age of eighteen in 1916. Enid was at Oxford when the SDRA was passed, and must have had high hopes that her chosen profession would quickly modernize to accept women on the same terms as men. It would not have made much difference if it had; unfortunately, she was one of those who failed to stay the course at Oxford, becoming 'mentally and intellectually restless', and never took her degree. She switched to the LSE to study the trade union movement, and for the short time she was there she loved it. She lived at the Warwick Club in Pimlico, a private residence for young women like her, and relished the racy social life of the LSE, where everyone danced of an evening in the common room, 'blacks and whites and yellows, all uninhibited and mixed up'.

In 1921 Enid was invited by the Lord Chancellor's department in the House of Lords to be a 'lady secretary'; she was still there in 1927, moving in 'high legal circles', developing a vague ambition to become a barrister – and having a great deal of fun. She occupied a little flat of her own at the club now, and led a heady social life, spending holidays abroad and going to balls at home with a succession of young men who presented her with roses. She was also a member of the University Women's Club, a fanatical theatre-goer and a keen fan of the flicks, going every Sunday afternoon with friends to a cinema in Regent Street to see the latest release.

Since 1924 she had been studying part-time, like her fellow St Hugh's alumna Gwyneth Bebb Thomson, at Lincoln's Inn; and in 1927 she was called to the Bar. She and her sister now moved to a bijou flat in Gray's Inn Square with a cat and a daily cleaner. What more could she desire? She was young(ish) and single; she had money and a profession and her freedom. 'I did not believe in aggressive feminism,' she confessed, 'largely because I had never had need to.' Apparently, she charmed her way to success.

Meanwhile, solicitor Carrie Morrison was practising *femme seule* in London, working like Helena Normanton for Poor Persons and on behalf of disadvantaged women and children. Who better than a woman solicitor, herself disadvantaged by virtue of her sex, to address their cases? For a while she and her husband lived in a tenement building in London's East End, partly – surely – as a gesture of solidarity. Carrie also campaigned for better facilities for female members of the Law Society. Her colleague Agnes Twiston Hughes had settled into the family practice in Conwy, where she and her solicitor husband lived over the shop. Mrs Twiston Hughes specialized in adoption cases, and is said to have been sought out more than once by people desperately trying to trace their birth families, assuming she must be their mother as her name was mentioned in court documents exclusively and often. It would not have occurred to them that she was the solicitor handling their case. She used to smoke like a chimney, by an open office window, cheerfully dressed in multiple cardigans to keep out those damp Welsh draughts.

Women doctors grew in confidence as a body of professionals during the 1920s, persevering in the face of diminishing opportunities at medical schools and the persistent refusal of chartered institutions to admit them as Fellows in any significant number, despite the provisions of the SDRA. Ida Mann had decided that eyes were 'clean and obvious', an opinion endorsed by Sir John Herbert Parsons who had taken her on as a junior and reckoned ophthalmology 'a very suitable line for a girl'.[23] Sir John, said Ida, was 'the Pope of my chosen religion' and an inspirational teacher. She learned to perfect cataract operations under his instruction, eventually taking only four-and-a-half minutes an eye. He encouraged her sub-specialty – embryos' lenses – and supported her application to Moorfields Eye Hospital in London, where she was appointed honorary ophthalmic surgeon in 1927. She remembered living a 'dedicated, masculine life' at this point in her career, 'virginal and fancy-free'.

Dr Helen Boyle was one of the Brighton set, struggling to establish progressive mental health services there, particularly for women. Having worked in slums, she was convinced that psychiatric patients are made and not born; that stress is a determining factor in 'madness'; and that mental patients deserve as much dignity and compassion as those with more obvious, physical complaints. In 1923 she co-founded the organization which later became MIND, then called the National Council for Mental Hygiene, and a year later was called to give evidence to the Royal Commission on Lunacy and Mental Disorder, which fed into the provisions of the Mental Treatment Act 1930. Her Brighton neighbour Octavia Wilberforce saw her point. 'I've got a patient [who is] suicidal every month,' she explained to a friend in 1920, 'and between times, a victim of asthma . . . When she's got asthma she's quite sane and a very nice girl – everybody loves her. When she hasn't [i.e. when she is menstruating] she's suicidal. I would like to cure her of one or t'other.' [24] There were several other notable women psychiatrists, whose success with patients must have owed something to a refusal to accept mental illness – any more than gender – as a weakness.

May Du Buisson qualified from King's College Medical School in the early 1920s, inspired by a period spent working as a VAD at Clandon Park Military Hospital in Surrey during the war. She was on her way to becoming a surgeon, having passed the membership exams for the Royal College, when she renewed acquaintance with a flamboyant young army officer while on holiday in Kenya and Uganda. May was with her cousin Evelyn at the time; they chaperoned one another on a railway journey with Captain Twining during which (the family legend goes) May was selected and duly proposed to. She agreed to marry in 1928 on condition that Captain Twining left the army and, one assumes, agreed to May's continuing to practise as a doctor. Both stuck to their bargains. Twining joined the Colonial Service and was posted to Gulu in Uganda, where May joined him. Here, and later elsewhere in Africa, in the Caribbean, North Borneo and Mauritius, she specialized in public health, holding clinics for women and children and educating them on the basics of disease prevention. She changed the way they lived.

It was cheering to hear of women like this – and the press was not slow to report on them. Precedent is powerful, and not just in the law. Pioneers in lines of work beyond the six core professions, too, were just as inspiring to ambitious women students and trainees. Lilian Lindsay (1871–1960) was the first woman to qualify as a dentist in the UK. Her headmistress had advised her to become a teacher but Lilian had other, stranger ideas. She applied to the London Dental Hospital in 1892 after serving a three-year apprenticeship; when one hears that her admission interview was conducted on the pavement outside the building one can't be too surprised to hear that she failed to get in – literally. Lilian tried the Edinburgh Dental School next. The city had just about recovered from the Sophia Jex-Blake episode, and accepted Lilian with reasonably good grace. She graduated in 1895; by the mid-1920s she was married and, though no longer practising, was publishing research papers and acting as librarian for the British Dental Association. Every dentist in the land must have known about Lilian.

Aleen Cust was the first woman to be awarded a diploma of membership by the Royal College of Veterinary Surgeons. By then, in 1922, she was aged fifty-four, and had been practising for years in Ireland, after graduating from Edinburgh University. That same year, Irene Barclay was the first to qualify as a chartered surveyor, though she was not elected a Fellow of her professional institute until 1931. Mary Harris Smith was seventy-two when she became a chartered accountant in May 1920; like Aleen Cust, she had been active and well respected in the profession all her working life, just formally unrecognized.

This record of accomplishment, impressive as it is, should not suggest that forging a career was straightforward for the pioneers. Personal circumstances and family pressure aside, there were plenty of external influences making their working lives difficult to negotiate. The price of training and of maintaining professional subscriptions was significant. In the mid-1920s it cost the equivalent of about £12,000 to read and qualify for the Bar (not including living expenses) and another £4,000 for each year of pupillage. That was followed by a period spent 'devilling' – basically, in unpaid work placement – so that you couldn't expect to cover your professional expenses, let alone start making a profit, until ten years or more after being called. That's partly why Helena Normanton turned her hand to journalism and Enid Rosser Locket kept on working for the House of Lords.

Solicitors could expect to pay sums that would now amount to between £4,000 and £40,000 as a premium for articled clerkship; architects, £7,500 for training and another £8,000 premium on qualification. Doctors spent some £14,500 on their five years at medical school, but could then start earning straight away. And after all that commitment of time, energy and money, professional women were often told they should be ashamed of themselves. One of Lilian Lindsay's professors railed at her for taking the bread, as he put it, out of some poor fellow's mouth. It took courage to withstand the passive – and not so passive – aggression of one's male colleagues at work. The educationalist Mary Bentinck Smith explained a phenomenon still recognized today. 'In most trades or professions in which women rather recently have entered into serious competition with men, it is a fact that in order to establish her claim to equality of opportunity and treatment with men the woman has . . . had to prove her superiority.'[25] But proving her superiority does her no favours either. Then she is considered aloof, conceited, 'too baggy for her breeches' and, worst of all, unfeminine. She needs taking down a peg or two.

Ritual has always been a prominent element of professional life – and just as it functions as a mark of belonging, so it also functions as a ready tool for undermining those perceived *not* to belong. So pioneering women found themselves humiliated by unwittingly contravening the rituals of the Inns of Court or the Senior Common Room that had not been explained to them – and this could be on a matter as mundane as the smoking of cigarettes. After her first lunch in post at Reading University, academic Edith Morley noticed everyone fidgeting with their pipes in the common room and looking shifty. As the only woman there, she did not possess a pipe; she assumed they were desperate for their tobacco but politely waiting for her to smoke, so accepted a cigarette for the first time in her life and nervously lit up. Shocked silence. No one had told her – while offering the cigarette – that smoking was forbidden before 1.45 p.m.

Archaeologist Margaret Murray was not allowed in the men's common room at University College London when she was elected a Fellow there in 1922. The space she was expected to share with her female colleagues was pitiful. It was later promoted to become a cloakroom. Margaret described it as long and narrow, with a slate slab down one side like a shelf taking up half the width of the room. There were two large, low basket chairs, too wide to stand side by side; a fireplace so tiny that the coal scuttle obscured it; and a gas ring for coffee on the slab. Margaret didn't mention how many female staff were required to share the room, but it was certainly more than the six (standing) and two (sitting) it accommodated. She made repeated requests for women staff to be assigned somewhere bigger in which to relax, do their marking and so on. Nothing happened until one day she had the bright idea of inviting the Provost to a post-prandial cup of coffee.

> The lamb came to the slaughter, quite flattered at having been invited, and when he arrived he was put in one of the big basket chairs at the far end of the little room and Miss Smith [one of Margaret's colleagues] in the other basket chair was put so that he was completely blocked in. Then all the members of the Common Room began to pour in and have coffee.[26]

Soon it was so crowded that no one could move. When he eventually managed to prise himself out, the Provost organized an upgrade: an ex-chemistry lab full of clapped-out cast-off furniture, where the coffee was brewed in the stink-cupboard.

Isolation was one of the Establishment's solutions to this very small invasion of professional women; if they must be included in day-to-day business, one could at least try to render them invisible, or ridiculous. Dr Gladys Wauchope remembered having to wear a uniform on the wards during her training, not for any practical reason but 'in order that we should not appear frivolous'.[27] It was a little like the traditional workhouse dress for women: a severe, boxy garment made of holland (a heavy, linen-like cotton) with capacious pockets. The rules on dress for women at Lincoln's Inn in 1922 were clear: 'dresses should be plain, black or very dark, high to the neck with long sleeves and not shorter than the gown'.[28] There should be no suggestion of glamour and not a whisper of 'come hither'. It was obvious that women were playing gooseberry in the professions; intrusive plain Janes gate-crashing someone else's party. They were the not-so-charming impostors in an exclusive and long-standing relationship between gentlemen and the Establishment.

The journal *Builder*, which in 1902 had published Ethel Charles's witty 'Plea for Women', also published a report of the RIBA president's annual address in 1920 – his first after the passing of the SDRA – which makes the terms of this relationship uncomfortably clear. The incumbent at the time was John Simpson – the designer of the old Wembley Stadium and of Roedean School for Girls. 'Architecture was an exacting mistress,' he told his members.

> She would tolerate no rivals; beware how they took her to themselves if they had not the strength to be faithful. Like a mistress, her pleasure was capricious; therefore be not discouraged by disappointment, for when they expected it least she would show her tenderest favour. Only to her lovers was disclosed the beauty of her symmetry and they, like Psyche, might not know its secret.[29]

6

Not Quite Nice

PROFESSIONAL WOMEN IN THE PUBLIC EYE

It is impossible for a man to serve under a woman
and retain his self-respect and manhood.[1]

THE ARCHITECT MASTERS his muse; the lawyer gives sight to blind
Lady Justice;[2] the doctor maps the disabilities of a woman's body,
while the priest reminds her of Eve's legacy. The engineer tames
the physical world; the academic orders the life of the mind. Neither realm concerns the weaker sex. It was Samuel Johnson who
said: 'Subordination tends greatly to human happiness. Were we
all upon an equality, we should have no other enjoyment than
animal pleasure.'[3] Sound chap, Johnson.

This was the patriarchal attitude, seasoned by centuries of self-
reinforcement, espoused by those opposed to women entering the
professions during the inter-war period known as Britain's 'long
weekend'. It really was: this isn't melodrama or some sort of feminist retrospectroscope in action. From the Age of Enlightenment
onwards, pioneering women were regarded by people of influence
as subversive, as social iconoclasts, as deviants intent on corrupting
the Empire, the country, the natural authority of men and the
future of the race. The press and popular culture caricatured, sen-
sationalized or ridiculed them, while the public considered them a
breed apart.

Naturally, not everyone during the period was a reactionary; the pioneers had their champions. The women themselves tried to be pragmatic, tending more to ignore such censure than to challenge it in any other way than by demonstrating it to be non-sensical. But in considering that post-war era when so much had changed – in many ways the first era of #MeToo – it is important to recognize the weight of prejudice against those pioneers, if only to appreciate their skill and grace in overcoming it.

I'll start at the bottom, with an essay published in 1926 by a prominent lawyer, Edmund Haynes. It begins promisingly: 'I was reared in the pure milk of feminism,'[4] he assures us, delivered by a female doctor and surrounded by aunts who were pioneers in the Post Office Savings Bank. He's been married to the same wife for twenty-one years and has three daughters, so – he insists – he's no misogynist (though in a passing reference he spells the immortal Jane Miss 'Austin', which immediately raises my suspicions). Having made these disclaimers, he lets rip.

He considers the modern woman too aggressive to be happy as a wife and mother, pointing out that this pugnacity is due to too many games lessons at school. He suspects female teachers have an unhealthy fascination with watching schoolgirls dangling about in gymnasiums or racing around the hockey pitch. That is because they are all frustrated virgins, which makes the current preponderance of spinsters in the profession distinctly unedifying. (Whose fault is *that*, given the marriage bar?) He suggests that in thirty or forty years' time we'll be able to choose the sex of our children, in which case he would recommend two boys to every girl. This would set education – and the wider world – to rights again.

He agrees that it must be irksome for women lawyers constantly to be captioned in the papers as 'modern Portias'; but he is sure that, if it were not for snobbery, most women would prefer domestic work to challenging men in the traditional professions, so the problem would not arise. By 'snobbery' he means unseemly jostling among educated women for public recognition, as though they were big-game hunters out for the most impressive trophy. If she is married, the modern woman too often produces only one or two children who are promptly consigned to a nanny while she pursues 'what is called a "career"'. It is true that the world would probably be a safer place if women had more influence; they have a horror of waste and destruction and 'hate each other so much that they logically prefer duelling to collective warfare'. But at what price?

The real nub of the problem, according to Mr Haynes, is the rise of the 'intermediate'. The suffrage movement (which he implies is at the root of many evils) was inspired by '"intermediates" or homosexuals' who were not sufficiently distracted by domestic occupation to keep them on the straight and narrow. He warns that there are more of these masculine women about these days than is generally imagined, and that they are better qualified than the more 'normal' woman to compete with men in the professional workplace. 'A woman who thinks of nothing but personal conquest or competition with men in male pursuits,' he concludes, 'or of money-making as an end in itself or of what may be called parasitic enjoyment, is much less useful to society than a common prostitute.'[5]

If Mr Haynes's tongue is not in his cheek – and there's no reason to suppose it is – then despite his protestations about the Post Office aunts and his mother's obstetrician, he is no feminist but falls fairly and squarely into the misogynist camp. There he mixes with like-minded gentlemen – and occasional ladies – who regard all ground-breaking females as lesbians. With curling lip, they call women medics 'she-doctors', as 'tough as old leather'.[6] Other professional women are repeatedly described as abnormal, dowdy, forceful and mannish or large and frumpy. Such individuals use their nominal femininity like a Trojan horse, to disguise their perversion while infiltrating the enemy. Haynes has their number.

The solution to the problem of the 'intermediate' invasion is not a corresponding excess of femininity; that is considered just as dangerous as the lack of it. A friend once commiserated with the academic Enid Starkie, who couldn't work out why her love life was in such disarray.

> Your tragedy is that you think like a man, indeed in many ways feel like a man, have need of development like a man, and yet are supremely a woman physically. If you were a les-bian it would be easier or if you were just a woman with desire to please [and] further [a] man's career. Or if you were frigid and intellectual. You have been made of bits and scraps, nothing properly put together.[7]

Some friend. One of the neatest back-handed insults I have come across, incidentally, appears in a 1936 report in the *Manchester Evening News* accompanying a happy picture of women medical students on graduation day. 'All alert and self-possessed, a large number are sufficiently good-looking to have no need of cosmet-ics, which they, naturally, eschew.'[8]

Just as successful women were berated for not appearing sexu-ally attractive to men, so they were blamed for trying too hard. They were accused of entering the professions solely to ensnare eligible men (or wreck the marriages of those already taken): 'He may have a face like a fruit salad, a figure like Epstein's "Genesis" [a pregnant woman] and as much sex-appeal as a jelly-fish – but if all's right with his bank balance, she'll marry him.' That was the Reverend George Braithwaite, dubbed 'the most outspoken Vicar in Britain', writing in the *Daily Mirror* in 1938.[9] At least the person he described had marriage in mind. Worse was the good-time girl with a high enough salary to tease her colleagues to distraction.

For she'll go out to dinner and go out to dance
Apparelled in priceless creations from France,
But she laughs when the victim begins on his dreams,
Though by no means averse to his chocolate creams.[10]

That brings us to another tranche of invective against women in a man's world – not about how they looked, but about their reprehensible behaviour. The word 'flapper' derives from a slang term for a prostitute. During the roaring twenties it was used to denote not so much loose morals as loose clothing (though depravity was often directly ascribed to a lack of disciplined corsetry). A flapper was a modern girl who knew how to have fun. She danced the Charleston all night, drank cocktails, smoked cigarettes, fraudulently impersonated boys with her short hair, flat chest and slender hips – or men, with her career. In other words, she broke the rules.

How could a flibbertigibbet like this hope to match the gravitas of a long-established member of, for instance, the Law Society – originally called the Society of Gentlemen Practitioners – with any degree of credibility? There is a reason why no feminine equivalent exists for the word 'fellowship' (or the word 'patronizing', come to that). In the face of women solicitors doing perfectly well when given the opportunity, detractors turned to playground insults. Women can't be good lawyers, they maintained, because their brains are tiny and their bodies feeble. Physically, they spend a quarter of their best years revoltingly mired in Eve's curse. Mentally they are illogical and inherently biased. They are bitchy to one another, flirtatious with men and completely unreliable, sharing a peculiarly feminine trait of 'seeing through a stone wall what is not on the other side'.[11]

The writer and journalist Winifred Holtby, on the other hand, thought the flapper a breath of fresh air, an antidote not only to the repressions of the Victorian era, but to the economic and cultural slump of the 1920s. Writing in 1935, she warned of the

dangers of quashing their enterprising spirit. Successful women
were even more impressive than they first appeared, handicapped
by having to do better than men to be acknowledged as anything
like equal, and by the struggle to reach the point where most professional men began. The modern girl might be criticized for
being rude to her elders and impatient of authority, neglectful of
her domestic duties, selfish about her pleasures and adventurous in
her desires (especially for chocolate creams), but every age had its
rebels. Rebellion was not in itself a bad thing. In Italy and Spain,
and most of all in Fascist Germany, professional women were
being forcefully repatriated to the kingdom of *Kinder, Küche* and
Kirche – children, kitchen and church – and it did not bode well.

There were plenty in Britain who wished Pandora back in her
box, regrettably opened by the exigencies of the First World War
and the suffrage campaign. They resented her (limited) success,
unearned by years spent in the purgatory of the trenches or, on a
lesser scale, the dormitories of public school. By the 1930s, some
of the young female pretenders in medicine or law, architecture,
engineering or the universities did not even remember the war.
Critics recalled the so-called atrocities of the suffragettes and
questioned the mental health of a sex whose members sought
political responsibility through violence, as though that were not
learned behaviour from men. Hysteria, by definition a feminine
affliction, was like a cancer: it upset the natural balance of things
and spread easily. In 1926 the *Illustrated Police News* reported a
sensational case in France in which a 'girl barrister' had shot herself 'in the heart' while at work. Mlle Juliet Goublet was (naturally)
remarkable for her 'studious features and striking beauty'. She
was madly in love with a male colleague who did not love her,
and had tried to end it all with a pearl-handled revolver. She was
rushed to hospital where her life was saved. With admirable and
lawyerly dispassion, she explained afterwards that her despair was
'purely sentimental'.[12] The implication of the article is that this is

what happened to women whose minds were warped by work beyond their natural capacity: they turned hysterical, posing a danger to themselves and to the public. It is why women students were subjected to medical checks every academic year, to make sure any financial grants they received were not in danger of being wasted. Men were not as rigorously tested because they were considered stronger than women in every way.

Paradoxically, I would argue, this presumption of a female's delicacy helped women more than it hindered them. It meant that at many universities, what we would now call mental health services for students were in place for women long before they existed for their supposedly more robust male peers. At Birmingham University there is a case file about a young woman I'll call Catherine, a collier's daughter in receipt of a miner's welfare grant. The first document is dated 2 May 1930 and is a succinct note from a doctor. 'Dear Miss Milne,' it says (Miss Milne was the senior tutor for women students). 'I think that [Catherine] should be sent home now. She is certainly not fit for university work.'[13] An accompanying report contains the diagnosis of 'an anaemia of nervous debility'. Catherine is unstable and excitable, and, having what was called a 'Derbyshire neck' – or goitre – is probably suffering from hyperthyroidism. Miss Milne informs her father, who replies with a note of desperation that he would help her if he could, but communication is not easy.

> I am willing for [Catherine] to come home, but she has written telling me not to expect her . . . I wish you could persuade her to go to Skegness for a few weeks, as she don't want to go . . . She mostly does what she thinks best.

There is no record of what became of Catherine, but her doctor thought it unlikely she could cope with a career in teaching, which is what her struggle to get to university was all about. Had her problems not been picked up, however, she might have suffered the same fate as a young woman – ironically, a doctor – found dead in her lodgings in Liverpool in 1938. 'Lone Woman Doctor Lost to Prejudice' ran the headline in the *Daily Mirror*, whose reporter reckoned a boycott of her practice, because of her gender, had led to her suicide. She was already suffering depression, being painfully shy and friendless; the shame of failure as a professional woman was ultimately too hard to bear.

We need an antidote to all this gloom. Veteran feminist Millicent Fawcett agreed with Winifred Holtby that the flapper was a Good Thing. Beneath her shingled head were an alert brain, a ready wit, an ability to make clear, quick decisions and an attractive tendency to laugh at obstacles. An article in *The Woman Engineer* published in June 1930 features just such a person. She is a ground engineer working for her engineer's licence at an aerodrome, and this is how her typical day unfolds.

It starts with her arrival at the hangar at 7.45 a.m. She is fifteen minutes late, and her boss informs her in the choicest of language (not reproducible) that she might as well go straight home again, if that's her attitude. After suitably abject apologies, she is physically kicked through the door to begin work with the boys. She clambers into her soiled overalls and arms herself with grease-gun, oil-squirt and spanner to service an engine. She washes it first, every minute growing dirtier as the machinery becomes cleaner. She breaks her last good nail trying to unscrew the petrol filter, and drops a hammer on her boss's foot before it's time to stop for a mug of tea. Her landlady won't countenance making breakfast at 7 a.m., so she is hungry. A huge cheese roll solves that problem.

The next job is to wheel out and fuel her aeroplane before warming it up ready for testing by a flying instructor at 10 a.m. Then it's back inside. Her companion is told to work on some pistons while she – nicknamed 'John' – is asked to sweep up and

tidy the hangar. She thought she had escaped housework by training to become an engineer; it seems not. With a broom bigger
than she is, she starts work. So efficient is she that there is still
time to begin decarbonizing a cylinder head before lunch.

Her break lasts an hour, spent eating, joking and talking shop.
The afternoon is fairly uneventful, except for the arrival of an
eager journalist asking for the 'Lady Engineer'. Everyone looks
blank. 'No lady here!' they assure him. John emerges to join in
the search, rubbing her grubby palms on the seat of her overalls;
no luck. When she washes her face before tea, her secret is discovered. She is the person they are looking for. But she doesn't play
the game. The journalist is not interested in what she's done, only
in what she's wearing. Overalls over her clothes, she snaps, and
over her overalls, grease, dirt and oil. He wanders off dissatisfied,
no doubt (she reckons) to make up the appropriate story for himself. Now a photographer appears. John is flustered.

> 'Oh hurry, where's my heart-shaped helmet, my manicure set,
> and my powder-puff?' Where can my powder-puff be? There's
> a spanner in my stern pocket, a few loose nuts, screws and
> bolts in every other pocket – but where, oh where, is my
> powder-puff pocket?
>
> You see, I must look nice for the photographer, for I've been
> told that every pilot has several proposals weekly, so I must
> spread abroad my beauty. (I've had no proposals yet, so I sup-
> pose I'm no pilot. But while there's life there's hope. Maybe the
> stronger sex don't like my brawny fist – or brawny arm, is it?)
>
> I don my smart flying suit and appear for once as others
> would have me be, but the minute the camera clicked off, off it
> comes . . . Hangar doors are closed, good-nights are said, and
> off we all go to our various pursuits. I to the pictures with my
> sweetheart? Oh, no, indeed. At 6 p.m. I have a lecture and after
> that I hope to do some reading for my next examination.
>
> A hard life, but Jove, it's a good one![14]

Had John managed to get to the cinema, with or without a sweetheart, during the summer of 1930, it's likely she would have sat through a newsreel featuring herself, for her real name was Amy Johnson (1903–41), one of the most famous women – and certainly the most famous female engineer – in the world. The article describes the time she had spent at the De Havilland works outside London three years earlier, working for the first licensed engineer's certificate awarded by the Air Ministry to a woman. This fishmonger's daughter from Hull was also learning to fly, having turned up at an aerodrome with a pound note in her pocket demanding lessons, and in May 1930 flew solo from England to Australia in nineteen and a half days. Her glamorous looks, picturesque back-story and unaffected courage catapulted her into the limelight, but she never lost her love of shop-floor engineering, serving as president of the WES from 1935 to 1937.

Engineer Amy Johnson in an unusually unglamorous pose.

What brighter example could there be of the lively flapper, the modern girl, the female professional who manages to be wholly feminine and wholly business-like at the same time?

Others like her were celebrated, or celebrated themselves, in less public ways. Barrister Helena Normanton was proud of the letters she received from grateful clients – especially, if her personal archive is anything to go by, if they came from those who recognized that it was not easy for a woman lawyer to be taken seriously. 'I do not know how to express my great gratitude to you for the endeavours you have made on my behalf,' writes a Mr James Mason. 'Working as you are under great difficulties makes my debt to you even greater.'[15] He can't do much for her in return, but offers to tackle any hard manual work, housework or clerical tasks she might need doing. Another gentleman writes from Parkhurst Prison on the Isle of Wight (perhaps she got his sentence commuted?). He might not see Helena again in person, but he promises never to forget that long talk they shared before his incarceration. He appreciates that she was never out for the money, unlike most of 'them' (i.e. male lawyers). It is clear that, unlike him, she was doing whatever good she could in the world. He needs to change. He's been handed his bill, he says, and will pay it. And then he'll come out and beat the cynics, with Miss Normanton for inspiration.

Countless women doctors must have been thanked by patients whose lives they changed or saved. The satisfaction of seeing a family living happily in a house you built in your head and then in reality must have been hard to beat. There were not many public fanfares, but the pioneers were quick to congratulate one another. They were particularly good at celebratory dinners. No personal or professional archive I have come across in the course of my research for this book has been without a handful of elaborately decorated menus for multiple-course dinners, marking various anniversaries of women's progress. The ritual of eating

together in a ceremonial setting has always been an important
part of professional life. Even after the passing of the SDRA,
women were not always invited to the main event – so they held
their own. Thank goodness stays were going out of fashion.

It would not be fair to suggest that all pioneering women
were joined in sisterly solidarity. They were human, after all.
Some were jealous of others' success, and could be snide. The
Principal of LMH in Oxford did not think much of Maude
Royden's choice of a career, considering her unwise and naïve.
Any success Maude enjoyed would soon fade, she warned, when
the novelty of hearing her preach wore off. A group photograph
of early women students in the archives of the MWF in Manchester is annotated with names and acerbic little comments by
one of their number about the rest, ranging from 'brilliant'
through 'intelligent' and 'harmless' to 'stupid to a degree'. Such
pettiness reminds us that these people were not superwomen, just
women, like us. I find that thought at once comforting – perhaps
we can achieve what they did – and depressing. Why are we still
fighting so many of the same battles, and still so apt to get caught
in the crossfire?

No amount of celebratory camaraderie or clients' appreciation
can conceal the fact that a great deal of institutional prejudice
against women persisted during the inter-war years. They were
handicapped by the limited terms and ambiguity of the SDRA,
which according to *Time and Tide* did not really remove sexual
discrimination at all. It might have allowed them to serve as
magistrates and jurors, but they were only appointed magistrates
when vacancies arose, and were exempted from jury duty if the
case was deemed too distasteful, or they were incapacitated by
some 'feminine condition or ailment'.[16] This was a travesty of
equality – indeed, it amounted to censorship. The number
of women students allowed at Oxford University was capped in

1927 at 840 (about one-sixth of the total student population), a limitation which lasted until 1956. At Cambridge, women were denied degrees and the free access to laboratories and libraries necessary for their studies. Their numbers were also capped. If women scientists did miraculously happen to be awarded competitive funding for research, it was often on the understanding that they did what they were told. There is a chance Maria Czaplicka might have continued in academia on someone else's terms, but she insisted on following her own interests. Biologist Barbara Dainton was assigned to slugs and potatoes and thought herself lucky – her female colleagues were fobbed off with wire-worms. A list of positions for women chemists published in the mid-1930s is curiously feminine, including work on fruit juices, confectionery, cosmetics and pigments: the jobs men – given the choice – did not want.

Of the thirty saints canonized between 1920 and 1939, nearly half were female, while living women of God were struggling for recognition. Maude Royden passionately believed Christ to be the first feminist, and God to be as much our mother as our father, but conceded that vocations like hers were difficult to realize when the church doors were kept so adamantly shut, and women were regarded by the clergy as lesser icons rather than human beings. During the 1920s it was estimated that the Anglican Church was at least seven hundred vicars short of the optimum number. The way to address this, according to the Establishment, was not – as Maude might have suggested – to appoint clergywomen, which would lower the moral tone, but for Christian women to relinquish worldly ambition and become better wives and mothers instead. Then society would have fewer problems, and consequently would require fewer priests.

Bankers explained their reluctance to appoint women at any level by insisting that customers would feel anxious if they knew someone's daughter or sister was looking after their money.

Women could not grasp the principles of finance (try telling that to Lady Rhondda or Gordon Holmes). That's why they could be refused mortgages on their own account until 1975, or any form of credit without a male guarantor until 1980. It's a wonder they were able to calculate that men were paid more than they were for the same work.

In 1925 the Civil Service allowed women to apply for posts in the higher administrative grades by open competitive examination – that is, on the same terms as male candidates – for the first time. Eighty men and twenty-seven women sat the exam that year; nineteen men and three women passed. The clerical and finally the executive grades followed in 1927 and 1928 respectively. During the next seven years, eighty-eight women competed, of whom eight were successful.[17] Coaching for the exams was expensive, and career progression for women in the higher echelons was slow. There was no compulsion to pay them the same salary as men, despite the intention of the Tomlin Commission in 1929 to offer all civil servants 'a fair field and no favour'.

A glance at the personnel files of female civil servants during the 1930s reveals what qualities their employers valued most. In November 1937 Hilda Martindale retired from her post as director of what was called the Women's Establishment at the Treasury. Although female civil servants were no longer physically segregated from their male colleagues (in most departments), they still had their own discrete administration. When the time came to choose a successor to this most 'biggish' of women, the post was advertised at Hilda's insistence not as the directorship of the Women's Establishment, but as an assistant secretaryship in the Treasury, with a focus on women employees. Hilda thought it counterproductive to continue viewing women as a subsection of the Civil Service. They *were* the Civil Service, no less than their male colleagues.

Twelve internal candidates were selected for interview. Miss A (45) of Cambridge and Manchester Universities had been an inspector at the Board of Trade since 1923; she was 'brilliant and charming', with good judgement and great courage, but perhaps lacked objectivity. 'I think she understands men better than she understands women,' commented a tight-lipped referee.[18] Miss B was a graduate of Royal Holloway College about whom the best that could be said was that she liked sports. 'Unruffled' Mrs C had an OBE and had been a civil servant since the war. She possessed 'exceptionally good judgement' – but, riskily, she was not a spinster. Miss D (42) had a similarly long record, having joined the Treasury in 1917. She had a 'very fine brain' but relied too much on logic and was 'a little lacking in the human approach'. Miss E had 'outstanding force of personality and generosity of heart'; her sense of humour saved her from being 'a prig or a bore' but her record was clouded by unspecified 'difficulties . . . on staff matters'. At the end of the list came Miss F – 'I hardly think [she] is the type you would want' and Miss G, who 'certainly is not'. The oldest candidate whose age is given was 55; the youngest, 35. Only one was a 'Mrs'.

The person appointed was Miss Myra Curtis, a Newnham alumna of Churchillian profile who came first in the Civil Service entrance exam and was a superintendent in the Post Office Savings Bank. Here is what was said about her – which we can take as a blueprint for the ideal female chief.

> Miss Curtis has energy, initiative and self-confidence. She has an exceptionally orderly mind and a flair for organisation. She is the most competent woman Civil Servant of everyone's acquaintance. It is on the personal side that one might have doubts as regards Miss Curtis. There is nothing by way of soft femininity about her. That, I reckon an advantage, enabling her the more readily to establish herself as an equal among equals.

In other words, she was just like a man.

Civil servant and academic Myra Curtis (right).

It is a fact of life that newspaper reports about women invariably supply their age in brackets and describe what they look like, either verbally or with the judicious choice of a photograph. A feature in the *Daily Express* in 1935 is startling to modern eyes: 'Do the Features of These Women Show Their Professions?' asks the headline. What follows is a sort of identity parade of six women, with the caption 'Professions Shown by the Expression. Tell-Tale Traits.' Their portraits have been given to a phrenologist, Mrs O'Dell, who has spookily identified in them the very characteristics essential to each woman's chosen career. The financier Gordon Holmes has strength, initiative and great powers of calculation; she's a gifted mathematician. Helena Normanton

has an unusually good memory; she is observant, a good communicator and 'a born judge'. The artist, dancer, politician and
musician photographed are identified with the same pinpoint
accuracy. To be honest, all the women look more or less the
same, except for Helena's scholarly glasses. But Mrs O'Dell has
proved beyond doubt, according to the *Express*, that 'a woman's
choice of a career will eventually mould her face'.[19] I can't help
wondering what a phrenologist looks like.

Canny career women were acutely aware of the phenomenon
of trial by appearance, and dressed accordingly. When applying
for a job, they were careful to look neat but unostentatious. A
good hat was as essential as paper qualifications. The popular
magazine *Miss Modern* ran a feature on job interviews in 1930,
advising its readers how important it was to sit nicely.[20] Your knees
and feet should be clamped together, not fidgeting all over the
place as though nothing to do with you. Concentrate on details.
A lost button could mean a lost job. Don't wear too much lipstick,
get rid of 'superfluous hair-flies' (a bafflingly euphemistic term for
a feminine moustache) and use your 'sex-weapons' with discretion. The assumption is implicit that the interviewer will be male.

Dress and appearance – and the use of sex-weaponry, which
we shall come to in due course – were all important strategies in
countering the prejudice faced by the pioneers. Some of them
were naturally chic and charming, like the tall and elegant Gwyneth
Bebb Thomson, who apparently loved a good hat, but the rest had
to make a conscious effort (unless, like eye-surgeon Ida Mann,
they took the view that practicality was the only criterion worth
considering). Self-possession and calmness were the looks to go
for, indicated by quiet confidence and good taste. The journals of
professional women's organizations advertised suitable under-
and outer garments for sober solicitors and unworldly academics
(who were notoriously eccentric). Engineers needed good cosmetics, as Amy Johnson knew, and architects, outfits suitable for

climbing ladders without hindrance or embarrassment. It was still unusual at this time for women to wear trousers – and unwise, unless compelled to do so for practical reasons.

A girl's crowning glory was her coiffure. You can chart the success of women in the workplace by measuring the length of their hair. When Amy Johnson cut off her long tresses as a teenager, impatient to be thought grown up, her father was so appalled that he forced her to stay on an extra year at school for punishment. My own mother Helen, born in 1925, had a classmate who moaned constantly about her parents' refusal to let her crop her hair. It was so long that when she sat down, her single plait reached well below the seat of her chair. Helen – a natural rebel – decided to take matters into her own hands, stop the whining, and catapult her friend into the twentieth century. She stole the kitchen scissors one day, took them to school, and chose the desk behind her friend. Leaning over in the middle of a lesson, she chopped the plait clean off. Helen remembered the irrevocable thud of the unravelling plait hitting the floor for the rest of her life.

Victorian girls put their hair up when they wished to be taken seriously as adults; inter-war women shingled it, or bobbed it with a Marcel wave. A *Daily Herald* critic once called Virginia Woolf 'dynamite in curlers'[21] – crashingly inappropriate in Woolf's case, but a good indicator of the eloquence of the hair-do. The barrister's wig was a gift to satirists out for an easy laugh at women's expense. One set of cartoons in the 1920s has a 'flapper advocate' dressed in a revealing little off-the-shoulder black robe, contemplating what style of wig is likely to suit her best. A pert little one like a fascinator? One with integral ribbons and bows? Or perhaps one so full and luxuriously long that it subsumes the opposition on the bench?[22] It is said, incidentally, that for centuries no lawyers thought of washing their horsehair wigs – until the arrival in court of the first women, to whom it came naturally.

One of the Establishment's favourite claims against professional women was that their health was not sound enough to stand the rigours of work. (There did not appear to be the same concern for women in the trades or industries.) It was therefore part of their strategy to prove this assumption wrong. It helped that sportiness and adventurousness were hallmarks of the modern girl. 'Less than half a century ago,' noted the economist Margaret Miller in 1927, 'women were as effectively barred from earning a livelihood in the higher ranks . . . as if femininity were an incurable disease with which they had been born.'[23] Now, supporters of careers for women claimed that even menstruation and pregnancy were no barriers to a full working life in themselves, though the marriage bar was another question. Erstwhile lawyer and industrialist Nancy Nettlefold was a first-rate tennis player, as was barrister Ivy Williams; Amy Johnson was a racing driver as well as a pilot, and leading stainless-steel engineer Cleone Griff – appropriately enough – an excellent fencer. Ray Strachey maintained that a woman who had six children, like her employer Lady Astor, need only be laid up for a total of twelve months of her life: no problem (as long as she also had the staff to cope). And anyway, men could be as weedy as women were supposed to be. A lady doctor used to tell a story of being asked to administer smallpox vaccinations to male clerks at a bank: they all fainted, one after the other, neat as dominoes in their black suits and white spats.

Dress, hair, behaviour and conspicuous good health: what was left in the arsenal of a professional woman hoping to defy prejudice and be taken seriously? Political activism was a risky strategy, given recent history, but potentially extremely powerful. After the Representation of the People Act was passed at the beginning of 1918, giving a vote to a number of women over the age of thirty, the National Union of Women's Suffrage Societies (NUWSS) was disbanded. Its heir was another campaign group, set up to lobby not only for equal voting rights for men and women, but for equal opportunities at work and equal status across the legislature. The National Union of Societies for Equal Citizenship (NUSEC) was born in March 1919; though its first chair was the former NUWSS leader Millicent Fawcett, she was soon succeeded by social reformer and sister suffragist Eleanor Rathbone (1872–1946).

Miss Rathbone was elected to Parliament in 1929, in the wake of the previous year's Equal Franchise Act, and went on to design the system of family allowances at the heart of the welfare state. There could not have been a more suitable figurehead to navigate the women's movement through its adolescence. NUSEC's first annual report in 1920 mentioned the impact Maude Royden and Edith Picton-Turbervill were making on London congregations and expressed optimism about the latest Lambeth Conference, the ten-yearly gathering of Anglican bishops. The Bishop of London had argued that the office of deaconess should be canonically recognized. A deaconess in the Anglican Church was essentially a low-paid lay-minister; a curate's curate. The bishop thought it time such women were ordained like male deacons, and allowed to administer certain sacraments. Good news – but it didn't happen until the 1980s.

The same annual report noted that, having reached a measure of political parity, the next target for British women was to achieve economic independence as workplace professionals and/or as wives and mothers. The tone of the report is optimistic. That optimism wavered a little during the following few years; to boost NUSEC members' enthusiasm, Millicent Fawcett wrote a pamphlet in 1926 summarizing the legislative progress made since women were first given a political voice.[24]

The list is impressive. In 1918 – before the first general election in which women could vote, and before there were any women MPs – the Registration of Midwives Act was amended and a new Act passed to increase statutory payments by fathers to single mothers in support of their illegitimate children. The

SDRA went through, as we know, in December 1919. The Women's Emancipation Bill it replaced would have been a more equitable piece of legislation, according to NUSEC, but the old suffrage adage of half a loaf being better than none still applied. That same year, 1919, saw the Nurses' Registration Act and the founding of the League of Nations within which all appointments were open to men and women alike. The Civil Service began to crack in 1920, with the first equal opportunity admissions exam held five years later. Also in 1920 Scottish women benefited from a Married Women's Property Act and another child maintenance Act was passed, improving the enforcement of maintenance orders relating to fathers abroad.

The pace picked up in 1922, despite there still being only two women sitting in the House of Commons (Lady Astor having been joined in 1921 by the Liberal Mrs Margaret Wintringham). The Married Women (Maintenance) Act was passed in that year, as was the Infanticide Act, ensuring that a woman could not be convicted of murder if she was found to be suffering from the 'effects of confinement' or what we would now call post-partum trauma. Married women were allowed to choose their nationality, without having to assume that of their husbands; the Criminal Law Amendment Act raised the age of consent from thirteen to sixteen, a material factor in cases of indecent assault, and extended the time limit for an alleged victim to report such an assault from six to nine months. There were various amendments to Property Acts between 1922 and 1925 affecting inheritance and marriage.

There was also the Matrimonial Causes Act 1923, permitting women to divorce their husbands on the grounds of adultery; in the same year, the Intoxicating Liquor (Sales to Persons Under 18) Act was piloted through the Commons by lifelong teetotaller Lady Astor. Women police officers were given powers of arrest. In 1925 mothers were allowed equal rights with fathers over the guardianship of their children; cruelty to children and habitual drunkenness became admissible grounds for a wife to request a legal separation from her husband; and the Widows, Orphans and Old Age Contributory Pensions Act was passed, improving the rights of an insured man's dependants.

This was a remarkable slew of legislation, justifying the familiar promise of suffragists that once women were given political influence, the world would become a fairer place for everyone – in time. For some, though, that was not soon enough. NUSEC's approach was considered too conciliatory by those concerned more with equality than with the sort of legislation designed to protect women's welfare. In a development echoing the progress of the suffrage campaign, a 'ginger group' was established to move things on. If NUSEC was the progressive but well-mannered daughter of the NUWSS, the Six Point Group, two years younger, was ruder and louder – the natural successor to Emmeline Pankhurst's militant Women's Social and Political Union (WSPU).

Lady Rhondda, a former suffragette herself, founded the Six Point Group in 1921. The 'six points' were six aspects of women's equality: political, occupational, moral, social, economic and legal. The group shared Lady Rhondda's intensely personal interest in the entitlement of peeresses to sit in the House of Lords; she was a peeress in her own right, having succeeded to the title on her father's death, and therefore should have been allowed to sit under the terms of the SDRA. In fact she was speciously prohibited from the Upper House, and never got to take her seat there, dying five years before the passing of the Peerage Act, 1963. Close friends Winifred Holtby and Vera Brittain were both members of the Six Point Group; Lady Rhondda's periodical *Time and Tide*, for which they wrote, was its unofficial organ.

Both NUSEC and the Six Point Group fought for gender equality of status and pay in the professional workplace. If their membership was not as numerous as the suffrage societies' had

been, it was only because more women were too busy practising
what they preached to attend meetings and sit on committees.
Further activist groups emerged, like the Open Door Council
founded in 1926 specifically to campaign for equal opportunities
at work, and the Married Women's Association to contest the
marriage bar. These supported more specific bodies like the WES,
the Law Society's '1919 Club' for women (which later became the
Association of Women Solicitors) and the MWF. NUSEC was
dissolved in 1928, but its ideology and to a certain extent its
membership continued in organizations like the Fawcett Society
that still exist. The Open Door Council closed in 1965; the Six
Point Group survived until the early 1980s and the Married
Women's Association until 1988. It would be nice to think they
all disappeared because the job was done.

According to Dr Louisa Aldrich-Blake, prejudice and counter-
prejudice were a waste of energy. We are all in this together, she
said of medicine. If you are good at your work you are certain to
succeed; if you are not, you are certain to fail. Was it brilliance or
naïvety that sped her on, stately as a galleon? Probably both. The
truth is that, in most professions at this time, being good at her
job was no guarantee of a woman's success. It might have been a
passport to potential success; but the borderlands between alien-
ation and acceptance were policed by public opinion, professional
jealousies and a host of personal insecurities. A friend of anthropologist Maria Czaplicka commented that she seemed to live
twenty lives in her short span on Earth. Perhaps that is an add-
itional skill the professional woman was forced to learn: to be at
once a 'womanly' woman and a welcome trespasser in a man's
world; to be a good wife and mother, if she chose, as well as a
reliable colleague at work; to be confident without being strident,
innovatory without being subversive. This mythical, multi-
tasking paragon, this woman of many faces, will be familiar to

many of us today. It is hard enough for professional women to negotiate the expectations of the twenty-first century. Think how much harder it must have been to be judged by a society traumatized emotionally and economically by the aftermath of one war and the portents of another; a society on the cusp of losing its imperial identity and unused to crediting women with a political voice worth hearing; a society in which boys were old chaps, girls were flappers and good mothers stayed at home.

The best advice offered to the pioneers to counter unhelpful attitudes came from their own ranks. It is noticeable that in the records of the UWC, members only started putting 'Dr' in front of their names with any regularity in the mid-1930s. Before that, we may infer, the ruling principle was: Do not show off; it's vulgar. Yet it was crucial to the campaign for women to be taken seriously in the professions that they should take themselves seriously – as Dr Louisa Aldrich-Blake obviously did. In a book sweepingly entitled *British Women in the Twentieth Century*, Elsie Lang assured her readers in 1929 that clever girls were endearingly human. She knew of one intellectually outstanding Oxford graduate who, when looking for something to draw the fire in her bedroom, ditsily chose her academic gown, which she then bundled into the cupboard where it smouldered for a while before bursting into flames. Our power lies in our ordinariness, insists Elsie Lang.

> It is universally admitted that women have brought into business, the professions and public life a freshness of ideas and feelings, and a grip on the realities of home, education and social well-being that are wholly beneficent and that have a stimulating effect on their masculine colleagues and competitors.[25]

This was a little disingenuous of Lang; 'universally admitted' it was *not* – but sometimes saying it makes it so. Thinking positive was another strategy for success recommended by the successful.

And taking inspiration from others who have quietly triumphed against the odds, like the political campaigner Una Marson (1905–65), who travelled from her native Jamaica to England for a 'long holiday' in 1932 and ended up speaking at the International Alliance of Women for Suffrage in Istanbul three years later. The *Manchester Guardian* patronizingly described her obvious intellect as astonishing. She was able to afford the trip to London because of the success of a play she had written; once there she became involved with the League of Coloured Peoples, members of which gave the first performance in Britain of a play – her play – with an all-black cast. Una went on to act as Haile Selassie's secretary at the League of Nations and to be the first Afro-Caribbean woman to work for the BBC.

The League of Coloured Peoples' librarian, incidentally, was another role model: Yoruba Nigerian Stella Thomas (1906–74) who in 1933 was the first west African woman called to the English Bar. Born in Lagos and schooled in Sierra Leone, she fought family expectation for the right to higher education. Fortunately she was supported by an enlightened father, who had the means to send her to Britain in 1926. Three years later she was admitted to Middle Temple. Following qualification, she courageously used her oratorical skills to campaign publicly against colonial oppression, before returning to Africa in 1935 to practise in Sierra Leone and Nigeria. At home she was awarded the title 'Ogboni Agba' – esteemed elder – in recognition of her activism and wisdom: while Britain might have been suspicious of her, Nigeria was proud.

Neither Stella Thomas nor Una Marson wasted her talent by submitting to the status quo. Vera Brittain once wrote that it was as outrageous for an ambitious and intelligent woman to be condemned to washing dishes, knitting woollies and making blancmange as it was for a brilliant male playwright – say – to be kept at home to darn stockings.[26] That's all very well, but if

society and your family expected you to spend your days surrounded by dirty dishes and woollies and blancmange – and holey
stockings – you had several battles to fight before you even
reached this 'fair field' with 'no favour' the legislators liked to
talk about. 'In the end,' sighed Winifred Holtby, 'what matters is
an attitude of mind.'[27] Not just your attitude, as someone desperate to climb ladders, but the attitude of those who would rather
reserve the ladder for their own exclusive use.

I mentioned families – and would like to close this chapter
about prejudice and expectation on a positive note. Although it is
true that women were more likely than their male colleagues to
be retrieved from a promising career for domestic reasons, home
support could be one of the most energizing things about a working woman's life. A good indicator of the level of that support is
the attitude of families now to what great-aunts and grandmoth-
ers achieved then. One elderly gentleman told me that of all the
names on his flourishing family tree, he was proudest of his medical mother's. He never knew how special she was until she died,
and people started paying tribute to her skills as a GP. To him, she
was Mum, apparently always there for him. To everyone else she
was the Lady Doctor who saved hundreds of lives and endeared
herself to the whole community. She never talked about her
training, about the obstacles put in her way or the difficulties of
achieving a work–life balance. She was too modest for that. So
modest that the gentleman did not want me to publish her name;
he thought she wouldn't like the recognition. But he has made
sure his own children and grandchildren appreciate what she did
and who she was.

I now realize that she was one of thousands during this 'long
weekend' in British history who were not talking about being
professional women, but doing it. We might not know their
names, but their actions helped to make us who we are.

7

Dynamite in Curlers

THE WORK–LIFE BALANCE, 1928–1939

Women Inspect Plane Parts. Engineer's Warning.
Possible Danger to Flying Public.[1]

THAT HEADLINE APPEARS in an edition of the *Morning Post*, published in 1936. It might raise half a smile now, but back then it probably seemed perfectly reasonable. The article to which it refers implies that engineers like Amy Johnson are feckless amateurs. Not the gorgeous Amy herself; the poster-girl of the modern age can do no wrong. It is her peers who are the problem: all those ordinary women sashaying into workshops up and down the country to play uninvited with boys' toys, and wreaking havoc. They might look decorative enough, but are lethal if left unsupervised by *real* engineers.

The hearts of those of us who know no better are apt to sink if all that is left in the dentist's waiting-room is the odd copy of the *British Medical Journal* or the *Investor's Chronicle*. Such professional organs are written by specialists for specialists; esoteric by definition. Yet had I been around during this period – engineer or not – I would cheerfully have gone out and bought my own copy of *The Woman Engineer*, just for the entertainment value. I might have treated that *Morning Post* reporter to a copy, too.

Published quarterly by the WES from 1919 onwards, it is full of fascinating information, surprising illustrations and spirited, endlessly energetic personalities. Reading it is like peering through the window of a bustling workshop peopled by women who individually and together, physically and metaphorically, are constructing a new world.[2]

The journal's first editor was Caroline Haslett, founder member of the WES. She had been a suffragette in her time, brave enough to answer back when Emmeline Pankhurst queried her ambition to become an electrical engineer. That is hardly a job for a lady, said Emmeline. What matters, retorted Caroline, is how well the job is done, not who does it. *The Woman Engineer* clearly reflects her wide-ranging interests and engagement with progress. Take the issues for 1928, for example. This was an auspicious year for Britain. The *Flying Scotsman* began its non-stop express service between London and Edinburgh. Two magnificent new bridges opened, the concrete Royal Tweed Bridge at Berwick and the Tyne Bridge between Newcastle and Gateshead, a great arc of steel rearing above its granite piers. John Logie Baird captivated the world with news of the first colour television transmission. Exciting times – and not just for engineers.

In July that year, the Representation of the People (Equal Franchise) Act received Royal Assent. At the next general election, all women would be eligible to vote on the same terms as men from the age of twenty-one: about time, given that the campaign for women's suffrage had been active since 1866. Some feared a political catastrophe as a result of what was dubbed 'the flapper vote' while others were overjoyed. No doubt Caroline Haslett welcomed universal suffrage with delight, mixed with exasperation that so many years of women's political influence had been lost.

Outside the professions, women were moving from the farms and factories of the north into busy city offices; from textile mills into department stores, and from domestic service into nursing and child care. The slump of 1931 was still over the horizon (though the 1920s had more than their share of economic hardship, with strikes, hunger marches and sporadically high unemployment). Women of all classes and – at last – of all generations were finally being offered true citizenship.

With a suitable air of confidence, 1928 numbers of *The Woman Engineer* celebrate the spirit of the age with articles on the physique of women workers, recently discovered by scientists to be superior to that of males; on commercial flying as a career; and on the high-octane sport of motor racing. There are abstrusely technical pieces on the Roseville Sewage Treatment Plant, for instance, and the problems faced by a naval architect who happens to be female. An invitation to purchase shares in the Women's Pioneer Housing Company promises a 60 per cent yield, which one might do well to invest in a 'Bachelor-Girl' pension scheme tailored to professional women by the Norwich Union . . .

Notable new members of the society are welcomed in print. They include Dorothy Rowntree, who has been working in Palestine, and Vega Willson, daughter of WES president Laura Willson, who is a buyer in her father's lathe business and responsible for all the clerical work there. Mrs Dunn runs a quarry in Hull; Mrs Rennie is the sales manager for a successful tool company in Manchester; Monica Maurice is our premier mine-lighting engineer. Entrepreneurs Pauline Gower and Dorothy Spicer recently started an air-taxi business which failed to prosper; now they have turned it into an air circus which tours the country giving death-defying displays. Incidentally (notes the editor), someone has unearthed the records of a Victorian engineering business in Leeds called Sarah Dixon and Son. Was she the first professional female engineer of all?

All this is interesting, but undeniably engineery. To prove that WES members are not narrow-minded, there are features in the following issues on women in finance; the application of psychology in industry; the very modern concept of 'anti-waste' in the professional workplace; conditions of pay in the Civil Service; how to apply for research grants; various pension and insurance schemes; and the work of the League of Nations in raising the profile of women around the world. For the purists, there is information about stress levels, piston temperatures or zonographs, tempered for others by lively biographical pieces on who is doing what in the profession, usually with a paragraph acknowledging the support of fathers or husbands – whose deaths, touchingly, are noted with personal obituaries. Members' weddings and other family landmarks are also celebrated, when there is room. There is even the odd burst of poetry, including 'The Machine', a contribution by electrical engineer Isabel Sloan which starts uncertainly, but then warms up.

> *I am the machine, the machine, the machine –*
> *I am not your master nor am I your slave.*
> *I am your child – you made me,*
> *I would be your companion and your friend.*

There are many more stanzas, one of which encapsulates the engineer's life mission in a vaguely biblical but moving way:

> *I give to your hands a million helpers*
> *And I will take from the bent backs of all men and*
> *   the children of all men*
> *The cross of toil, the weary sordidness of their days;*
> *And they will walk straight and their raised eyes will*
> *   see life and its loveliness.*
> *With my strong hands I will bring bountiful bread,*
> *And your hands will be free to gather roses.*[3]

One of the most intriguing illustrations from this period accompanies an article by Margaret Partridge on a new invention doomed, surely, to failure. It is called the Dynasphere, something like a souped-up zorb ball. The construction, explains Miss Partridge, is perfectly simple.

> It consists of an outer light, hollow sphere, with its opposite cheeks cut off; inside that a loose tramway-track, and inside again, a heavy truck running on the smooth tramway track. Running straight, the truck runs up a little way . . . along the track, and gravity starts the sphere in motion. Running round corners, the track is shifted to right or left of the sphere and the vehicle turns . . . The solid portions of the lattice work spherical shell pass before the eyes so fast that they become invisible, and only the picture of the country in front affects the eye, just as the shadow of the shutter of a cinema projector which constantly blacks out the picture on the screen is unseen owing to its rapidity of motion.[4]

The photograph shows four Dynaspheres hurtling round a bend on a steep hill, the leader apparently about to career into a five-bar gate. There is one vital question, of course – which Margaret neatly ignores: how you actually stop the thing.

The Woman Engineer is not all about business, diverting as that business often is. There has always been a social element to the WES. A dinner marking ten years since the passing of the SDRA was held at the Lyceum Club in 1929. Professor Winifred Cullis of the Royal Free Hospital was there; she managed somehow to make a talk about new radium treatments for cancer 'very witty'. Gertrude Leverkus was also present, as was Helena Normanton, who gave a short but heartfelt speech about how far women still had to go in the professions. Yes, they could become engineers, but they could not become Church of England ministers; they were forbidden to enter the Stock Exchange and the House of Lords; they could be appointed Cabinet ministers (as Labour politician Margaret Bondfield was that year), but not ambassadors.

Helena considered all women diminished while any one of them was held back from the position to which her talents drew her.

The advertisements in *The Woman Engineer* are eloquent. They reveal who was interested in targeting this growing market of independent consumers, and what the editor thought suitable temptation for her readers. Thus there are plenty for Castrol oil, endorsed by famous female air aces or motor racers; several for pieces of equipment like steel cables, 'coiled-coil' lamps or a complete hydro-electric plant; a few for other publications – *Time and Tide*, of course, and bedside classics such as *An Electrical Adventure* by Peggy Scott – and one or two unclassifiable: for a 'dream house in Bristol', a lantern lecture on 'The Romance of Hatton Garden' or Miss Florence Blenkiron's 'Valet Motoring' business whereby she can drive you, for a fee, in her eighteen-horsepower seven-seater deluxe saloon to Africa.

Almost everyone, in every photo in the magazine, is smiling; not in a saccharine way, but genuinely smiling. This appears to be a vibrant world, a good-humoured sisterhood happy, by and large, in its work.

That level of solidarity was enviable. As Helena Normanton pointed out, women attempting to enter the Church continued to get nowhere. There was little to buoy their spirits. The report of an Archbishops' Commission on the Ministry of Women in 1936 exposed the ideological chasm between the Establishment and campaigners like Maude Royden. The archbishops congratulated themselves that the Church had always been a pioneer in exalting womanhood. They graciously saluted women for advancing into previously forbidden territory in the other professions, and had no doubt that they were spiritually capable of ordination. But it would be practically inconvenient to admit them to the priesthood just now (the old argument of the ladies' lavatory) and might offend traditionalists, therefore risking schism. Best to leave things be.

The League of Church Militant was a Christian campaign group founded in 1909 'to secure for women the vote in Church and State'. By 1928 the latter was done and dusted, but the former seemed a hopeless cause; so much so that the League was disbanded in despair. Individuals, male as well as female, continued the campaign as best they could. They acknowledged that the Church had indeed exalted ladies: that was the problem. Real, live women did not require to be worshipped like saints and angels; it held them back. Meanwhile a Professor of Divinity at Cambridge, Canon Charles Raven, publicly made the point that working women (skilled and unskilled) were being spiritually short-changed. Most clergymen knew nothing of a working woman's cares, and were ill-qualified to act as confessors. Clergywomen would be far more suitable. This was agreed in theory, but still nothing changed.

Maude Royden attempted to practise what she preached – indeed, to preach what she practised – by co-founding a non-denominational fellowship of prayer based at the Guildhouse in the wealthy London district of Knightsbridge. Her Sunday-evening sermons there drew crowds from all over the capital city. Her friend, the Congregationalist minister Constance Coltman – now sharing a parish with her husband in Oxford – was an enduring role model for other women whose religious vocations were stymied. Similarly inspiring was the former missionary Edith Picton-Turbervill, who took her campaign to Parliament as the Labour member for the Wrekin in 1929, while Edith Gates (the first Baptist woman to be given a parish, in 1918) and Violet Hedger (the first to be officially trained for the ministry, the following year) quietly got on with their jobs as rural pastors as though such a thing were nothing new.

Less visible pioneers joined the Society for the Equal Ministry of Women and Men, established in 1929. Campaigners toured the country giving lectures and, if invited to by sympathetic vicars, preaching from the pulpit. As ever, Maude was the most eloquent of them, especially when expounding her 'theology of friendship'. This was fundamentally a doctrine of inclusion, recognizing that we are all God's creatures whether Christian or not, heterosexual or homosexual, men or women; even British or foreign. We should love and respect each other as equals, stop seeking outcasts, and honour each others' talents as God-given, not to be squandered.

A secular version of this philosophy was slowly gaining traction elsewhere. In medicine, the third and fourth cohorts of qualified women were beginning to establish themselves in every specialty, rarely eliciting comment from the Establishment, as long as they didn't interfere too much. What would be the point of arguing against them? They were demonstrably successful with their patients and tolerated by all but the most reactionary of colleagues. One of the criticisms levelled against them in the early days was that newly qualified women had no inkling of how unromantic a vocation medicine was. It was not all ladies with lamps soothing grateful brows. Mass swoonings were to be expected when these women realized what their work would involve – and mass desertion from the profession, after a costly and exclusive training. This did not happen. They were neither squeamish nor aloof when faced by the realities of disease and death.

After the war there was an increased incidence of syphilis, a grisly souvenir of brothels on the Western Front. In an unhealthy spirit of denial, no medical student, male or female, was routinely taught about its diagnosis and treatment before 1922. It must have been shocking to learn subsequently about the extent of the disease and witness its devastating effects – but women coped. The extreme poverty of patients in the slums meant that home visits were sometimes harrowing. Obstetrics trainee Octavia Wilberforce found some of her duties sickening. She was once called to a confinement in Dublin, a 'long trudge' from home.

It was too early for the trams to have started running and I had to walk. I arrived at my destination and found endless stone stairs to climb. I reached and knocked at the appropriate door. 'Come in,' called a weary voice. I did, and found a sandy-haired woman lying on a mattress with only newspapers covering it, and no sign of either blanket or sheet. Several children were playing on the floor which had little puddles all about, and one child was squatting and opening her bowels. A pigsty smelt cleaner. Luck was on my side and the hefty noisy baby arrived almost at once . . .[5]

Again, she coped, partly because women doctors were less 'soft' than their male colleagues assumed, but also because they were less soft than we are today. The inter-war period was a harsher age for everyone; an age when a baby born with terminal deformities could be drowned (by one woman doctor I have come across) 'like a kitten'.[6] It is not that doctors today have an easier time of it; just that contexts change over time.

In 1933 physician Christine Murrell became the first woman elected to the General Medical Council. She had been the first on the British Medical Association's Central Council before that. Thanks to the political efforts of the MWF, inroads were even being made in the matter of the gender pay gap in medicine. Women doctors learned to expect equal pay for equal work, to demand it, and in many cases to get it – except when working for local authorities, which adhered to differing pay scales and conditions for men and women in their employ.

When Dr May Thorne applied to Huddersfield Health Board before the Great War for a job described as 'diminishing infant mortality', she was told explicitly that if a male doctor got the position, he would naturally be paid a higher salary than she would. She complained, and received the following response – which still held good, in principle, for several decades afterwards. First, a woman is physically capable of doing only 75–80 per cent of the work a man can do. Second, this is a newly created position, so who knows what the pay should be? And third, how dare she be so ungrateful? She has no idea of the lengths to which the chairman of the Health Board has gone, personally, to obtain this opening for her, against prejudice and opposition of every kind, 'and now you fling this back in my face; that is not pleasant but it is a small matter'.[7] The chairman, with his quivering bottom lip, was obviously a master of the passive-aggressive. May refused the post.

The very first generation of medical pioneers was disappearing now. Sophia Jex-Blake died in 1912; Elizabeth Garrett Anderson in 1917; Louisa Aldrich-Blake in 1925; Frances Hoggan two years later. Ophthalmologist Ida Mann, though, was still going strong. After her appointment as Honorary Surgeon at Moorfields in 1928 she embarked on a lecture tour of America. In 1930 she became the first woman to be awarded the prestigious Nettleship Medal by the Royal College of Ophthalmologists and settled into a private practice in Wimpole Street which she cheerfully admitted was making her a nice, fat living. She began research into contact lenses, developed an interest in neurosurgery, and looked set to conquer her own corner of the professional world – until, in swift succession, her brother suffered a fatal heart attack and both her parents died.

Ida was knocked off balance – and caught in the (metaphorical) arms of Kamala, an Indian student of hers, 'a tiny, perfect image of beauty and intelligence',[8] whom Ida grew to love. In 1936 Ida travelled to India to meet Kamala's family, and proudly learned to chew paan, made from betel leaves and areca nuts, for 'relaxation'. When she returned to London she felt renewed and ready for the next chapter in an increasingly eccentric personal and professional story.

Dr Louisa Martindale – now popularly known as 'Lulu' – maintained her general practice in Brighton throughout the

1930s, developing a specialty in the treatment of breast and cervical cancers. She spent a good deal of time in London as president of the MWF and an active member of the Six Point Group. When she resigned from the latter in 1937 she endearingly threw a party for every patient on whom she had ever performed major surgery, and hired a conjuror to entertain them. She and Ismay Fitzgerald still lived and travelled happily together. Lulu seems to have got the work–life balance just about right – as did Dr Elsie Sacks, who was so sanguine about the division between home and work that in 1933, while teaching a lecture-hall full of students about infant nutrition, she whipped out a breast and started feeding her baby son Oliver. This was 'show and tell' at its most practical. When Oliver was a little older – eleven – he was encouraged by his mother to have a go at dissection, not on the usual frogs or rabbits but on stillborn, malformed foetuses she brought home from the obstetric wards. He went on to become a fine neurologist.

One of Lulu and Ismay's closest friends on the south coast was Dublin-born Dr Helen Boyle, who ran a general practice in Hove with her partner Dr Mabel Jones. Helen's medical mission in life was to treat psychiatric patients *before* their condition reached crisis point. Formerly, they were entitled to medical help only once they had been certified as insane; when Helen founded the Lady Chichester Hospital for Women with Nervous Diseases (later the New Sussex Hospital for Women and Children) it was with the intention of preventing them from being certified at all. Dr Louisa Aldrich-Blake had been the hospital's first consulting surgeon, adding this to all her other roles, and Lady Rhondda its honorary treasurer. Dr Gladys Wauchope was a physician there and described Helen as small, humorous and very Irish. She was also relentlessly positive in outlook: when a bomb fell in her garden during the Second World War she was delighted. She had always fancied a rockery.

Staff at the pioneering Lady Chichester Hospital for Women with Nervous Diseases.

It is a measure of Dr Boyle's reputation that patients were dis-patched into her care from all over the country. There is a letter in the archives of a university in the midlands, dated 1932, about a female student who has suffered a nervous breakdown. She is worried that she might not have enough money to pay for the medical treatment arranged for her by the university at the Lady Chichester, some two hundred miles away. Don't fret, she is told: Dr Boyle will decide when you are ready to leave; nothing else matters. The implication is that the fee is not important.[9]

When Professor Winifred Cullis visited a medical-school society in 1939, the students were incredulous at the tales she had to tell of prejudice and distrust in the olden days when she first trained. That is a good indicator of progress – although students today are similarly appalled when they hear that most London medical schools remained closed to females until the mid-1940s. Qualified women were getting on well in medicine, but it was still comparatively difficult to qualify.

Progress was also being made in the law, though not quite as rapidly as in medicine. Newspapers remained inordinately fond of a good 'Portia' story. The *Daily Sketch* conceded in a 1934 report that yes, more lady barristers and solicitors were appearing in court all the time, but it was only because they were good at exams. They could learn easily, but found it tricky to apply knowledge appropriately. It was unthinkable that those Portias should ever become Solomons, or judges. Helena Normanton had other ideas. Buoyed by the success of a high-profile case at Newcastle Assizes in 1930, when she defended someone on a charge of murder, she applied to be considered as recorder for the north-east circuit. Becoming a recorder is the first step on the judicial ladder towards becoming a judge. No woman had been appointed before. She was refused.

Meanwhile a dynamic young Liverpool graduate, Rose Heilbron (1914–2005), began to attract attention. She achieved a Master of Laws (LLM) degree at the age of twenty-two and won a scholarship to Gray's Inn three years later. Her father was a Jewish immigrant who worked for the Cunard shipping line; her mother died of breast cancer ten days after the LLM ceremony. In 1939, after borrowing money from the Union Bank in Manchester and from relatives, Rose was called to the Bar. A decade later, she and Helena were the first two women to take silk in England, following the appointment of Scottish lawyer Margaret Kidd in 1948 – and Rose went on to even greater things. A celebratory photograph of these two brand-new King's Counsel shows them side by side like representations of the old world and the new, Helena looking haughty and slightly old-fashioned while Rose is glamorous and immaculately made-up: the Amy Johnson of the law courts.

We last saw Carrie Morrison living in a Whitechapel tenement and practising as a self-employed solicitor, often on behalf of those who could not pay. She and her 26-year-old solicitor fiancé Ambrose Appelbe were married at Stepney Register Office

Helena Normanton (left) and Rose Heilbron on their appointment as the first women King's Counsel in England, 1949.

in April 1929, holding a church service a few days later at Maude Royden's Knightsbridge Guildhouse in 'truly up-to-date style', as the papers put it. This was a story worth reporting, involving the first woman to be admitted on to the roll as a solicitor in Britain and 'the most famous woman preacher in the world'.[10] The church was full; the bride wore georgette with a veil and an orange-blossom head-dress, and carried a daffodil bouquet. There was an extravagant number of bridesmaids – eight – who wore frocks of hyacinth blue.[11] Astonishingly, Carrie's age was not divulged by the press (though she was described as 'dark and attractive'): she was forty.

After their marriage Ambrose and Carrie worked together. Carrie specialized in conducting divorce cases, and supporting those she considered to be disadvantaged by dint of their gender or poverty. They were a progressive couple, embracing popular causes, like divorce law reform, and more esoteric ones, including the movement against tyranny in women's fashion (one of her articled clerks reckoned she and supportive underwear were strangers). Ambrose, in fact, was so progressive that he began to make a name for himself as an eccentric. In 1935 he founded the Smell Society, claiming that 'the national sense of smell was dying from neglect'.[12] Its meagre membership included George Bernard Shaw, always game for a laugh.

Perhaps it is ironic that in 1937 Carrie divorced Ambrose on the grounds of his adultery with a woman he went on to marry. However they remained close for the rest of their lives, and despite the stigma surrounding a broken marriage – compounded by her being a woman – Carrie's reputation did not appear to suffer. In fact, as a divorced divorce lawyer, it probably improved.

The number of women practising as architects increased throughout the 1930s. By 1935 there were nearly thirty practices run entirely by women.[13] No one attracted as much public attention as Elisabeth Scott, an early graduate of the Architectural Association School. Elisabeth had an enviable pedigree, both as a professional – iconic architect Sir George Gilbert Scott was her great-uncle – and as a member of the sisterhood. She designed a house for a lady doctor in Surrey; in 1938 she was responsible for additions to Newnham College in Cambridge; and she also worked on the Marie Curie Centre in London. All this was solid stuff – but her greatest achievement was winning an open competition to design the new Shakespeare Memorial Theatre in Stratford-upon-Avon, just two years after completing her training. The old one had spectacularly burned down in 1926. Seventy-two plans were submitted for the competition by architects from Britain, Canada and the United States; six were shortlisted 'blind', and of these, Elisabeth's was the judges' unanimous choice. Imagine their consternation when it was realized that design number three was actually by a dainty 29-year-old woman fresh out of school.

The new theatre was opened to great acclaim on Shakespeare's birthday in 1932. The dashing Prince of Wales, later (briefly) Edward VIII, arrived at the helm of his own monoplane to perform the opening ceremony, which was broadcast live by the BBC. The event was relayed to North America, where most of the funds for the theatre were raised. It was an impressive and somewhat blockish edifice, unmistakably art deco in style and built in bright red brick. Stratford residents nicknamed it 'the jam factory' with more or less affection; the fragrant George Bernard Shaw admired it publicly, but composer Edward Elgar refused to set foot inside, calling it unspeakably ugly and just plain wrong.

When the theatre was revamped in 2010, elements of Scott's original design were incorporated into the new building, notably

The Shakespeare Memorial Theatre at Stratford, designed by Elisabeth Scott and opened in 1932.

the cocktail bar and wonderful curved staircase. It is fitting that something remains of the first ever important public building in Britain to be designed by a woman. Female colleagues of Elisabeth worked on other high-profile sites – the Sydney Harbour Bridge, for example, or Liverpool Cathedral – but none achieved the same level of recognition as this young woman who was not even old enough to vote when she bagged one of the biggest architectural prizes in the world.

By 1939, thirty-seven women had been elected as Members of Parliament, including two medical doctors, two academics (one of whom became a civil servant), a schoolteacher and an unofficial preacher.[14] Suffragist Eleanor Rathbone succeeded Sir Alfred Hopkinson as member for the English Universities in 1929. In his valedictory speech Hopkinson offered barbed congratulations. 'In many ways, I think the modern girl of today is brilliant . . . But in spite of her brains I cannot ever imagine a woman Prime Minister. There is something lacking in her which a man leader has. It is perhaps what I should call mental tact. She is too interfering.'[15] Ellen Wilkinson MP held a different view of the modern girl. She was tired of constant references in the press to women who habitually beat flying records, carried off 'the architectural prize of the year' and bested men at their own game all along the line. One began to wonder whether males were doing anything at all, mused Ellen, who as well as being a feminist was a champion of working men's rights.[16] She also objected to the lazy assumption that successful women were like circus performers rather than valuable members of a society trying to improve itself.

The teaching profession remained sharply divided between male and female practitioners, the former paid more than the latter. A Miss Biggs was appointed the first woman District Inspector of Schools in 1932, which was encouraging, but in general the 1930s were unpromising for ambitious schoolmistresses. Sara Burstall was head of Manchester High School for Girls from 1919 to 1924. When she retired, she had little faith in the future for professionals like her. 'Don't ask me about educational principles,' she complained wearily. 'I have long abandoned them. I seek only to administer regulations to do the least possible harm to my children.'[17]

A young lady called Gladys began her career as a pupil–teacher in east London before qualifying from Islington Day Training College. During the 1930s she worked at a junior boys' school and kept a diary, which I should like to share with you in the interests of equilibrium. Gladys is here to prove that not every professional woman was a textbook role model for others, or necessarily pleased with her choice of career. It makes hair-raising reading in our modern, child-centred age.

> Wednesday 2 October. To school. A new class and the children know nothing despite the marvels (alleged) of Miss H's teaching. She's NEVER in her room. She is the slackest woman I ever met . . .
>
> Friday 13 November. An angry mother at school today because I had rapped [her] boy's fingers with a stick of pencil yet no-one comes to complain of Mr K who hits boys' heads with a screwdriver! . . .
>
> Wednesday 8 September. I *have* stormed at the poor brats today. They are so lazy. One boy . . . I bailed [*sic*] so unmercifully with tongue and rod his mouth grew dry and he could hardly speak and I was ashamed at my own harshness . . .[18]

Gladys describes a school manager as 'toady, a pop-eyed woman in spectacles with thick lenses and wearing stockings that concertinaed round her ankles'. She thinks refugee children a nuisance and panics when her punishment of a pupil draws blood. She's worried not about the boy's health – his nails were already bitten to the quick, so he's damaged goods – but about the possibility of a summons for assault.

Nearly 86 per cent of women graduating from Manchester University in 1930 became teachers.[19] The front of a classroom remained the most popular destination for educated young ladies. This popularity in terms of numbers should not indicate, however, that everyone who taught was happy. It is safe to say that Gladys was a square peg in a round hole, a predicament of which careers advisers for girls (when you could find one) were well aware. Live careers advice was still in its infancy during this period. But organizations like the Women's Employment Federation were beginning to reach out, supporting schools' and universities' careers services for young women, and arranging 'milk-round' visits from prominent potential employers such as the Gas Light and Coke Company, the LMS Railway or the BBC. They published case studies of alumnae who were making their way in the world, showing how they had got to where they were.

Miss Q, for example, appeared in a glossy brochure designed to inspire undecided 'undergraduettes' at Birmingham. She was twenty-eight; she was a graduate of Oxford and London universities who trained for and was called to the Bar and now worked as a police detective.[20] Miss B (24) was even more adventurous. She was a keen photographer who left university with a history degree and good French and German. 'For experience' she took a position as a house parlourmaid in Australia, sailing there on a tall ship, and was currently working as a copywriter for a firm of photographic agents . . . *You* could be like Miss Q or Miss B.

By the end of the 1920s there were few no-go areas for females in search of non-professional employment (except, bizarrely, taxi-driving: on this, advisers were agreed). The cultural climate was changing, and now women were not accused quite so regularly or vehemently of stealing the bread from men's mouths. It was generally acknowledged that they must look for work where they could, so that the state wouldn't be obliged to pay them the limited unemployment benefits to which they were entitled.[21] Yet more jaunty books were published with titles more or less along the lines of *Careers for Girls*, suggesting occupations to match different personalities. Do be realistic, their readers were urged: it might be a fact (as one author claimed) that about 50 per cent of young women these days wanted to be mannequins or ships' stewardesses,[22] but try to recognize that for you, such tinselly sophistication might be too ambitious – or not ambitious enough. How about film? Alfred Hitchcock's Nottingham-born wife Alma Reville was a film screenwriter and editor. Continuity announcing, like the glossy ladies in the popular magazine *Radio Pictorial*? Pharmacy, for those of a serious turn of mind? Ballroom dancing? Goat farming, anyone?

The professions gradually relaxed, too. By 1930 there were more than eighty women dentists on the register;[23] eleven (out of 650) British university professors were women;[24] there were around a hundred women barristers and sixty-six solicitors on the roll;[25] and approaching six thousand women were qualified medical doctors.[26] Though the majority of them were from prosperous backgrounds, applicants were encouraged by careers advisers not to be afraid of working their way up the ladder. Cabinet minister Margaret Bondfield used to be a shop assistant and Dr Ella Pringle, the first female Fellow of the Royal College of Physicians in Edinburgh, was once a typist.

Throughout this period, however, messages to women graduates were mixed. On the one hand, vestiges of the old Victorian regime dictated a curfew for women students, with humiliating punishments for being caught out of college after hours. Unrelated men were not allowed into their rooms; if fathers and brothers visited, bedroom doors were required to be propped open – and at some institutions, the bed removed, just in case (of what?). These adult schoolgirls could be turned away from restaurants if they had no gentleman in tow to guarantee that they were neither ladies of the night nor short of funds to pay the bill.

At one women's college the principal, who lodged in the same building as her undergraduates, used solemnly to put on hat and coat and take an umbrella whenever she wished to pay one of her students a visit, even if they lived on the same floor. Standards, dear girls; standards. Yet at the same time, the same students were being encouraged to step out into the working and professional worlds with confidence and comparatively high expectations while using their femininity, or 'sex-weapons', not only to advance their careers, but to secure an eligible mate.

This confusion of purpose was not the only obstacle in the way of a career girl's progress. During the 1920s and 1930s the popular press sizzled with stories of young women in danger. Few people can have been more self-possessed than the feminist writer and wartime nurse Vera Brittain, yet her father was convinced that whenever she stepped outside her front door she was likely to be abducted and sold into the white slave trade. Scotland Yard had a White Slavery Suppression branch, and though few if any incidents of sex trafficking of the kind Mr Brittain imagined were authenticated, fear and ignorance combined to cast a shadow over the independence of 'unprotected' working women. It was all part of their evolution; a century before, no young lady was allowed to set foot outside her house without a chaperone.

Women who chose to work abroad deserved whatever they got, according to some press commentators. There is a scrapbook of random cuttings in the Women's Library in London dating from the early 1930s. It is labelled 'Women in the Professions' and includes the chilling news that a female anthropologist conducting some research on an Indian reservation in North America, living in a shack while dressing like and consorting with the locals, has just been found 'outraged' and murdered by an Apache brave. Silly girl. That isolated and freakish episode is supposed to stand as a lesson to all professional women who think a risk worth taking.

Such terrors were a far cry from the polished-wood corridors of the Civil Service where the original 'biggish' women like Hilda Martindale were even bigger now – and more numerous, despite what were called 'reconstruction' policies reserving certain posts for men. By 1939, forty-three women worked in the élite administrative grades; that is 3 per cent of all civil servants (including female clerical workers, of whom there were thousands).[27] It was reported in *The Times* in 1932 that this tiny but influential minority was proving a considerable asset. The Joint Committee of Women in the Civil Service had just held a celebratory dinner (naturally) at which their guest, a gentleman from the upper echelons of the Home Office, had acknowledged that ladies were now a necessary and integral part of the fabric. 'Wild horses, or wild women, however, would not drag from him his opinion on the subject of equal pay. (Laughter.)'[28]

Mary Somerville (1897–1963) knew exactly what the current thinking was on equal pay. She was one of the first powerful women at the BBC. Mary was born in New Zealand but brought up in her father's Presbyterian manse in Scotland. Money was not plentiful and Mary's health was bad; both factors limited her early education and prevented her starting at Oxford (where she was a member of Somerville College, appropriately enough) until the age of twenty-four. Mary was diabetic. She was too ill to sit her finals in 1925 but was awarded an *aegrotat* degree in English Language and Literature by virtue of past performance, and went straight into a job at what was then known as the British Broadcasting Company, formed three years previously. In 1927 it became the British Broadcasting Corporation, which it remains.

Mary was appointed as an assistant in the education department, and was swiftly promoted. In 1929 she was put in charge of schools' programmes; shortly after the Second World War she became Assistant Controller and then Controller of the vast

'Talks' section – the first woman to achieve such dizzy heights within the Corporation. Her success was attributable to a lifelong engagement with the philosophy of education; her enthusiasm for teaching and learning at the highest possible level; and a genuine passion for the brand new and endlessly adaptable medium of radio. It was *not* attributable to her acquiescence at work. 'She is very clever, capable of immense activity, full of courage & energy, push & go,' wrote a colleague, before continuing that she also possessed 'the defects of her qualities', being 'rather masterful & difficult'.[29]

In fact Mary was notorious for her bolshiness. She rarely neglected an opportunity to challenge the BBC's attitude to and treatment of its female employees. As an organization claiming to offer equal opportunities, it did not perform well, according to her. The following letter from the BBC Archives demonstrates her point. Mary is expected to travel for work, visiting schools in various regions. She has her own vehicle, but can't afford to run it. Why isn't she paid enough to do her job properly?

> I am so badly clipped [short of money] that I think I'll have to sell that damned car. Heaven knows how I'll get along without it, but as my Kent visits are pretty well over I suppose I will somehow. Anyhow I've got to raise some cash somehow, and I don't want to make a fuss at home at this juncture.
> What will happen about my loan if I do sell it? I still owe the BBC £86. Will I have to settle that all in a lump?
> You people really are ungrateful critters to let a pore [*sic*] defenceless female work more than you let her earn![30]

There is obviously a twinkle in her eye, but she means what she says. We do not have the BBC's response to that query, but there is an affectionately exasperated answer to another complaint she lodged in 1934, about meagre expenses. A BBC bigwig wrote that he could not see a case for giving Miss Somerville an increase in salary to cover the entertaining she did. She already received an allowance of about £100 a year to cover fifty-six lunches and thirty-two dinners; beyond that her commitments were 'so intangible as to be incapable of being expressed on an expense sheet'.[31] And as for her plea for an increased clothes budget (she claimed that she could only afford cast-offs): that betrayed financial mismanagement on her part, not miserliness on the BBC's. The following year, Mary was awarded an OBE for services to broadcasting, presumably on the recommendation of her colleagues. They recognized her talent and loyalty, while dealing with her 'masterful and difficult' outbursts as best they could.

Would such outbursts from a man at her level have been tolerated, indulged or admired? The question of how women should behave in the professional workplace, now that they were populating it in greater numbers, was a matter exercising the minds of specialist associations. Should a journalist complain, for instance, if, like Phyllis Deakin, she was refused her own byline in *The Times* for the whole of her 48-year career? Or should she keep her shingled head below the parapet so as not to cause trouble or give women journalists as a whole a bad name? On a wider scale, did women who joined protest marches for equal rights risk losing their jobs? There were several such mass demonstrations during the 1930s; not as widely publicized as the 'hunger marches' like the one from Jarrow to London in 1936, but well supported. Where should the line be drawn between personal indignation and professional duty?

The Federation of British Business and Professional Women's Clubs was set up to offer its members safety in numbers in their campaign for women's rights, especially those who had no trade union representation. It held its first meeting in 1933. Caroline Haslett, editor of *The Woman Engineer*, was in the chair; also present were members from an impressive array of organizations including the Women's Advertising Club, the Au Pairs' Association, the

Society of Women Housing Estate Managers, the Chartered Society of Massage and Medical Gymnastics (whom we would recognize as physiotherapists) and the Association of Women Clerks and Secretaries.

It is clear that professional and business women were digging into their new environment, manufacturing their own infrastructure within which concerns might be raised and success encouraged, and embedding the sense of entitlement we take for granted, as working women, today. It is not easy to imagine individuals like Mary Somerville as team players; but what she did share with the most junior of junior house officers in hospital, or the newest of new pupils in a barrister's chambers, was an awareness of natural justice. Women had a right to work where they chose, and to be rewarded for that work, just as men did. Politician Eleanor Rathbone went one step further, championing the right of housewives and mothers to be rewarded for their domestic careers, not as second-class citizens but as dedicated architects of Britain's future. Motherhood was as crucial to national prosperity as any of the traditional professions.

But were domestic and professional careers mutually exclusive? It was time to ask the Big Question. *Could* a woman have it all? Virginia Woolf, who had no children, was cynical about the apparent desire of women in the professional workplace to metamorphose into their male colleagues. Behind us lies the patriarchal system, she wrote in 1938, centred on the home and reeking of hypocrisy and servility.

> Before us lies the public world, the professional system with all its possessiveness, its jealousy, its pugnacity, its greed. The one shuts us up like slaves in a harem; the other forces us to circle, like caterpillars head to tail, round and round the mulberry tree . . . It is a choice of evils.[32]

★

So why make the choice at all? Why not combine home with work and create a new model, a new world from the best of the old? These were challenging questions at the time, as they are still. The period leading up to the outbreak of war in 1939 was in many ways a testing-ground for a pattern of work and life for women which, if we are honest, has yet to be defined.

8

Wives or Workers?

Relationships and the Marriage Bar

*In the absence of a possible husband, a girl can
always prop up civilisation.*[1]

In November 1932 the Vice-Chancellor of Liverpool University
wrote to his lawyer, as one chap to another, to ask for some advice.
There was a personnel problem at work, he explained, 'a minor
but entertaining question',[2] and he was unsure how to resolve it.
The tone of the note suggests it was something quite trivial: a
persistently forgetful professor, perhaps, or a clumsy charwoman.
In fact his enquiry concerned the so-called 'marriage bar', a measure responsible for calling a halt to the professional careers of
millions of women nationwide. Hardly minor or entertaining.

Four months earlier he had received a letter from two of the
university's lecturers, Dr Margaret Miller and Dr Jean Wright, who
planned to marry their fiancés during the summer vacation. They
courteously informed him that they intended to return to their jobs
in the autumn, as usual. They would not be changing their names,
which should make life easier at work, and looked forward to continuing their promising academic careers.

Vice-Chancellor Hetherington's problem was quite straightforward: these two women were obviously mad. This is the sort

of letter they should have written, sent by a female academic to her boss at another university in 1920:

> I beg to send in my resignation of the post of History Lecturer in the Training Department of this University, to take effect at the close of this term.
>
> I regret very much having to put the University to the inconvenience of appointing a new Lecturer so soon after my coming here. But when I came I did not know that I should be staying for one year only. I am going to be married in the course of next year and I fear, therefore, that I am under the necessity of resigning my post at the end of this term.
>
> I am very sorry to have to sever my connection with the University. During the short time I have been here I have found the greatest interest and pleasure in my work.
>
> Yours faithfully,
>
> H. Stella Watson.[3]

Very nice: a well-brought-up young lady sensible of the privilege she had enjoyed as an academic, but properly mindful of her principal duties as a wife and in time, no doubt, a mother. Her resignation was accepted 'with regret' but no arguments. How had Margaret Miller and Jean Wright got the script so wrong?

The bar, requiring women to give up their jobs when they married, was an entrenched feature of working life for women in the Civil Service and the teaching profession, and for female employees (including doctors) of local authorities around the country. For practical reasons it could be troublesome for married women to work as resident medical officers in hospitals, or as circuit lawyers, but it was not impossible. In those professions, as in architecture and engineering, the handicaps of marriage were dealt with on a case-by-case basis. There was no marriage bar for women who wished to become ministers of the various churches, partly because there was no job specification at all for such mavericks; if you had gone so far as to countenance a woman preacher, it would hardly make a difference whether or not she was married – although Congregationalist minister Vera Kenmure felt herself compelled to resign from her Glasgow parish in 1933 when hostility after the birth of her son became too hard to bear. She could not agree with the members of her congregation who had sent her poisonous anonymous letters implying that the divided loyalties of work and family life would lead to her ruin and theirs. 'On the contrary, I am convinced that my ministry, and indeed any ministry, will only be enriched and made more useful by the added experiences which these relationships bring.'[4] She offered to resign solely because of her 'strong feeling that the deep opposition and active hostility of a section of the congregation make honest cooperation impossible, and prevent me from continuing a successful ministry among them.' Vera overcame this check to her career by setting up her own parish, as Maude Royden had; a sort of para-Congregational church in a neighbouring area.

There was nothing in the statutes at Liverpool University about the marriage bar. It was a matter of decency; staff should know what was expected of them, and do it without coercion. It was extraordinarily ill-mannered of Drs Miller and Wright to make a fuss. But Margaret Miller had good reason to fight for what the SDRA implied were her rights. She had published well-respected academic papers (including one claiming that femininity was treated in the professional workplace like 'an incurable disease') and planned further research in collaboration with her husband, a fellow economist; her mother was financially dependent on her, and she was a staunch feminist. On these grounds, and on the grounds of natural justice, she refused to give up work.

This is the point at which Vice-Chancellor Hetherington sought advice. It was delivered in pompous legalese, full of weighty phrases about the dubious desirability of continuing the employment of women lecturers who marry, and whether wedlock

constitutes a condition preventing women from attending ad-
equately to their academic duties. By February 1933 the university's
statutes were amended to include a clause about compulsory resignation on marriage (of women, of course; not men). Drs Miller
and Wright were sacked and told that although there was nothing
to prevent them from re-applying for their former posts, 'prefer-
ential consideration' should not be expected.

Fifteen of their female colleagues signed a letter of protest following the news, deploring the idea that the private lives of any
members of the university should be a matter for general legislation, and accusing the Vice-Chancellor of a breach of moral
justice. The British Federation of University Women passed a
resolution in support of the women, and the Six Point Group and
Open Door Council took up their cause with vigour. A mass
meeting at Central Hall, Westminster, in November 1933 was
supported by twenty-nine official women's groups and a number
of high-profile politicians including Lady Astor and Gwyneth
Bebb Thomson's friend Lord Buckmaster, all demanding that
married women be given the same rights as any other citizen.
Even Ethel Smyth was there, hard-line suffragette and famous
composer of the stirring anthem 'March of the Women' which
was resurrected for the occasion. Now that the university had
officially articulated its stance, there were hopes of bringing a test
case against its ruling body for having broken the law by contravening the terms of the SDRA.

The offending clause in Liverpool's statutes was hastily sus-
pended the following month and withdrawn soon afterwards, but
with bad grace. It is not known what happened to Dr Wright, but
Dr Miller left Liverpool soon afterwards, anxious to find security
of tenure in another field. It would be comforting to think that
the Liverpool affair changed the way professional organizations
dealt with married women, but that was sadly not the case.

The bar had been in place in the teaching profession for

decades, officially or otherwise. There were always exceptions, especially for widows, but for as long as there had been women teachers, the majority of them were spinsters. This rule was relaxed, like so many others, during the First World War, but even then there was a grading system for the employment of wives. Top of the list came the spouses of impoverished or injured ex-servicemen; then came women whose families were dependent on their earnings; then women in rural areas; and finally, the rest.[5] In 1921, Nottingham City Council announced that henceforth it would not appoint any women whose husbands were still alive. Any single woman it currently employed would be expected to resign in advance of her wedding, and though she might be eligible to apply for supply teaching thereafter, that would only ever be a temporary measure: as soon as a spinster became available, the wife would be replaced. This policy did not affect teachers exclusively, but as a significant proportion of single professional women *were* teachers, and most teachers were employed by a local authority, they bore the brunt.

The policy backfired somewhat in Cannock, Staffordshire. The council there sacked all its married women teachers in July 1922 but embarrassingly had to invite them back after the summer holidays because of staff shortages. Elsewhere the authorities were draconian in their application of the bar. The NUWT protested, suggesting that employees should respond to the imposition 'even to the point of making themselves a nuisance'.[6] The MWF suggested the same to its affected members. There were a few skirmishes, but nothing on the scale of the campaign for the vote or, later on, for equal pay. Perhaps working women were too busy actually working to spend time organizing the sort of industrial action that would in all probability result in instant dismissal.

It did not help that working wives were caught in the crossfire whenever they raised their heads above the parapet, facing missiles both from those whose main concern was to keep them out of the professions (but who were not particularly bothered about what they did instead) and from those determined that they should be kept at home to breed, come what may. Both camps used the same weapons. Ideologists insisted that too much money corrupted women; too much freedom turned their heads; too much independence transformed them into unmarriageable monsters. Amateur biologists (and real ones) repeated the old 'use it or lose it' tag. If not enough women stayed at home as wives and mothers, the fairer sex might somehow become barren by evolution, paradoxical as that sounds. Then where should we be? The economic argument was apparently compelling: that as unemployment figures rose, it was only right that the last into the professions should be the first out, to clear the field for traditional male breadwinners.

In a post-war world it was not easy for women to counter these points without either losing the dignity and gravitas necessary to succeed as pioneers at work, or appearing heartlessly selfish. The semantically jesuitical SDRA was of little help, as we have seen. Saying a woman is not disqualified from working by marriage can be interpreted to mean that employers are free to choose married employees if they like, but are under no compulsion to do so.

The eugenics movement was popular during the 1920s and 1930s. It was about designing an optimal society based loosely on Darwin's theory of evolution by natural selection, popularly rendered as 'survival of the fittest'. Only the strongest and most intelligent members of society should be encouraged to have children: educated women, for example. In the United States, degree courses were offered in how to be a fruitful wife: they culminated in the award of 'Bride Certificates'.[7] The theory was enthusiastically propounded in *Motherhood and its Enemies*, a book by Charlotte Haldane published in 1927. The burden of her song was that if too many clever women went into the professions, the modern cult of contraception which she (rather randomly) claimed was rife in the workplace might spread out of control and render them unproductive sexual 'intermediates'. The implication was that the production of the next generation would thereby be left to inferiors, with a catastrophic impact on the balance of global power.

It was not particularly challenging to argue against people like Charlotte Haldane. They were generally considered eccentric, even then. Former suffragette Cicely Hamilton was not alone in shooting down their theories, claiming in her book *Marriage as a Trade* that the business of wedlock was closely managed by men and complicit women who systematically arrested females' 'mental growth' and thus controlled them. She declared that 'the degradation of woman's position and the inferiority of woman's capabilities are chiefly due to the compulsory restriction of her energies and ambitions to the uncertain livelihood and unpaid trade of marriage'.[8] Thus Hamilton joined a long feminist tradition that included Virginia Woolf, who called marriage 'the one great profession open to our class since the dawn of time',[9] and Jane Austen, who agreed that 'it was the only honourable provision for well-educated young women of small fortune, and however uncertain of giving happiness, must be their pleasantest preservative from want'.[10]

Today, it would seem simple common sense to oppose such a discriminatory measure as the marriage bar. So it appeared to many people then, frustrated by its rank injustice. Men enjoy a normal family life; why can't we? Married women have succeeded in the past – Professor Marie Curie, who won two Nobel Prizes, had a husband and two children, for heaven's sake. If we are required to train for a profession, why are we forbidden from practising it? The cry of an unmarried NUWT member in an article published in 1935 was strikingly simple: 'Where are my children?'[11] However, it was difficult to ignore members of one's own profession publicly maintaining, as gynaecologist Dr Emily Dickson did, that marriage and motherhood were the most élite

professions of all. In an article she wrote for a girls' school magazine, she did not recommend her own choice of career. A woman's
first priority must always be the patient, she wrote – day or night.
A married woman's first duty was to her husband and family. So
to whom should a married doctor give precedence? 'One must be
first in her heart, and whichever it be, the other will suffer.'[12] I
take comfort in the fact that within a few years of writing that,
Dr Dickson and her husband had five children and she happily
continued her medical career.

The marriage bar tended not to apply to female wage-earners in
large organizations like the Civil Service, ICI or the BBC. Only
salaried women were expected to obey its strictures. (The difference is that a wage-earner is paid a fixed rate per hour, multiplied
by however many hours she works, while a salary-earner receives
a named sum per annum.) That meant that cleaners and catering
staff were exempt. It was also possible for 'exceptional' or 'indispensable' women to side-step the bar. Those are vague enough
terms to accommodate an entirely subjective judgement. Alice
Jennings, a principal in the Ministry of Labour, was the first
woman in the Civil Service to be retained on marriage, in 1937.
There were ways to avoid or evade the bar. One was to live
secretly with one's fiancé. It is impossible to appreciate today how
serious a step that was. Only a generation or two ago, it signalled
complete moral degeneracy. One young teacher admitted later in
life to having lived 'in sin' with her lover, also a teacher. Fortunately her headmistress was both progressive and sympathetic,
letting the couple use the school as a decoy home address. 'It
would have been really serious if they had found out . . . [A]s you
were sinful you weren't the right sort to have anything to do with
children, so you both would have lost [teaching] Certificates . . .
We lived in a state of constant terror.'[13]

  She was right to be afraid. Local authorities were zealous in policing the regulations, as were all establishments with a bar in place. The *Sunday Chronicle* reported an 'extensive and expensive espionage system' at the BBC, which prompted this response from a staff member in the Corporation's magazine *Ariel*.

> *Do they snoop and sleuth and follow me round*
> *If I go by bus or the Underground?*
> *Do they chalk it up or write it down*
> *When I'm 'working late,' and I stay in town?*
> *Then they know, it seems, the friend I meet*
> *At half-past five in Hallam Street;*
> *And they're quite aware that I live with Mother,*
> *Or if I don't, with A. N. Other . . .*
> *Are they aware of my secret sins,*
> *Like football coupons and drinks at inns,*
> *Or cutting off crusts when they're rather tough,*
> *And picking my golf-ball out of the rough? . . .*
> *Or that I go over the twenty mark*
> *When driving my car through Regent's Park!*
> *And as for things I cannot mention –*
> *I'd have to leave, and lose my pension.*[14]

At the same time, the press was mounting a campaign against single women teachers, 'embittered, sexless or homosexual hoydens', corrupting their pupils.[15] What was a girl to do? Gladys – she who rapped her pupils' knuckles until they bled – had a pragmatic solution. She took lovers, though more in desperation than in rapture. ('I am so sexually hungry,' she complained in her diary.) She realized that schoolmistresses were not considered glamorous. 'A woman teacher obtained 20 gn. [guineas] cost from a landlord who kissed her twice. I should have thought any landlord who kissed a school marm deserved 20 gn. reward!'[16] But that did not prevent her from being disappointed when her thighs were not squeezed in the dark by 'strange men' at the cinema. Luckily, a middle-aged office worker of her acquaintance rose to the challenge, providing jaded Gladys with 'a wild orgy of love-making' from time to time to distract her from the drudgery of her job.

Certain large-scale organizations instituted a system of appeal against the marriage bar, resulting in tribunals. The BBC was one of them. In 1928, three years after Mary Somerville joined the schools section, she said 'yes' to Ralph Penton Brown, a journalist. 'Miss M. Somerville has just announced her engagement and approaching wedding,' reads a handwritten note in her staff file. 'She will be a great loss as she has grown up with the business and has largely influenced it.'[17] Mary, you will remember, was the forceful personality who tried to squeeze extra expenses out of the BBC for her clothes and car. She also elicited much admiration from its Director-General, Sir John Reith; so it is no surprise that she was considered 'exceptional' and was retained on marriage. Not only retained, indeed, but allowed leave when her son was born in 1929 and whenever he was sick. This exercised some of her seniors; why did not her husband fulfil the wife's role in such circumstances and look after the boy himself? Or at least pay for a nanny? Mary was having her cake and eating it.

It helped that she and Ralph were married before the bar was made official at the BBC in October 1932. Opinions were taken at the highest level about the advisability of instituting it.[18] Arguments against included the acknowledgement that women 'presumably' had the right to live as they thought fit; that married employees probably enjoyed 'an experience and balance lacking in certain single women'; and that wives were likely to be more stable, lacking the restless or skittish outlook of so many girls contemplating a wedding. In favour: it was unfair, given the current level of unemployment, for married women supported by their husbands to hog jobs which could be taken by unmarried women forced to support themselves. Also, it would seem unfeasible for a married woman to devote the required time to home and family while at the same time doing her work satisfactorily. Something would have to give: her business, her health, her husband or her children. If she were a working wife, she might choose not to have children to make life easier (now that contraception was more widespread), which would be damaging for her and for society at large. The arguments in favour won the day.

A general memo published in April 1933 explained, somewhat tardily, why the bar had been put in place.

> Experience has shewn [*sic*] that after marriage, women find it more difficult to perform their duties satisfactorily as servants of the Corporation, even if they have no children to look after. In future, therefore, the retention on the staff of women who marry will be entirely dependent on the circumstances of individual exceptional cases.[19]

What this 'experience' was is unclear. Anyway, the default position was that women about to marry should resign, whereupon they would receive a gratuity commensurate with their finishing salary. A leaving present.

As part of the Corporation's preparation for taking this step, a list was produced of married salaried women in its employ, accompanied by little notes about their status, presumably with a view to assessing who was likely to cause trouble.[20] Mary Somerville – now wed to Mr Brown – 'would be an exception even under present rules'. Mrs A's husband 'suffers from wounds, and has a precarious income'. Mrs B's is a subaltern in the Army, but they are separated and he pays her no allowance. Mrs C, on the other hand, has 'no hardship' and allegedly does not want to go on working indefinitely; and Mrs D's husband is earning a perfectly good salary. There would be no chance for Mrs E, who 'is known to have won several thousands in an Irish Sweep[stake]'.

Two years later, new regulations were laid down very carefully, in an attempt at transparency. This may have been to combat the opinion expressed in certain elements of the press that the BBC was acting like a dictatorship (as Helena Normanton wrote in a piece for the *Daily Mirror*[21]) and heartlessly outlawing motherhood.

The BBC's Married Women's Policy, set out in 1935, was broadly as follows. A married woman could be kept on if it was too inconvenient to replace her; if she was indispensable in terms of experience, ability or 'goodwill', or on compassionate grounds; if she was particularly distinguished by long service and good conduct; if her personality was such that she was likely to cope with 'the strain of combining married life with office work'; or if it was clear that she intended to make a lifelong career in broadcasting. Everyone was entitled to appeal decisions at a tribunal. Each tribunal panel included both men and women, and consisted of three BBC employees and two lay members. Points were awarded for each category, and an average calculated to produce an overall score for each individual at the end of the proceedings.

Between 1933 and 1937, thirty-one tribunals were held; sixteen women were allowed to stay on and the rest had to go, though one of the latter postponed her marriage in consequence and stayed a little longer.[22] The panels' notes make fascinating reading. Comments in favour of retention include: 'Mrs F's personality and appearance were such that it would not be easy for her to get as well paid a post outside.' (As far as I am aware there was no official score for how an applicant looked.) Another woman is about to marry a stoker in the Navy, who is due to be posted abroad for two and a half years. They won't marry if she can't stay. Mrs G would not have married had she had known she couldn't return to work – she never realized there was a bar in place. She supported her mother, who looked after things while Mrs G was at work so she didn't have to juggle professional business with housework. Her husband was an accountant, but a low-paid one. Rashly, she mentioned at her tribunal that 'it seemed unfair to contemplate terminating married women's appointments when there are so many single people working here with private incomes'.[23] I am unsure if she was retained.

Being a panel member was not straightforward. What follows is a verbatim transcription of some case notes (with names redacted, as in all of these quotes from the BBC Archives), dated 6 March 1935. How would you respond?

I forward herewith minutes of a recent marriage Tribunal summoned to re-consider the cases of Miss X and Miss Y and to consider an application from Miss Z.

With regard to Miss X and Miss Y, the issue is quite a plain one, but rather difficult to decide. Miss Y has been ten years in the Music Library . . . She knows her work very well and is a useful and responsible person. In that sense, it is inconvenient to replace her, and we should lose temporarily by doing so, but after a few months, it would make no difference, provided we got someone of equal efficiency.

Miss X is secretary to Mr Anon . . . and is the first satisfactory secretary that he has had, he being a very difficult person to work for and hard to please. From that point of view, it would be extremely difficult . . . to replace her, and we might run through several other secretaries before anyone was found as a permanent incumbent of the job. On the other hand, Mr Anon. will be retiring in a few years' time, and the permission for a girl to stay on is for all time.

In both the above cases, we are up against the compassionate element, which is simply that neither of the girls can get married as things are. It is over a year since they originally applied, and neither of them has in fact been able to get married. Here we are up against a very difficult policy question of our action preventing early marriages.

Putting ourselves in Miss X's place, with a fiancé whose salary is limited to £3 a week, what is she to do? She is faced with the alternatives of (1) getting married on that sum and lowering her standard of living, and being permanently extremely hard up [£3 is equivalent to about £150 today], (2) staying on unmarried almost indefinitely, (3) leaving the BBC and getting a less congenial job outside. Obviously in many ways (3) is the best alternative, but it involves risk, and so far no-one has attempted it except Miss H, in whom we lost a very useful member of the staff purely because of the ban.

Then take Miss Y's case. She is not as young as she might be (age 35), and delay is therefore all the more important. Looking at it as a human problem, one might say that at her age her chance of marrying is a relatively poor one and by staying on unmarried she is running something of a risk of never getting married, and yet the compassionate circumstances are such that she cannot get married unless she is able to earn her own living and support certain dependents[sic].

In neither Miss X or Miss Y's case are we in my opinion intrinsically justified in keeping the girls on if we interpret the Governors' ruling according to its intention, but we cannot ignore the fact that our decision is actually stopping these girls getting married. In point of fact, although there is no reason to suppose that this is the case, one of the most probable effects of such decisions is a secret marriage.

Looking at the matter from the narrow point of view, are we better served in the long run by [a female employee who is] an embittered, because compulsory, spinster, or by her as a contented married woman allowed to remain on the staff?

Alternatively is it our object to avoid having old or oldish women on the staff? This is a practical objective, which has something to commend it, but in point of fact a ban on marriage is probably not the best way of achieving it, as in most marriages there would come a time when domestic life (I don't necessarily mean babies) would claim the services of the wife. This time would normally be dependent on their financial means. After a certain point, it would be natural for them both to wish her to stop work and look after the home in a way which cannot be done by proxy or as a spare-time job in the evenings. With spinsters, of course, this tremendous motive does not operate, and we are virtually faced with their services to the age of retirement . . .

With regard to Miss Z, the position is quite different. In view of her special experience, her present position, and the Tribunal's recommendation, I have no hesitation in recommending that she should be allowed to stay on the staff after marriage. The only difficulty is that she happens to be a secretary in the Internal Administration Branch and people would tend to say that she got through the Tribunal by virtue of that position. I think we are bound to face this and ignore it.[24]

In the event, all three women were retained.

Marriage was a tricky enough question for working women and their employers; when it came to children, things became even more confused. There was no statutory maternity benefit for working mothers until after the Second World War. During the inter-war years they were dependent on the whims of an employer and/or the support of family members. Gwyneth Bebb Thomson's husband made it possible for her to read for the Bar while a young mother; between them they arranged for baby Diana to be cared for. The pioneering architect Jane Drew ran special classes for mothers wishing to return to work after having had a family, and across the professions higher salaries meant easier access to child care, provided mothers were able to keep working. An unnamed member of the WES had eleven children *and* a career. Academics were not as well paid as doctors or lawyers; when the literary scholar Elsie Duncan-Jones became pregnant while working at Birmingham University in 1937, she asked for a few weeks' leave after the birth of the baby. This was refused by the Vice-Chancellor on the irrefutable grounds that a man would never ask for such a thing. Female colleagues covered for Elsie when her absence was unavoidable; otherwise she carried on, returning to work as soon as she was physically able and had organized some ad hoc child care.

There were more life-choices than marriage and motherhood, of course. And the two were not indivisible: Maude Royden adopted a war orphan, Helen, in 1918, and also fostered an Austrian boy whose family had suffered during the post-war famine in Europe. She was thus a single mother. Dr Frances Hoggan, as we have seen, took her illegitimate daughter to live with her, disguised as a younger sister. Given an inevitable post-war shortage of eligible men, however, certain choices had more to do with necessity than preference. Perhaps it was this shortage that engendered the forthright new attitude among working women noticed by, among others, Winifred Holtby. She observed signs of recognition that they were not inherently disadvantaged by their gender and that, despite the edicts of history, men were not more important than women. Lady Astor is credited with this Wildean quip: 'I married beneath me. Most women do.'

Those who did not marry were no longer the piteous figures they used to be. The inferiority complex bred into them by generations of Victorian and Edwardian censure was beginning to dissipate. A male barrister writing in 1928 noticed the same phenomenon. The pendulum has swung, he remarked; now many young women are wedded to independence with no intention of contemplating conventional wedlock or being tied down by children.[25] Vera Brittain commented that certain 'advanced' young women demonstrated, by refusing to marry, that 'the fire is not the only alternative to the frying pan'.[26] This sort of modernism recalls the plea of the Russian diarist Marie Bashkirtseff, who wrote in 1890 – answering someone who assumed she wanted to marry and have children – 'Any washerwoman can do that . . . What do I want? I want GLORY.'

The writer and scholar Muriel St Clare Byrne spent most of

her working life editing a dense body of Tudor correspondence. She embarked on the project in the early 1930s; the resulting six volumes were eventually published on her eighty-sixth birthday in 1981. For her, the characters in those thousands of letters became both friends and family. They sustained her, and brought her the academic glory she had always craved. In an unpublished 'Envoi' to the edition, however, she wondered whether she might have sacrificed along the way something even more precious.

> This book is about human beings
> And for human beings.
> It has been made and written
> Because I have enjoyed the society of these people
> Almost as much as I have enjoyed anything in my life.
> I have had the privilege of their company
> For over forty years.
> They have become the dear familiars
> Of heart and thought.
> They have moved me, delighted me, surprised me;
> And some things they have revealed to me
> That I ought to have known –
> Things about human beings
> And what it is that makes them tick –
> Which I suppose I should have learned from life itself,
> And for one reason or another
> Had just missed.[27]

Journalist Margaret Bateson had no such qualms. She said she loved coming home in the evenings to a peaceful house, especially one containing, as hers did, a cook, a parlourmaid and no husband. Some professional women lived with one another in companionable harmony, sisters in all but name. Doctors Ruth Nicholson, Fanny Toza and Helen Duval worked together at Liverpool Maternity Hospital for years; they were great friends, nicknamed the 'three musketeers', and retired together to Exeter in Devon. So did my own aunt, a teacher who lived all her life with a female colleague (my honorary aunt), not as a lover but as a dear friend. They shared the bills, each others' families, holidays and hard times, and were never lonely. Businesswoman Gordon Holmes recognized the need for this sort of relationship. It was completely suitable and natural, she insisted, for all human beings to form deep and tender attachments, irrespective of sex or age.

Women like my aunts may not have chosen spinsterhood, but they did choose celibacy. They were of a generation who believed sex was a function of marriage. An increasing number of career women rejected that assumption. Others were happy to delay the obligations of the marriage bed, making the most of life on the shelf. When trainee barrister Enid Rosser received a proposal of marriage in 1923, she was not even tempted to accept.

> Matrimony to me I knew would be the end of life as I wanted it to happen, and there were many things I wanted to achieve before renouncing independence and all that marriage would mean. My life was, I fear, much too glamorous for any young man to compete with successfully.[28]

She eventually capitulated in 1944, marrying an arachnologist, George Hazlewood Locket. Comparatively wealthy, confident, with a wide social circle and probably armed with a copy of Marie Stopes's *Married Love*, many women like the young Enid relished the single life. Dr Stopes was not a medical doctor, incidentally; she was originally an academic, a palaeo-botanist who became the first female Doctor of Science in England. Her fame grew after 1918, when *Married Love* was published. Forty thousand copies of the book were sold by 1923, and birth-control clinics bearing her name began to appear around the country – publicly endorsed by the unfailingly surprising Maude Royden. The book, and the clinics, were aimed at married women who, like Marie when she first became a wife, had no idea about sex. It would be interesting to know how many of those forty thousand copies went to sexually active spinsters.

Civil servant Jenifer Hart (*née* Williams, 1914–2005) was a thoroughly modern woman. She talked about sex in her memoir without any sense of embarrassment; for her it was simply part of

MARRIED LOVE
A NEW CONTRIBUTION TO THE
SOLUTION OF SEX DIFFICULTIES

*A BOOK FOR
MARRIED COUPLES*

BY

MARIE STOPES, D.Sc., Ph.D.

With a Preface by
Dr. JESSIE MURRAY

Fourteenth Edition. Revised and Enlarged

Six Shillings Net

TO the married and to those about to marry, provided they are normal in mind and body and not afraid of facing facts, this should prove a most helpful book.—
British Medical Journal.

The title-page to Dr Marie Stopes's sensational
Married Love, *first published in 1918.*

life as a single professional woman in London during the 1930s. Jenifer was a pupil at Downe House School while the enigmatic Maria Nickel was working there as resident caretaker/gardener/chauffeur/science teacher/violin coach in the 1920s. Miss Nickel made a deep impression on the girl. In 1931 Jenifer passed a scholarship exam for Somerville College, Oxford, but was considered too young at seventeen to take up her place, which was deferred for a year. To pass the time she went to work as an au pair for British friends of her parents stationed in Geneva.

During her stay, the wife was called home to look after a sick son. Jenifer and the husband, who was twenty years her senior, had an affair. He claimed to espouse the deliciously unconventional morality of the Bloomsbury Group: that anything went, as long as no one got hurt. Ideologically Jenifer was gladly seduced, though she found the sex act less than thrilling. Nevertheless, she had various other adventures during her stay in Europe, and was thus probably much more experienced than most of her sister 'freshers', or first-years, at Somerville. She must surely have caught young tutor Enid Starkie's attention as someone different, and strikingly charismatic.

Oxford was a barren hunting-ground. Jenifer claimed to have met only three men during her entire university career. Two were disappointingly stolid; the third paper-aeroplaned a note to her in the Bodleian Library to invite her for a walk in the woods. He turned out to be a railwayman's son from the midlands (which was exciting) whose main concern seemed to be the lack of sex available in Oxford (which was not).

Jenifer wrote about how another Somervillian fell in love with her and 'extended my horizons' (it was exclusively a women's college at the time). During the vacations she experimented with older men, including her brother-in-law. On leaving Oxford she joined the Communist Party and promptly embarked on a relationship with a married, unemployed Communist milkman.

Ever since hearing Hilda Martindale give a talk about it, she had yearned to join the Civil Service. Perhaps the milkman encouraged an unlikely plan she hatched to act as a left-wing mole while she was there. She sat the entrance exam, passed easily (coming third out of 493 candidates) and chose the Home Office for her field of operations. She even had the odd meeting with a Communist controller during her first year, but the novelty wore off. She found she valued the camaraderie of her colleagues more than skulking about with a metaphorical cloak and dagger, and by 1939 had left the Party.

She enjoyed her job. Office hours were flexible, lunches were long, she worked on Saturday mornings but had six weeks' holiday. Her boss was urbane and interesting. There was only one problem: the marriage bar. Jenifer was in her mid-twenties and rather wanted a child – which meant finding someone to marry. When she enquired whether she was 'indispensable' yet and thus likely to be retained afterwards, she was told that it would take another ten years at least to reach that dizzy height. So she left the Home Office for the Treasury, which was rumoured to be more lenient. By this point war had broken out, which aided her cause; in 1941 she married an Oxford don and the following year became a mother. Even that was not as simple as it sounds: according to Jenifer, Herbert Hart had always thought he was gay until he fell in love with her. Turns out he was a suppressed heterosexual all along.

The term 'lesbian' was not used to identify someone's sexuality until 1908; and although male homosexuality was a criminal offence throughout this period, female homosexuality has never been legislated against. Because of the institutional naïvety promoted in girls' schools by a lack of sex education, many young women at university and beyond had no idea what a lesbian was, nor any terms of reference for an explanation. Gordon Holmes, for example, said she was not told the most basic facts about the birds and the bees until she was well into her twenties. Yet crushes, 'pashes' and intense, intimate friendships between women were neither unusual nor shameful. My research for this book leads me to believe that long and faithful 'marriages' between profes- sional women, like Dr Louisa Martindale's with Ismay Fitzgerald, were also not uncommon. Perhaps it was easier to kick over the traces personally and sexually if one had already done so professionally.

Given that they were by definition unconventional, it would be intriguing to know how many pioneers in the professions con- formed to the traditional pattern of femininity current at the time. In other words, how many worked, then married, then resigned to become housewives. But that could only be done if it were possible to categorize them, which it is not. They defy pigeon-holing, as we all do if you look closely enough. It is pre- cisely why they are so attractive, and why most of us can recognize something of ourselves in them and their colleagues. Some mar- ried, gave up work, then slipped back in through a metaphorical side door; others worked, married, then set up their own busi- nesses, perhaps in partnership with their husbands. Some didn't marry at all − in fact some, one suspects, went into one of the professions precisely in order to live a blamelessly single life.

We could take those who have appeared most frequently in this book as a cross-section. By no means would that be an admis- sible scientific or academic exercise, but it might suggest how idiosyncratic they were. We started with Ray Strachey. In her mid-twenties she married Oliver, a divorcé thirteen years her senior. They had two children. Ray did not give up her work or her activism, her extensive sporting, literary and architectural interests, or her public service committee work. In fact, she seems hardly to have drawn breath. Her husband had affairs; he assured Ray that they did not mean he loved her any the less, and that she was still the light of his life. Nevertheless, they must have been damaging. Perhaps they explained her frantic work rate. Or perhaps the fact that she worked so frantically led to the affairs: we cannot know.

Gwyneth Bebb Thomson was a hard-working mother, as was Dr Frances Hoggan, even though – for different reasons – neither would be recognized by her offspring. Margaret Partridge lived with sister engineer Dorothy Rowbotham, her partner in business and life, in Devon from 1927 to the end of her days. Maude Royden's personal life was more complicated. She did not marry the man she loved – and who loved her – until she was nearing seventy and he, recently widowed, was eighty-five. She told the unusual story of their relationship (outlined briefly here in an earlier chapter) in a memoir, *A Threefold Cord*, published in 1947. Maude and George Hudson Shaw fell in love at first sight in 1901, when she heard him speak at a summer school in Oxford. They corresponded, Maude grateful for his guidance on her spiritual odyssey and Shaw simply acknowledging that this eloquent young graduate, so eager to do the right thing by God, did him good. According to Maude, at this stage it never occurred to either of them that they had become romantically involved; if it had, they would have parted immediately. Naïvety? Denial? It is not clear.

Maude worked near her family home in Liverpool for two years after leaving Oxford; Shaw returned to his parish in Rutland. They kept in touch. After what she describes offhandedly as her breakdown, he suggested she come to stay in the countryside with him and his wife Effie. A change of scene might cheer her up. Gradually Maude evolved into Shaw's unpaid curate, even giving a sermon on one occasion when he was unable to do so. After three months, she went home for Christmas. Do you want me back, she asked Shaw? ' "Want you?" he cried with a voice of sudden passion that shook me. "*Want* you? If you could know the chill, the horror, that falls on me when I think you won't come!" '[29] She stayed for three years, Jane Eyre with her Mr Rochester.

Shaw's wife Effie realized what was happening and, astonishingly, encouraged Maude and Shaw to consummate their
relationship. Maude believed, she wrote, 'that I could never have
all I needed as long as Hudson gave to me, and I to him, no more
than affection, no more than friendship'.[30] Effie loved them both:
hence the 'threefold cord' binding the trio together. Yet despite
Effie's urging, Maude suggests that her relationship with Hudson,
though intense, remained platonic.

The Shaws moved to London in 1912; Maude lived with them
on and off until her own marriage, which was announced in *The
Times* on 3 October 1944. She proudly kept the letters of con-
gratulation that poured in. On their wedding night, George
Hudson Shaw suffered a heart attack; two months later, he died.

Maude's close friend Constance Coltman led a comparatively
orthodox personal life. She met her husband Claud at Mansfield
College, Oxford, and they married the day after their joint ordination in September 1917. They had three children. Constance,
like Vera Kenmure, believed that marriage increased her spiritual
understanding and made her better at her job. Barrister Helena
Normanton would agree; she was not a mother like Constance
but found it easy to empathize with her married clients. If one
appreciated the mechanics of a successful relationship, one might
better understand what made it fail. She believed passionately
in a woman's right to divorce her husband if married life was
insupportable – making what she termed a 'surgical clean cut' –
though the only argument she and her husband Gavin ever had,
she remembered, was over the correct way to carve a salmon.

Academic Enid Starkie had affairs throughout her working life,
but none appears to have been satisfactory or even helpful – though
perhaps that is not, in any case, the primary purpose of an affair.
Lady Rhondda, having endured three 'seasons' as a debutante in
search of a husband before going to university (which she left after
her first year), was twenty-six when she married an eligible but

unsuitable man in his late thirties. She tried her best to do her duty as a wife in the minor gentry, but neither her personality nor her politics sat comfortably in the role, and in 1923 the couple divorced. After that, she enjoyed a series of close friendships with women and in 1933 met her life partner Theodora Bosanquet, an author and the secretary of the International Federation of University Women.

Pioneering solicitor Carrie Morrison, as noted earlier, also went through a divorce when she and Ambrose Appelbe parted in 1937 – but they continued to work together and remained close for the rest of her life. Glamorous aviator and serious engineer Amy Johnson married glamorous aviator and 'playboy' Jim Mollison in 1932, at the height of her fame. The relationship foundered within two years and they divorced in the full glare of celebrity in 1938.

Contemporary records tend to be coy about personal and sexual relationships, and in many respects these attachments were not relevant to professional achievements; nevertheless it is frustrating to curious social historians that so little is known of the private lives of 'biggish women' like civil servant Hilda Martindale or surgeon Louisa Aldrich-Blake. Hilda's sister Louisa lived happily with Ismay Fitzgerald; Hilda herself never had any recorded relationship, let alone children of her own, though she was keenly interested in child welfare and a faithful benefactor of Dr Barnardo's Homes. As for Dr Aldrich-Blake, those who described her, usually with affection, noted that she was not really built for romance. She loved young people; she kept the same maid, Florence, for twenty-five years; and she and the friend with whom she shared her house, Rosamond Wigram, used to go out for drives together on Sunday afternoons in Louisa's beloved motor car. She obviously inspired loyalty and lived a pleasant life. Whether she and Rosamond were lovers is a moot point; her biographer thinks not.

As we have seen, Mary Somerville of the BBC was married in 1928, though like Helena Normanton and Drs Miller and Wright at

Liverpool University, she kept her maiden name. She and her husband had just the one child, and divorced in 1945. In 1962, after
she had retired, Mary married again. She was sixty-six years old.

One of Mary's colleagues at the BBC was Hilda Matheson, who
became the Corporation's first Director of Talks. Like Mary, Hilda
was brought up in a Presbyterian manse in Scotland; after taking a
degree in History at Oxford she worked as a secretary, a clerk in the
War Office, in the Special Intelligence Directorate (which later
became MI5), and as an assistant to Lady Astor MP. She joined the
BBC in 1927 and was soon on a salary of £900 per annum. (The
average salary of a woman teacher at the time was £100.) Hilda's
mission was to enrich the intellectual output of the Corporation,
inviting high-profile public figures to give broadcast talks, thus provoking intelligent debate (it was hoped) among the listening public.
Her department was known as 'the University of the Air'.

One of her guests was the author, politician and Bloomsbury
Group figure Harold Nicolson, husband of Vita Sackville-West –
herself a lover of Virginia Woolf. Hilda also engaged Vita to give
a talk. The two women appear to have spontaneously combusted
on meeting; eight hundred pages of Hilda's love letters to Vita
survive, charting an intense relationship which burned brightly
for three years.

Unusually, Hilda did not strive to hide her sexuality. It tickled
her to imagine what colleagues would think if they could read some
of the correspondence between her and Vita, sometimes naughtily
written on BBC headed notepaper. 'By Jove, what a shock all these
good people would have if they could see what thoughts and long-
ings are filling my head!'[31] She felt no compulsion to be discreet. In
1931 she resigned from the BBC, primarily because of a clash of
personality and politics with Sir John Reith, and went on to work
under Virginia and Leonard Woolf at the Hogarth Press. A year
later, Hilda took another of Vita's lovers, the poet Dorothy Welles-
ley, as her new partner – as it turned out, for life.

All that sounds rather exhausting – but is nothing compared to the private life of ophthalmologist Ida Mann. When Gertrude Leverkus was warned by her tearful mother that a man did not want a wife who wears glasses (never mind one who is a qualified architect), Gertrude was unperturbed. Now that she could see, life was going to be too exciting to worry about that sort of thing. So it was with Ida Mann, when embarking on her medical training. 'No one will ever marry you now,' mourned her father.[32] Ida's response was unexpected. So what? 'I could get as true a physical thrill from my channelled libido while gazing at a microscope slide.'[33] Later in her career she fell in love with a married professor with three children. He was widowed soon after they met, and they began a technicolour affair. 'We did the oddest things, like going to bed with a microscope and arising to watch the ecstatic wiggles of Bill's spermatozoa on the slide.'[34] She did not long for children, and always assumed she would never marry – but she and her professor did tie the knot in 1944; at this point she became a stepmother of three, as well as looking after her brother's children when their parents died young.

Ida touchingly quotes one of her own poems in her autobiography. It must have been written before she met Bill.

> I asked of life adventure without end.
> I asked of Death that he should be my friend.
> I asked of Love that he should pass me by . . .
> Life said, 'I give if you have strength to take.'
> Death said, 'Then live adventurous for my sake.'
> Love cared not overmuch for such as I.[35]

In the end, both Ida and her father were wrong: she became one of the most distinguished specialists of her generation, *and* found love.

9

Butterfly's Wings with Blue Stockings

SPENDING-POWER AND LEISURE

The root of modern feminism is . . . the desire for money.[1]

IT IS ABOUT 11 a.m. on a weekday morning in 1920. Middle-class housewives across the British Isles are taking a well-earned break. They have supervised a hearty breakfast; waved hubby and the children off to work and school; taken the Highland terrier for a walk while the 'help' has made the beds and done the dusting. There's some shopping to do and the library books to return later, and Baby will have woken from his morning nap soon. But now it's time to sit in that patch of sunlight in the kitchen, enjoy a cup of Camp coffee and a Kensitas cigarette, and read the latest copy of a favourite magazine.

This chapter is something of a digression, which is appropriate given that it's about a change being as good as a rest. Everyone needs something to distract them from the rigours of the working day: even professional women. And one of the most gratifying aspects of earning a salary is the freedom to spend it. Many of the pioneers had dependants to support, loans to repay and fees or premiums to meet. Even so, there was usually something left over each month – and a little spare time – for themselves. Women's magazines not only entertained the reader in the short term, but inspired her with suggestions for the weekend, the next holiday, the next job, and that dream man just about to drop into her life.

There were several titles to choose from. *The Queen* was rather high-class, with news (or superior gossip) about the Royals and glimpses into the home lives of famous Ladies. *Vogue* was not exclusively concerned with fashion; it covered highbrow arts and literature too. *Woman's Life* was more homely, offering unambitious recipes and tips on how to make the most of oneself – with straplines like 'Miss Fluffy Femininity carries off the prizes'.[2] *Home Chat* ran serialized stories about charismatic heroes falling for girls who hid their lights under bushels, only revealing their beauty when whisking off their spectacles and liberating their crowning glory from its hairpins. *Woman's Weekly* often included paper patterns, modelled by a man wearing a Fair Isle sweater and a faraway look, or an approachable-looking young woman with lipstick and dimples. *The Lady* appealed to fantasists. Perusing its many classified advertisements for domestic staff, readers could pretend they had enough money to employ and accommodate (probably in the South Lodge) a married housekeeper and gardener, as well as a neatly starched nanny and a gentlewoman companion for grandmama.

None of this reading stuff appears at first glance as though it would attract the sort of women who people this book: 'fluffy femininity' and all-consuming domesticity were not what the modern age was about. These magazines belonged to a pre-war era when most journalists were men and very few women had any appreciable spending-power. We all have our guilty pleasures; maybe Dr Louisa Aldrich-Blake read romances about rugged war heroes smitten by secretaries and Margaret Partridge spent her evenings cooking meat-paste pies and jellied milk (by electricity, of course) while dreaming of the perfect perm – but it is hard to imagine.

As the new decade progressed, a brisk wind blew in from the west, bringing with it the promise of American innovation: new

music, new dances, a new way of speaking, new things to read –
and lots of new gossip about film stars and socialites. *Good
Housekeeping* had been going strong in the United States since
1885. In March 1922 the first British issue appeared, promising its
readers a taste of the 'higher life'. At first glance the cover of volume one, number one, is not convincing, with its soppy illustration
of an apple-cheeked toddler in a red frock, pouring a saucer of
milk for a kitten. The list of contributors beneath the picture is
more robust, however, suggesting that this is, after all, a women's
magazine fit for a post-war world.

Clemence Dane was the pseudonym of feminist Winifred
Ashton (1888–1965), already a notable novelist and playwright
whose first book, *Regiment of Women* (1917), was a story of lesbian
love and suicide in a girls' boarding school. Her debut play, *A Bill
of Divorcement*, was staged in London in 1921. *Good Housekeeping*
commissioned her, appropriately enough, to write an article about
women negotiating a marriage break-up. Marie Corelli (Mary
Mackay, 1855–1924) was another high-profile contributor: a
best-selling author for more than thirty years. John Galsworthy
joined her on the fiction pages, a year after completing his fabu-
lously successful series of novels, *The Forsyte Saga*. Lady Astor MP
wrote a piece on temperance, a cause she supported throughout
her political life. No doubt it was included to counter any accusations of excessive sensationalism that might be levelled at the
magazine, and to lend it gravitas.

The opening editorial set the tone of *Good Housekeeping*. 'Any
keen observer of the times cannot have failed to notice that we
are on the threshold of a great feminine awakening,'[3] it ran. The
days of dullness and drudgery in the home were over: coming up
in the next few numbers were exclusive articles on careers for
women – controversially including housekeeping – and news on
the latest trends in electrical engineering, domestic architecture,
fashion, cookery and interior decor.

It becomes easier now to imagine Helena Normanton or Maude Royden leafing through a woman's magazine like this when they paused for a moment's rest; to see its potential appeal to activist Ray Strachey or engineer Cleone Griff, a pioneering member of the WES dubbed the Queen of Stainless Steel. And indeed, all of them wrote for *Good Housekeeping* on various occasions: Helena most regularly, on feminism and legal matters,[4] Maude on double standards in morality, Ray on designing and building one's own house, and Cleone on careers in professional engineering. Other contributors included Millicent Fawcett, alerting readers to the fact that they still could not vote until the age of thirty and suggesting they do something about it; an economics tutor from Girton College, Cambridge, explaining how to manage household budgets; and Lady Rhondda taking a break from *Time and Tide* to discuss rosy prospects for women in business.

Publications like *Good Housekeeping* were soon a part of professional life for career women, offering opportunities to boost their personal income and profile through writing – as well as the pleasure of reading. Publishers and advertisers alike were quick to recognize a ready market. From the mid-1920s onwards, more titles emerged for the educated reader in charge of her own purse-strings. *Britannia and Eve* was founded in May 1929 as 'a Monthly Journal for Men and Women'. The first number, running to over two hundred pages, cost one shilling (four times the price of a pint of milk). It is loaded with advertisements, some of them in colour, for cigarettes, 'shadow-garments' (lingerie), hats, insurance policies, Ryvita to eat, champagne to drink, fancy kitchenware, cars and cosmetics (startlingly including 'radio-active hair restorer'): everything a modern woman of the world could possibly need. And nothing much for men at all; in fact, it did not take long for *Britannia and Eve* to be marketed exclusively at women.

The magazine is a strange mixture; progressive features about sex and the single girl, financial independence and the advantages of a good divorce sit side by side with beige recipes for boiled lettuce with breadcrumbs, curried apples and Bismarck herrings.[5] A piece about racing cars is followed by tips on how to knit your own bathing-suit ('a short-cut to chic'); a feminist critique of the psychology of fashion precedes an anodyne article by Daphne du Maurier on 'Women and their Pets through the Ages'. Perhaps the publishers hoped there would be something for everyone – and perhaps they were right: *Britannia and Eve* ran until 1957.

Miss Modern (from October 1930) is aimed at a younger readership, with a film supplement and regular advice on health and beauty: how to deal with blackheads, disappointing teeth or flabbiness. This magazine seems to be obsessed by the concept of sex-appeal. An article on applying for a job is not about building an impressive *curriculum vitae*; it is about how to arrange your limbs during the interview (assuming the interviewer will be male); how much make-up to wear; and how to move in and out of the room effectively. 'Pity the Pretty Girl in Business' is the title of a jauntily illustrated feature on using 'sex-weapons' with discretion in the 'battle of a career'.

> Should you use your good looks in order to help your career, or shouldn't you? Is it wrong to bring sex into business or isn't it? What ought to be your attitude to your chief if he shows signs of admiring you (a) if he's married and (b) if he isn't? . . . In my opinion you would be foolish not to use your good looks discreetly in order to help your career. They are a fortunate accident of birth and part of your capital. If you had been born with £500 a year no-one would expect you not to use it, and good looks may be worth more than £500 a year. Besides, if you want to carve a career, some day you must graduate beyond secretarial work to something more important, and then you may have to compete with men, and men have better brains than women.[6]

You can imagine what the magazine made of the American Mrs Wallis Simpson and her sex-weaponry. She was the ultimate sharp-shooter, and Edward, Prince of Wales, the most willing of targets. Their relationship from 1931 onwards was manna from heaven to the gossip columnists.

This inter-war period was when the pattern for the modern women's magazine was established. Rebecca West, Agatha Christie and Somerset Maugham wrote short stories for them. Female interior designers, architects and engineers suggested how to live with economy and style, not just in the family house, but in your own private bedsit. In a 1923 issue of *Good Housekeeping* Helena Normanton explained how to persuade a bank manager to give you a chequebook, and what to do with it when he did. If you were married, you would naturally need your husband's written permission to open an account of your own (this remained the case until 1975). You could not secure a mortgage unless your husband or father applied on your behalf, nor enter into a hire-purchase agreement without a man's counter-signature. Credit cards did not exist, and a bank account would not be available if you earned less than £3 per week.[7] But if none of the above applied, chequebooks were definitely the way forward.

Helena advised that the possession of a bank account was an easily recognizable sign of independence and responsibility. Practise a sensible signature before you open yours (elaborate flourishes make it easier for forgers to copy, not the reverse), and do not take your chequebook and fountain-pen with you wherever you go, in case you are tempted to over-use it. Watch your balance carefully. Being an account-holder has several advantages: you can store valuables at the bank, and your manager (whom you will come to know personally) will act as a character referee if necessary.

This was useful information, imparted in a safe and familiar forum in one's own home. There is no doubt that women's magazines performed a significant service to their readers as well as entertaining them. The most basic information on nutrition, for example, could be revelatory. It is easy to forget how ignorant a young woman living alone could be, after leaving home, university or a place of training where she was housed, fed and generally looked after. One cheerful working girl admitted that she regularly lunched on 'half a pound of mixed chocolates and two aspirins'.[8] When Myfanwy Gipson was reading for the Bar in London in the late 1920s, it never occurred to her to worry about what she was putting into her body.

> One night I started vomiting blood and had severe stomach pains, and sent for my Doctor, Dr Ledingham. He asked me all sorts of odd questions, even about my companion, Meg, and after he had gone, it suddenly dawned on me that he must think I was being poisoned! Horrors! That gave me furiously to think: what could it possibly be? Then the penny dropped: Iron and Arsenic pills! I was still taking them without prescription, just buying them over the counter, ever since some Doctor said I was anaemic and needed iron and arsenic. I nearly put paid to my existence.[9]

It is to editors' credit that their recipe and health-care sections do not generally come across as patronizing. Cartoons and elegant art-deco illustrations lighten the mood, and there are recipes for cocktails as well as advertisements for Ovaltine; features about the latest night-club dances as well as the new-born Women's League of Health and Beauty with its bracing motto – 'Movement is Life' – and alluring gym-knickers.

The staple diet of most women's magazines then (as now) was fashion. Virginia Woolf highlights the significance of dress as a statement in *Three Guineas*, a parable about how a responsible, socially aware woman spends her money. She describes the sartorial habits of professional men, whose clothes make us 'gape with astonishment'. To signal how superior he is, a bishop wears a long, violet dress with a jewelled crucifix at his breast; a judge's shoulders are festooned with lace and his robes edged in ermine; lawyers' wigs froth with self-importance; and hats are infinite in their variety, 'boat-shaped, or cocked; now they mount in cones of black fur; now they are made of brass and scuttle-shaped; now plumes of red, now of blue hair surmount them'.[10] Yet these same men criticize women for a vacuous love of dress! Woolf's implication is that men are as jealous of their professional ritual and the associated finery as they are of the professions themselves. They want exclusive use of the dressing-up box. And it is true, I have found that a woman's proudest moment is often the first time she dons a mortar-board, a surgical gown, the bright robes of a Doctor of Philosophy or a tickly, tightly curled barrister's wig. These are outward signs of arrival and belonging.

In 1925 *Success through Dress* was published, a book about making sure one's personal shop window is as effective an advertisement as possible. 'Now that woman has secured so much that she has striven for,' writes the author, the Hon. Mrs C. W. Forester, 'I would impress upon her not to neglect, in her newly found freedom, those feminine arts and niceties which are in these, as in all times, associated with an attractive and intelligent personality.'[11] Mrs Forester differentiates between fashion and style. Fashion is the commodity; style is what you do with it. She advises 'advanced feminists' to throw away their headwear: bonnets and berets are *not* radical. The trick is to look smart, confident and self-possessed. You can't go wrong in a crisply tailored navy serge suit with a neat, white collar. Avoid at all costs seated skirts, blowsy necklines, down-at-heel shoes and bedraggled hats: only 'clever women' favour those.

By the time *Success through Dress* hit the bookshops, artificial fibres were becoming available to the mass market, thus widening the variety and lowering the cost of off-the-peg outfits. In 1930

Courtaulds developed a new fabric unfortunately called 'Cour-gette'. Rayon, or artificial silk, was more successful – especially for lingerie, which underwent something of a revolution, and a drastic loss of weight, during the inter-war period. Mirroring the political emancipation of women, 1920s fashion waved a tem-porary farewell to restrictive stays and whale-boned corsets, welcoming light camisoles in their stead. Jupons were 'warm and dainty' garments worn beneath one's *crêpe-de-chine* knickers in the winter, with a fine woollen vest if necessary up top, over one's *brassière* (if one possessed such a fashionable piece of equipment). Corsets diminished into girdles and suspender-belts, with the dual purpose of keeping one's tummy in and stockings up. All this felt liberating.

Come the 1930s, however, things were changing again. An advertisement for Harrods department store stated confidently that 'women are going to be their normal feminine selves in 1934. Parisian dressmakers have decided in favour of a sweetly feminine silhouette for the coming spring which will accentuate a woman's charm by means of ruffles, frills and delightful artifices.'[12] English designers like the young Cambridge graduate Norman Hartnell were thinking the same; meanwhile, however, Italian Elsa Schia-parelli produced gorgeously fluid trouser-suits and long-lined, highly wrought gowns. It is difficult to picture Amy Johnson, for instance, in a nip-waisted Parisian frock; being the epitome of the stylish, go-getting modern woman, she oozed art deco charm whenever she emerged from her flying overalls. She was surely a Schiaparelli girl. Lady Astor designed her own sober but smartly cut suit for work in the House of Commons and beyond; so strik-ing did she look that clothes manufacturers copied the pattern, naming their version 'the Westminster'.

Even academics were not immune to the fickle charm of fash-ion, despite being what Mrs Forester witheringly called 'clever women'. We know about Enid Starkie's peculiarly maritime sense of dress; Maria Czaplicka was more conventionally dashing, and knew how to wear a hat with panache. She belonged to a group of intellectually and visually brilliant women distinguished, according to a contemporary journalist, by their elegant ability to team 'butterfly's wings with blue stockings'.[13] At Oxford, when female undergraduates were finally allowed to wear academic dress in 1920, a mannequin parade was held to model different designs of headwear. They might as well not have bothered: the Tudor beret women ended up with was universally scorned.

Enid Rosser Locket's diary of the years she spent training for and practising at the Bar reveals how important it was to her not to appear dowdy. Female barristers faced enough problems without being labelled frumps. She remembers the day she 'cast off' her black stockings in 1922 and wore pale fawn silk ones for the first time. As she walked down Curzon Street in London's Mayfair she felt as though she were almost naked. And she tried every new hairstyle going: bobs, shingles, perms, and finally Marcel waving, which involved creating regular, glossy undulations with the aid of heated curling tongs. She spent any spare time during the day (admittedly, there wasn't much) having lunch with her old university friends and going shopping; in the 'gin-soaked' evenings she enjoyed midnight treasure-hunts and paper-chases, danced to jazz bands in an ever-increasing variety of night-clubs, went to the cinema – which anyone in work could afford to do at least once a week – or talked about the latest novels and radio programmes over cocktails and smokes. Cocaine would certainly have been available at the sorts of venues Enid frequented, but there is nothing in the diary about that. Popular tonic wines were infused with it – to go with the arsenic pills, perhaps, as a punchy pick-me-up – and women were encouraged to smoke pipes of tobacco instead of cigarettes because it calmed the nerves more swiftly. Kensitas cigarettes were positively good for you, *and* helped you lose weight.

American influence was everywhere: imbuing the music at dance-halls, choreographing the dances themselves – the 'Kickaboo' or the 'Black Bottom' as well as the more familiar Charleston – and saturating films. The first 'talkie' arrived in 1927, but cinemas were habitually full well before that. It might be unusual for a woman to go on her own (unless, like the disillusioned teacher Gladys, she was hoping to find male company there) but it was a perfect, inexpensive outing for groups of female friends. By 1939 there were five thousand picture-houses in the UK, with about 19 million customers each week: a staggering statistic given that the total population of Great Britain at the time was roughly 45 million.[14]

Those with higher cultural aspirations went to the theatre, where ticket prices ranged from a shilling to 4 guineas, or to the opera. Bacteriologist Emma Mason worked as an analyst in a creamery in Manchester and counted her regular visit to the Opera House there a necessity of life. She always sat in the cheapest seats, up in the gods, which meant she could just about afford the other essentials: rent, food, clothes, the odd tea-time visit to the Squirrel Restaurant near her digs, and a riding lesson on Sunday mornings. 'The root of modern feminism is . . . the desire for money,' wrote the novelist Arnold Bennett in 1920. He was wrong. The root of modern feminism was the quest for political, financial and emotional independence. Money was the means to that end.

It is one of those things we all remember: what we did with our first pay cheque. In a perverse fit of domesticity I find slightly unsettling now, I went out and bought a sewing-machine with mine. It sits reproachfully in its original box in the loft as I write. The first thing Virginia Woolf bought with money she earned herself was a cat. It was a beautiful Persian cat, who looked divine but soon involved her in bitter disputes with her neighbours. Fortunately she already had the means to provide herself with a roof over her head, food for the table and clothes. During the 1930s, the instinct of many a working woman on receiving her salary was to treat herself to something unnecessary from a department store – perhaps Lewis's in Liverpool; Marshall and Snelgrove in Manchester; Fenwicks in Newcastle; Jenners in Edinburgh; Howells in Cardiff; Beatties in Birmingham – or any one of scores of others up and down the country, most of which have since been subsumed by chains or completely disappeared. Between them, they turned shopping from a chore into an art, with attractions rivalling the circus, the cinema and the seaside promenade.

Bentalls in Kingston-upon-Thames had its own Palm Court orchestra, serenading customers who had come not just to spend their money, but to enter their infants into Bonny Baby competitions, watch twice-daily mannequin parades, or purchase a Hollywood makeover in the cosmetics department and then perform a pretend screen test in front of a real, live movie camera operated by a real, live movie cameraman. Every summer the store somehow managed to acquire the floral decorations from the Royal Box at Ascot Racecourse; these adorned various different departments before being sold to anyone who cared to share the King's flowers. At Christmas, Bentalls had its own menagerie with elephants, and a lion who lived in the lift-shaft. An in-house peep-show featured 'Marsana the long-necked woman' – a Karen, perhaps, from Thailand.[15]

Elsewhere, department stores hosted dance shows that were broadcast on the BBC; engaged live models to sit in shop windows saucily changing their stockings; booked popular actresses to glide around the shop floor looking entranced, or circus performers with their animal side-kicks – like Koringa 'the Female Fakir', who brought five live crocodiles to work with her, the beefiest of which was called Churchill.

The most exotic of all attractions must surely have been Miss Annie Kittner from Sweden, who appeared in the escalator hall at Bentalls twice daily for a fortnight wearing nothing but a swimming costume, a bathing cap and a pair of shoes. First she took off the shoes; then she climbed a specially erected ladder with a diving board teetering at the top of it, performed a handstand on the board, and dived into a small pool some 19 metres below. On one particularly memorable occasion, her costume split. The management couldn't have asked for more.

All this effort was directed at persuading more women (who were the majority of customers) to spend more money, more often. Like magazine editors, those who owned and ran department stores appreciated this lively new market, and did what they could to milk it. The leisure industry, in its infancy before the Second World War, soon learned the same lesson. It is clear from Adèle Mager's diary – the one I found at the antiques fair – that an important element of her and her husband Len's weekend was 'going for a spin'. Sometimes it was described as taking a turn in the car, or simply motoring. I remember it from my own childhood in the 1960s: at about three o'clock on a Sunday afternoon, when we were all drowsy after a roast lunch and low-spirited at the thought of Monday morning, my father would announce that it was time to go. For the next hour or so we would drive aimlessly around the lanes of north Yorkshire, occasionally encountering other glum-looking families doing exactly the same but in the opposite direction.

So it was for the Magers, except that they appear to have enjoyed the exercise more than I ever did. The opportunity to get away from home relatively spontaneously, however briefly, was a novelty in the 1920s. Dr Louisa Aldrich–Blake adored her car and was a skilled mechanic. Sundays, for her, were made for driving. Enid Rosser Locket used to motor over the Chiltern Hills from London to visit Oxford at weekends, and architect Gertrude Leverkus chugged to visit her sisters Dorothy and Elsie in their house (which she had designed) in Oxfordshire. Elsie was a gifted amateur artist, trained in Paris; she now kept house for

Dorothy (known as Dolly), who was a doctor. Gertrude enjoyed chauffeuring Dolly on her rural rounds.

The Woman Engineer is unsurprisingly full of hints to lady motorists: what vehicle to buy (some were marketed directly at women), how to look after it and where to drive it. Motorcycles were also in vogue. In 1928 two more sisters, Betty and Nancy Debenham, published *Motor-Cycling for Women*, which gives practical advice on this adventurous new sport and recommends taking a dog with you – preferably (like Gromit) in a side-car – as a substitute for a man. They carried Poncho almost everywhere they went. Perhaps the best-known female motorcyclist of the era was Beatrice 'Tilly' Shilling. Tilly bought her first machine at the age of fourteen, three years before she answered an advertisement

The dashing Debenham sisters on their BSA *motorcycles, minus dog Poncho.*

Margaret Partridge enterprisingly sent to girls' secondary schools across the country, inviting applications for a traineeship in her electrical engineering enterprise. Tilly got the job, and while working as an apprentice took a BSc and then an MSc in engineering at Manchester University; then in 1936 she joined the Royal Aircraft Establishment (RAE) at Farnborough, working on the design of aircraft carburettors.

Tilly never lost her love of motorcycling. Her first machine, a Royal Enfield, had fascinated her, but it was not particularly powerful; once she had taught herself how to dismantle it and put it back together in slightly better fettle, she was ready for something new. This time she bought a Norton 500cc monster, modified and tuned it herself, and went racing. By the mid-1930s she had become the fastest female ever around the circuit at Brooklands, winning a coveted 'Gold Star' award for topping 100 mph for an entire lap. In fact, Tilly achieved 106 mph. When RAE colleague George Naylor proposed to her, she is said to have accepted him on the condition that he, too, won a Gold Star. He promptly did so. Dr Gladys Wauchope was another keen motorcyclist, but only at the sort of speed suitable for visiting patients in obscure Norfolk villages.

The travel company Thomas Cook owed its early success to women. When its eponymous founder set up the business in the mid-nineteenth century, offering personally conducted tours on the continent and in Egypt, a large part of his clientele consisted of 'unprotected' ladies eager to see the world but lacking a husband, brother or son to chaperone them. Travelling alone risked one's reputation; who better to be one's guide and companion than a thoroughly respectable, teetotal family man like Mr Cook? Cook's Tours offered women three things. The most valuable was a precedent for travel. Before his intervention, lone women travellers attracted a good deal of suspicion and mistrust. Going abroad was unsuitable for *ladies*. But once the first few cohorts of Cook's tourists had arrived back home again safe and sound, attitudes began to change. The second of his gifts to women was confidence, and the third, a taste for adventure.

Mr Cook's first conducted tour of Europe took place in 1855. It was widely publicized, and its success, frequently repeated in subsequent years, could well have influenced Mrs Martindale, for example, when she decided to take her daughters Louisa and Hilda around the world some twenty years later; the parents of Dr Frances Hoggan when they sent her to Paris and Düsseldorf as a schoolgirl (though what happened to Frances in Paris hardly vindicated their decision); and even the Irish architect Eileen Gray, who chose to live and work in Paris. She grew up the daughter of a painter in Ireland and in London, where she attended the Slade School of Art in 1901. Surprisingly, there were 168 female day students there in her time, and only 60 men.[16] One of her closest friends at the Slade was Kathleen Bruce, the sculptor who went on to marry Captain Scott of the Antarctic. Together the young women travelled to Paris in 1902, inspired by the glasswork of René Lalique and Emile Gallé to enrol at art school there.

They made an arresting pair, Kathleen with her strong jaw-line and extraordinarily luxuriant hair (which she sometimes wore loose, like a cloak) and the willowy Eileen, always snappily dressed and elegant. It was rumoured (according to Kathleen) that there was madness in Eileen's family, which lent the young Irishwoman an air of edgy exoticism. From the age of twenty-nine to that of ninety-eight Eileen lived in the same apartment in Paris, decorated with the lacquer-work in which she specialized. Not all of her influences were European; for pleasure, as well as for work, Eileen travelled in the United States; and she collaborated with a Japanese artist. One of her clients as an interior designer was Elsa Schiaparelli.

None of these people were aristocrats steeped in the tradition of the Grand Tour; it was indirectly thanks to Thomas Cook and

his legacy that they had the courage to step away from the familiar and look at the world with new eyes. Ophthalmologist Ida
Mann loved going abroad. Before her marriage, as we have seen,
she re-invented herself in India as the honorary member of a traditional Hindu family. She regularly attended international
conferences, and in 1930 completed a lecture tour in America.
Maude Royden also toured America; indeed, most people involved
in the network of professional women at the heart of this history
will have spent at least some of their customary six weeks' annual
holiday abroad. It seems to me that a good many of them spent
the remainder marching up and down mountains in Snowdonia
and the Lake District. These pioneers were great walkers. Lady
Rhondda even had a special outfit for the purpose, consisting of
a battered pair of ex-Land Army breeches worn beneath a
respectable-looking skirt. As soon as she was far enough from
civilization for no one to be offended, she would discard the skirt
with a flourish and stride off into the misty distance.

Other popular sports included the usual tennis and hockey; I
have not come across a professional ladies' football team (as in a
team of ladies from the professions), though the thought of barristers in full fig versus gynaecologists, or chemical engineers
versus church ministers, is appealing. Before 1921, working-class
women's football was a major participatory and spectator sport in
Britain. A team in Preston, drawn from employees at the Dick,
Kerr engineering company, regularly attracted tens of thousands
of supporters. But, just as at medical schools and in professional
practices, so on the football pitch: a few years after the war it was
decided that women should relinquish their places to men, and go
home. The official argument put forward by the Football Association was that the game was too rough and dangerous for girls.
Almost overnight, women's football all but disappeared, and is
only now beginning to approach its former glory a century later.

Ladies' cricket was acceptable; so was golf – all the more so because of its comparatively genteel history. Women's golf never achieved the arcane social cachet of the men's game, which operated a little like an eighteen-hole version of Freemasonry. But it was certainly a fashionable pastime for modern young women who could afford it, and a sociable one, less overtly competitive than alternatives. Inevitably, extra rules were put in place for ladies, to keep them in check. They included a ludicrous decree that women should not be allowed to drive the ball beyond 70 yards. Any further, and they were liable to swing their arms above their shoulders, making an inelegant and possibly embarrassing spectacle of their upper torsos. And on no account should they mix with gentlemen in the clubhouse – or even set foot in there, in some cases. Does this remind you of anything? Climbing ladders, perhaps, or having to make do with a dingy common room at the back of the building?

Holidays were not just about taking a break and broadening the mind in a cultural sense. They offered the prospect of romance. Medic Peggy Kenyon was spending some off-duty time in Hampshire when she met her future husband. Her contemporary at King's College Hospital, May Du Buisson, was wooed and won in Africa. Civil servant Jenifer Hart met lovers abroad; and when architect Eileen Gray opened an interior design shop on the rue du Faubourg Saint-Honoré in 1922, she had already been initiated into the louche secrets of Parisian night-life, having visited bars there with a female friend, both dressed as men, while training at the Académie Julian in the early 1900s. Organizations like the WES and the MWF held conferences around the country and occasionally abroad, as well as regular 'socials' (they still do). The chance to meet new people was always welcome. There was a sense during the inter-war period that women had literally earned the right to enjoy themselves, and intended to do so. Besides, if relationships at work were frowned upon, where else were they to meet a partner?

With this in mind, magazines like the ones discussed earlier started hosting increasingly explicit columns discussing the art of flirting. Maude Royden was concerned about this.

> Let us be honest. As long as girls are taught that to attract men is the first duty of woman, and to attract one sufficiently to persuade him to marry her is the vocation of woman; so long as a woman who fails in this vocation is regarded as a maimed and wasted being who, whatever her work and value, is really 'superfluous' . . . so long will the temptation to hang about those places where men congregate exist.[17]

But surely, the movement to repopulate the traditional professions with women was all about women hanging about the places where men congregate — and doing so *on their own merits*? The counter-argument to Maude's uncharacteristic plea for decorum had already been expressed in *Miss Modern*: use your sex-weapons to your own advantage, to empower rather than appease. But do not go too far. An office worker writing in the *Daily Express* in 1923 was positively brazen.

> My one terror in life is the thought that the time will come when my skirts will have to be at least two inches longer than they are now . . . I know that my shapely legs are the admiration of pale young City men . . . I make my own pleasure, supply my own enjoyment, manufacture my own thrills . . . No ordinary natural man can resist me. I have made it my study not only to attract, but also to hold in bonds that no-one can break. I am a flapper, a coquette, and every man is my slave.[18]

Most magazines encouraged readers to set their sights a little lower, with inoffensive articles on 'How to Kiss' (accompanied by an advertisement for 'kiss-proof lipstick'); on keeping control when sex, 'the most explosive thing in life', threatened to take you hostage; and on the perils of over-plucking your eyebrows. *Radio Pictorial* was first published in 1933 as a weekly magazine ostensibly offering 'news and views of the radio world'. However, it was more wide-ranging than that. As well as British and Continental radio schedules it included, like other popular journals, short stories and regular helpings of celebrity interviews. It is particularly significant from our point of view because it also ran an 'Agony Aunt' feature, dealing with the problems of working women.

Anna of Harrow wrote for help in 1936. 'I am far too short for my age and don't seem to be growing any more.'[19] She was desperate to join the Civil Service as a telephonist, but did not meet the height requirement: what could she do? Auntie told her not to worry: she would send Anna a 'stretching exercise' which would easily do the trick. Someone else shamefully confessed to being forty-five years old and forced to earn her own living; how could she fool potential employers into thinking she was younger and therefore more desirable to them? It's all about your skin, replied Auntie. And there are plenty of preparations to help with that.

Radio Pictorial ran a series of features about high-achieving women in the BBC, including Mary Somerville; it also displayed photo galleries of the most attractive (female) secretaries – and, in the interests of impartiality, of tweedy-looking 'BBC Bachelors on Parade'. Tucked away in a corner of the BBC's own in-house magazine, *Ariel*, is a satirical glimpse of how aware the Corporation was of its own shortcomings as far as gender stereotyping went (even then).[20] A special edition of the children's board game *Snakes and Ladders* has been produced, it reports, where one of the squares is labelled 'marriage'. If a female player lands on it, she retires from the game; males just carry on as usual.

For a number of the pioneers, work itself was a source of relaxation as well as a career. When the establishment of the National

Grid threatened to put local entrepreneurs like her out of business in the late 1920s, Margaret Partridge entertained herself by designing and running an electric bus – well ahead of its time – in Exeter. It is tempting to think she drove the thing herself; sadly, I can't corroborate that. Helena Normanton corresponded with prisoners, sending encouraging letters and Christmas cards, especially to those who had no families of their own. Financier Gordon Holmes became a spokeswoman for the International Federation of Business and Professional Women, inspiring colleagues around the world to take heart from her own success and follow in her smartly shod footsteps. 'Thrilling for an old suffragette!' she said. Officers of the MWF did the same when work allowed, as well as holding copious numbers of lunches and dinners to celebrate past medical achievements and network for future success.

Lady Rhondda was never content unless she had a cause on the go. The most personal of these was the campaign to be allowed to take her rightful place, as an hereditary peeress, in the House of Lords. After her father's death in 1918, Margaret inherited his title of Viscount as his only heir. When the SDRA was passed the following year, she assumed that her right to sit in the Upper House was assured. It did not happen automatically; in 1922, after an appeal to the Committee of Privileges, permission was granted – but then immediately rescinded, quashed by twenty votes to four. The Lord Chancellor ruled that sitting in the House of Lords could not be proven a 'public function' as specified by the Act.

This decision not only felt like a personal insult but offended Lady Rhondda's well-developed sense of fair play. It sparked off a wider campaign, backed by the Six Point Group and publicized in *Time and Tide*, for the terms and implementation of the SDRA to be held to account. Why was there still blatant sexual discrimination in the Civil Service? Why were wives disadvantaged in so many professional workplaces? And when would the House of Lords become a House of Ladies too?

No satisfactory answers were forthcoming. Legal casuistry continued to obfuscate progress, and though she campaigned for the rest of her life (activism on this subject being her default mode) Lady Rhondda never did take her seat. One wonders whether she would have been equally vigorous in her campaigning had she not had this personal battle to fight; necessarily, perhaps, she thrived in opposition.

Voluntary work appealed to veterans of the suffrage campaign, especially those with a strong sense of commitment. One gets the impression that they regarded it not just as a social duty, but as an act of gratitude. Various frameworks accommodated them. The Soroptimist group was founded in Britain in 1923 as a sister organization to men's Rotary clubs. Members met together not so much for the purpose of mutual support (though this was a welcome by-product) but to raise money for and awareness of women less fortunate than themselves; to set up vocational training schemes for the under-educated and offer welfare support to the disadvantaged. Gordon Holmes was an enthusiastic pioneer. The London National Society for Women's Service (formerly for Women's Suffrage) was a similar organization, working particularly in the fields of employment and training. Millicent Fawcett and Ray Strachey were linchpins, continuing their activism for the rights of women of all classes and backgrounds to realize their own potential. The National Council of Women similarly campaigned for better conditions for working women, and was indirectly responsible for the appointment in 1919 of the first women police officers in Britain. All of these organizations relied on the energy and expertise of volunteer committee members.

Other professional women became magistrates, councillors, governors of schools or other institutions, and mentors. They took their responsibilities as pioneers seriously. Dr May Du Buisson

was a real crusader, joining a mission with her friend Dr Peggy
Kenyon to the hop-pickers of Kent during their medical training.
May described five 'very happy weeks' near Canterbury in a talk
to the mission organizers afterwards.[21] Whole families, mostly
from the East End of London, had been spending the summer
hop-picking for generations. They numbered about six thousand
when May joined them in 1923. This was a chance for them to
escape the hot, smoggy city for some fresh air; to spend time
together, and to earn some extra money. After the terrible summer of 1849, when cholera broke out in Kent and forty-three
workers died on one farm alone, harvest time became a chance to
access medical care for chronic as well as acute conditions. Practitioners volunteered to run makeshift surgeries for the workers
and their families, offering first aid, limited treatment and sound
public health advice.

May and Peggy were not prepared for the arrangements they
found when they arrived at the village of Boughton with their
bicycles and little else at the end of August. Their camp was one
of twenty within a 12-mile radius. The workers were crowded
into aged wooden huts with straw spread on the floor for bed-
ding, holes in the roof, and nowhere to go when it rained. The
young doctors were split up as soon as they arrived. May was
allotted a hut of her own to fit out as best she could. This she did
by balancing wooden planks on packing-cases for shelves and
cupboards, and begging a quantity of empty Oxo tins from a
local grocer, which she sterilized by boiling them up and then
stocked with dressings and bandages. She was also lent two small
stoves (essential for sterilizing linen and heating up poultices) and
a couple of hurricane lamps. The floor, being of mud, got rather
slippery whenever it was wet; that could not be helped.

In her talk to the organizers, she described a typical day. In the
morning she did the rounds of the workers' huts to see who had
been left behind while the others had gone to the hop-gardens.

The reason for their illness was frequently some sort of low-grade fever. May comforted them and kept them warm with a heated brick wrapped in a clean rag or some hot water sealed in a discarded beer bottle. If they needed medication, she visited a pop-up dispensary run by a trained nurse in the next village, and brought it back for them.

Then she joined other volunteers in the hop-gardens, watching as men on stilts deftly pulled the plants from their tall frames, letting them drop to the ground where the women and children stripped them of their flowers. There was usually something to attend to: an average of 150 cases a day would typically include fractures she could splint with a rolled-up newspaper and odd bits of wood, or fingers and toes inflamed by hop-splinters. She also had to deal with isolated outbreaks of influenza, three cases of pleurisy and one of pneumonia. Sadly, five women miscarried their babies during the summer.

The busiest time of day was between six-thirty in the evening, when the pickers returned to their camps, and bedtime at nine or ten. May was surprised by how many burns and scalds she was asked to treat, mostly affecting children who had tripped and fallen on to camp fires or got in the way of water boiled for tea. At weekends, trainloads of family and friends arrived to visit the pickers; they joined the surgery queues, as it was easier to access treatment here than at home. Anything May felt beyond her capabilities, she referred to more senior doctors in the locality. After all the weeks and months spent in lecture theatres and anatomy demonstrations, this was *real* medicine, and she relished it.

Social scientist Leta Jones was a postgraduate student at Liverpool University when she volunteered for a similar mission in 1934. She and some of her peers set up a summer camp near Wrexham, on the Welsh borders, for unemployed women, much like Eleanor Roosevelt's 'She-She-She' camps in the United States, founded the same year. It was well supported, which allowed a

generous ratio of two 'campers' to every student. The whole
enterprise ran for three months, but only a dozen women attended
at any one time, each staying for a fortnight.

Leta immersed herself in the project. Before the camp opened,
she wrote to all the businesses she could think of to beg for support.
She was promised fresh fish from Grimsby, jam from Liverpool
(probably courtesy of local firm Hartley's), sanitary towels from
Boots the Chemist, coal from Gresford colliery just down the
road and cakes from local bakeries. This was at a time when the
Depression still cast a deep economic shadow. Leta's powers of
persuasion must have been extraordinary.

For the first of their two weeks' holiday, most of the women
simply ate and slept. When they surfaced again, they were invited
to dances held at the corresponding camp for unemployed men
12 miles away at Mold. There were regular picnics and walks
through the countryside, a chance to talk and befriend one
another, and opportunities for the students to suggest some constructive advice for the future. Leta kept some of the letters
she received after the camp was over. One is from a woman –
obviously educated – who apologizes to her for 'displaying her
emotions' on parting. The fortnight meant so much to her.
Another, less articulate, thanks Leta for finding her a job at a convalescent home. 'I am getting on alright . . . the matron and staff
are very nise [*sic*].'[22] Yet another simply thanks Leta for 'the happiest of holidays'.

Missions like this were apt to politicize those involved. Familiar names crop up throughout this period in reports of deputations
to Parliament and public protests. The so-called 'hunger marches'
of the 1920s and 1930s (most famously, the Jarrow march of 1936)
attracted the support of the educated and the socially aware.
NUSEC and the Six Point Group either supported or organized
events involving high-status women from across the professions,
armed with a confidence born of their new responsibilities and a

special understanding of what it was like to be society's under-dog. They fought old battles, joined new ones, and gained strength as their numbers grew. But after each victory (political enfranchisement, the passing of the SDRA . . .) another challenge lay in wait (the marriage bar, equal pay, financial independence . . .). Perhaps the pioneers' greatest ally was not their ambition, but their stamina.

10

Modern Women

THE PIONEERS' LEGACY

To no man, I think, can the world be quite as wonderful
as it is to the woman now alive who has fought free.[1]

THE SECOND WORLD War did not exactly catch people unawares.
Twenty-five years previously, conflict had seemed to flare out of
a perfect blue summer like a bush fire. This time it was more of a
slow burn through the 1930s, a sickening glow on the horizon
which somehow never receded. Maude Royden joined a new
organization, the Peace Pledge Union, in 1936. Its members,
including Canon Dick Sheppard, Vera Brittain, Siegfried Sassoon
and Aldous Huxley, were committed to pacifism, mindful of the
profound inhumanity of the Great War and desperate to quell an
appetite for renewed militarism. They distributed white poppies
on Remembrance Day and campaigned, if not for appeasement,
then – to pre-empt Winston Churchill – for negotiations 'jaw to
jaw' rather than for war.

This was all very well before 3 September 1939; when hostilities began and the extent of Hitler's aggression was revealed, Maude
resigned her Peace Pledge Union membership. Some things have
to be fought for, being more evil than war itself. And some battles –
like the struggle for equal pay – must wait their turn in the face of

greater urgency. Now in her sixties, she became a frequent religious broadcaster on the BBC, while also caring for George Hudson Shaw and his increasingly ailing wife Effie. She kept writing, the books, papers and lectures she produced during the war swelling a lifetime's output on Christianity, feminism, politics and autobiography, all revealing her originality of thought, her refusal to be labelled and her moral courage. Like other old-school suffragists, she was a positive thinker; not in a Pollyanna-like way, but upholding a belief in the transformative power of optimism. There was little to be joyful about between 1939 and 1945; a high point for her was the maverick ordination of a woman priest in 1944 into the Anglican Communion in Hong Kong. Experience had taught Maude that war could be a crucible for change; perhaps the time had arrived, at last, for women to be ordained here at home?

In 1941, females between the ages of twenty and thirty were conscripted as auxiliaries to the forces, or to work in civil defence or war-related industries. By September 1943, 90 per cent of able-bodied women aged eighteen to forty were in some form of employment.[2] In many ways, not much had changed about the wartime workplace since the last occasion: millions went into munitions factories, worked on the land or deputized elsewhere for absent men. It should come as no surprise to learn that the indomitable engineer Margaret Partridge, now in her late forties, set up her own business employing women – Exeter Munitions Ltd – and later worked as a technical officer for the south-west of England, advising other factory managers on how to recruit, train and accommodate a new female workforce.

Her former apprentice, Tilly Shilling, was ensconced at the RAE, where she became, and remains, famous as the inventor of the 'RAE restrictor'. During the aerial dogfights which became a feature of hostilities, it was soon found that British Spitfires and Hurricanes were at a disadvantage. While German Messerschmitts had a fuel-injection system, the Rolls-Royce Merlin engines in

British planes were gravity-fed, which meant that when they suddenly dived into 'negative gravity' to avoid or instigate an attack, the fuel could not keep up and the engines cut out. Tilly developed a brilliant quick fix, a washer on the fuel line which instantly solved the problem. A 'restrictor' might have been the official name for this piece of kit, but it was universally and affectionately known as 'Miss Shilling's Orifice'.

The journal of the Women's Engineering Society was characteristically forthright in discussing the role of WES members during the war. On the one hand, it celebrated the achievements of individuals like Margaret, Tilly and countless others able to contribute materially to the war effort. Right from the outset, however, its editor was anxious that professional women – not just engineers, but career women across the board – were likely to be under-used as a resource. They must not be content to remain backstage in the theatre of war. The part they played before had surely qualified them to enter the professional workplace on their own merits in 1919. Their performance since then meant they deserved an opportunity, at the very least, to work alongside men at the highest level.

As *The Woman Engineer* pointed out, there was no call for street lighting in a country locked down in blackout every night. No one in her right mind would demand a bigger, better oven in the kitchen or an elaborate heating system when there were weapons to be developed and codes to be broken. Yet while their male counterparts smoothly transferred into the forces or into military establishments as executives, many women engineers were left stranded. Those qualified to do so worked in munitions, on the construction of ships and aeroplanes, as mechanics and ambulance drivers or, like Amy Johnson, as pilots in the Air Transport Auxiliary. After years of specialism and commitment to finding a niche, however, it was not always easy to drop everything and change direction.

The WES worried for the future, remembering how reluctant employers had been during the last war to pay women the same as the men they replaced, and how wary the trade unions were of a female workforce consequently threatening to undercut the men in peacetime. On the very first page of the December 1939 issue of *The Woman Engineer* is an article simply entitled 'After the War', arguing that professional women's contributions to the war effort in the coming months (which turned out to be years) should be recognized and invested in a fairer working environment afterwards.

That early wartime issue also reports WES support for the British Federation of Business and Professional Women's deputation to Parliament in November 1939. This stated that dangerously high numbers of well-educated and fully trained women, who were normally self-supporting, had found themselves redundant and in 'desperate straits' since the declaration of war in September. Would the government therefore undertake to consider them first, when recruiting 'executives . . . in existing administrative staffs and in setting up new ones'?[3] Shortly afterwards, a new register of previously high-earning but now unemployed women was compiled, with the support of Lady Astor, who also hosted monthly meetings at her own home for women MPs and business or professional women.

Not every female engineer – or lawyer, architect or academic – remained for the duration in the profession for which she had qualified. She might join the forces in whatever capacity she was allowed, or find herself mysteriously occupied at top-secret establishments like Bletchley Park in Buckinghamshire, where her mathematical, linguistic or analytical skills would help to win the information war. Margaret Allan was 'in Intelligence' at Bletchley Park; like Tilly Shilling, she drove racing cars before the war, then ambulances during it. Of the other 'Bletchley girls', Rosalind Hudson was a trainee architect, Miriam Rothschild a marine biologist and Margaret Rock an economist. Most of the women working on cryptanalysis at Bletchley Park were in their late teens or early twenties and had not had time to start training for a professional career before the war broke out, moving straight from university – or even from school – into one of the secretive huts, blocks and other on-site structures where they would spend the next few years.

After the war, however, they shone. Cicely Mayhew from Hut 8 went on to become the first female British diplomat in 1947 (until she married, when her pension was summarily converted into a dowry and she was waved goodbye). Joy Tamblin progressed to university after Bletchley and rose to the rank of air commodore in the Women's Royal Air Force, which she directed between 1976 and 1980. Jean Barker left Hut 4 to become a

Women working at Bletchley Park, home of the Government Code and Cypher School during the Second World War.

prominent politician in both Houses of Parliament as the redoubtable Baroness Trumpington. Indeed, we shall probably never
know to what extent the corridors of power echoed to the feminine but business-like footsteps of Bletchley Park graduates. More
than we imagine, for secrecy is a difficult habit to break.

Medicine was a reserved occupation for men and women during the Second World War. Those medical schools that had closed
their doors to female students after the last war perforce opened
them again, and were glad of the extra numbers. Qualified doctors were now basically paid the same, whether male or female,
largely thanks to a sustained campaign on the part of the MWF.
While many worked abroad, those who stayed at home were
expected to pick up the slack. Dr Ivy Oates qualified in July 1941,
'when the war was going very badly', and was sent to a children's
hospital in Hull.

> Hull was especially devastating because it not only had the
> raids other towns got, but it was a port. Planes came over to
> mine the Humber Estuary. Outside my bedroom door was a
> school; in the schoolyard was a naval gun. This went off twice
> every night. My bed vibrated across the room and the win-
> dows fell out. I don't know why they bothered to replace them.
>
> Poor doctors nowadays, if they work at night, they have to
> rest in the day. What would they do if they had an air raid
> every night, go to bed? There were supposed to be two house
> physicians. I was the 'two house physicians'. There was one
> house surgeon. The casualty officer had gone in the forces.
> The two of us shared the casualty officer's work. The anaes-
> thetist had also gone into the forces. The house surgeon
> assisted at the operations. So, who were the anaesthetists? The
> two house physicians; all this for 10 pounds a month.[4]

Dr Louisa Martindale continued practising in London and
Brighton while taking on executive duties on the council of the

Royal College of Obstetricians and Gynaecologists (she was the first woman to be elected) and as president of the Medical Women's International Federation from 1937 to 1947. Ophthalmologist Ida Mann, ever ground-breaking, was evacuated with the rest of Moorfields Hospital's staff to Oxford in 1941. There she became the first female professor to be appointed at Oxford University, teaching students and researching the effects of war gases on the eye, while frequently nipping down to London to perform surgery. And getting married.

The architectural profession in its purest form suffered considerably. There would no doubt be a glut of opportunity afterwards, but that was cold comfort as the bombs fell. Gertrude Leverkus was quick to diversify, volunteering as an organizer of evacuees before her appointment in 1943 as housing architect in West Ham, an area of east London devastated by the Blitz. She explored the possibilities of pre-fabricated dwellings, and learned to design new types of buildings quickly and with limited resources, to keep bombed-out residents as safe as possible. Meanwhile the Irishwoman and modernist Eileen Gray, living and working in Paris, was interned as an alien for the duration, which marked the beginning of a professional decline.

Universities kept going as best they could, attempting to attract more female students to pay the fees necessary for academia to function. Qualified women were needed to stop gaps among the academic staff, and could conveniently be paid less than the men they replaced. By now, the first woman to qualify as a barrister in England, Dr Ivy Williams, had been teaching law at Oxford for some twenty years; she carried on doing so until the end of the war. Enid Starkie must have been aware of increased numbers of young women at Somerville, but between January 1940 and September 1941 she was in the throes of a torrid affair, so probably preoccupied. It was a feature of this war that fewer female undergraduates left university early to volunteer at the front, as Vera Brittain and Winifred Holtby had done. The previous two decades had taught them the currency of a degree: they were more valuable to society with one than without, so it was important to keep going. Every women's college and hall of residence in the country had a programme of war work anyway, which it was compulsory to join. Tasks included fire-watching; digging for victory in the grounds, replacing flowerbeds with vegetable patches; working in local forces' canteens or children's nurseries; and learning and/or teaching first aid.

It has been said that the success of certain female lawyers during this period can be attributed to the lack of any meaningful competition. As before, solicitors' offices were bereft of conscripted men and the Inns of Court even raised their own regiment. Rose Heilbron was called to the Bar in 1939 and appointed to sit on the northern circuit the following year, attracting attention from the start. Yes, the fact that the profession was less crowded must have helped; but Rose's colleague Helena Normanton was intensely irritated by any assumption that Rose and others like her had triumphed overnight. In fact, as we know, their success marked the culmination of sixty years' struggle to be taken seriously by the Law Society and the Bar Council. This war did not create good women lawyers; it gave them the opportunity to demonstrate just how good they were.

Apart from that one clergywoman in Hong Kong – who was asked to resign after two years, or somehow to de-ordain herself, because of episcopal opposition[5] – the story of women in the traditional profession of the priesthood continued much as before. Those already in the ministry in nonconformist churches carried on their parish work at a time of greater need than ever, yet none was given extra recognition. They were the churches' spiritual mopper-uppers, but for most of them working as lay women or missionaries at home and abroad, their vocations were flatly denied.

*

What happened next? Did the exigencies of the Second World War de-materialize that crystal ceiling holding down the careers of professional women? It would appear not. There was a backlash afterwards, as there had been in the early 1920s, born of a fear that women had deviously sidestepped their way to the top while their male colleagues' backs were turned. Tragically, far fewer men returned from the battlefields in 1945 than had set out; those who did survive, it was insisted, deserved their proper place in the judiciary and in hospitals, in architectural practices, professorial chairs or pulpits, and at the head of construction businesses. Of course they do, agreed the women, but in the modern world there will (eventually) be enough work for everyone. Even if that proves so, responded reactionary employers, we will never be able to afford to pay everyone the same. Ladies must accept less than gentlemen: it's only right. 'Though the trumpets have sounded,' wrote the economist Gertrude Williams in 1945, 'Jericho's walls are still standing.'[6] What she meant is that despite the SDRA, despite political enfranchisement, the conferral (by most universities) of degrees, and the conspicuous contribution of working women to winning the war, the male-dominated Establishment was still the most potent influence in the professional workplace.

I explained a long time ago that this was not a book about firsts. With a few exceptions, the pioneers were not motivated by competition with other women for its own sake. 'If asked about becoming a "first woman" by another woman,' confessed the first female Director of Public Prosecutions, Barbara Mills, 'my instant reaction is to say "Don't do it" . . . The proof of true equality will be when a woman is appointed to a top position and no one comments on the fact that she is a woman.'[7] It does help illustrate the pace of change, however, to point out a few post-war milestones. We have already noted Helena Normanton's and Rose Heilbron's appointment as King's Counsel in 1949 – the first women to take silk at the English Bar. Rose was thirty-nine, Helena fifty-six.

The first female High Court judge was Elizabeth Lane, appointed in 1965. The first woman to be elected president of the Royal College of Physicians in England was Margaret Turner-Warwick in 1989. The Royal College of Surgeons in Ireland elected its first female president, Eilis McGovern, in 2010 and the corresponding College in England in 2014: Clare Marx. Mary Horgan became president of the Royal College of Physicians in Ireland in 2017. Still, at the time of writing, neither College in Scotland has ever had a woman at its head. Perhaps the ghost of Sophia Jex-Blake is too alarming.

The marriage bar was abolished in the teaching profession in 1944 and in the Civil Service in 1946 (at home) and 1973 (for

Dame Elizabeth Lane.

diplomats). The first women were allowed to trade on the floor of the London Stock Exchange in 1973 and the first female pilot for British Airways got the job in 1987. The first female priests in the Church of England were ordained in 1994. Ruth Reed was elected president of RIBA in 2009. The Institute of Civil Engineers welcomed Jean Venables to the corresponding position the previous year. All British Army combat roles have been open to women since 2018.

The wheels of the women's movement have always turned slowly. That might be because we constantly have to position chocks under them to stop them sliding backwards: it's an uphill struggle. It did not help that there was a period of neo-Victorianism immediately after the Second World War, when the model of contemporary femininity portrayed by the media comprised an attractive, neat and shiny housewife, proud of her tiny waist and lovely, labour-saving new home; of her 2.4 children and, most of all, her heroic hubby. She was a modern Angel in the House. It had become unfeminine again to plan a career and shameful to have a working wife (Can you not afford to keep her? Call yourself a man?). These images acted as a societal comfort blanket, a reminder of the old order when the globe was still predominantly Empire-pink and everyone knew their place. They were reflected in the advertisements of the 1950s, with slogans like 'By moonlight, no doubt, you care very little about whether she can cook. But you will, my boy, you will' (Nestlé's milk) or 'In a man's world, a woman needs . . . Camay – for the skin men can't ignore' (soap).

Women in the 1960s, aware of continued discrimination, were more likely to assert themselves – as, in part, the flappers had done – as independent people in charge of their own future. While popular culture portrayed them as mini-skirted dolly-birds (or, in the case of intellectuals like Joan Bakewell, 'the thinking man's crumpet'), career women were trying hard to consolidate their position in the professions. Still the road led uphill. Practices and offices might have a 'skirt' or a 'bird' or two among the staff, but they were only tokens, a box ticked. One woman in chambers meant there need not be any more (nor any extra plumbing). One female senior lecturer in the faculty obviated the requirement for a female professor. It was a common assumption that part of a woman's role at work was to look decorative – yet those who were promoted were habitually accused of sleeping with the boss.

Someone told me recently that when she became a member of the Institute of Industrial Managers, the in-house magazine printed an article about her unusual achievement. Throughout, she was lip-lickingly described as a 'blonde bombshell'. This harks back to the reaction in the press a century before, when the first women graduates in Britain received their degrees at the University of London in 1881. They were congratulated not for their academic accomplishment, but because they had sewn their own *very* attractive academic gowns, and chosen such alluring colours for the hoods. Women at work during the 1960s and 1970s remember how wearying was the constant propositioning by men who had decided that because they were economically independent, they must naturally be sexually 'liberated' too. It was as though, having elected to break out of the domestic sphere, they were fair game.

A contemporary advertisement for managers at Unilever buys into the stereotype. It is in the format of an application form.

> **Line of work.** Marketing. I approve those things they squeeze between television programmes when people hurry to the kitchen for a glass of milk.
>
> **But what would you really rather do?** Nothing. I don't mean not to do anything. There just isn't anything else I'd rather do.
>
> **Driving force.** The usual one. A hungry wife. Two hungry children. A hungry cat and a hungry dog. Besides, I get hungry too.

Most paradoxical quality. I'm lazy. I can watch my wife
mow the lawn without a qualm of conscience. Yet at the office
I work hard.

The terrible temptation. About 5 feet 6. Blonde. Blue eyes.
Luckily I married her.[8]

It continues in the same vein.

Women were routinely asked at their own job interviews
whether they intended to start a family while in post.

During a critical interview for a head of [department] job I
had to admit that I was expecting the result of a pregnancy
test as the job was an internal promotion. I was appointed to
the job and two days later when the result of the test was positive, [was] asked to resign my promotion, or rather withdraw
my application and a man was appointed instead. It took me
17 years to get back to that promoted position.[9]

That person was talking about the 1970s, which was a critical
decade for women. The British Women's Liberation Movement
was formed at a conference in March 1970 with four demands:
equal pay, equal education and opportunities, 24-hour nursery
provision, and free contraception with abortion on request. Those
demands echo the ones listed at a League of Nations 'Status of
Women' day held at University College London more than thirty
years previously, in 1937. They include equal pay (at the top of
the list again), parity with men in national insurance and unemployment benefits, the removal of the double standard in legislation
concerning prostitution and sexual assault, and separate taxation
for men and women.

The Equal Pay Act was passed in 1970, after the famous
machinists' strike at Dagenham's Ford works when 187 women
downed tools for four weeks. With the Minister for Employment
Barbara Castle on their side, they *almost* won the right to be paid

as much as men doing similar work: from 87 per cent of the male rate, their wages rose to 92 per cent. The Act stated a duty on employers to ensure that 'for men and women employed on like work the terms and conditions of one sex are not less favourable than those of the other'. That sounds straightforward. It did not come into operation, however, until January 1976, giving recalcitrant employers plenty of time to engineer job descriptions and pay grades in such a way that women's jobs could be differentiated from men's, making them less costly. We know this is true: even after the passing of the Equality Act in 2010, the gender pay gap is still an issue.

In 1975 the direct descendant of the SDRA was born. One can spot the family resemblance: much like its ancestor, the new Sex Discrimination Act was intended 'to render unlawful certain kinds of sex discrimination and discrimination on the ground of marriage, and establish a Commission with the function of

Sewing machinists on strike at the Dagenham Ford plant, 1968.

working towards the elimination of such discrimination and pro-
moting equality of opportunity between men and women
generally'. And, like the SDRA, it was open to interpretation;
the casual disregard of its stipulations did not automatically lead
to prosecution. Just as in 1913, when Gwyneth Bebb Thomson
challenged the Law Society, the 'law of inveterate usage' came
into play again: despite the efforts of the previous decades, to a
greater or lesser degree (depending on how enlightened one's
principals or clients were) discrimination was still customary in
the professional workplace. There was a breakthrough at the top
of the political tree in 1979 when Britain's first female Prime
Minister was elected, setting hundreds of old anti-suffragists
whirling in their graves. But Margaret Thatcher was not exactly
a feminist. She was more inclined to haul up the ladder after her
than hold it steady for the next tranche of women to come along.

On 3 July 1956, the newspapers reported a tragic discovery in
Suffolk. 'The Heiress Who Hated Spending: Rich Race Woman
Murdered' ran the headline in the *Daily Herald*. A 71-year-old
lady, 'one of the richest and most eccentric women in Britain',
had been found bludgeoned to death in the huge, squalid man-
sion she owned in Newmarket. She kept a string of sixty-nine
racehorses (along with twenty-two cats and a dog called Bruce)
but was so difficult an employer that no trainer ever stayed with
her long enough to enter them in races. Domestic staff were soon
frightened off by her miserliness and her insistence on living in
one room, with the odd foal and piles of horse fodder and manure
occupying all the rest. She looked extraordinary, though the
inhabitants of Newmarket were used to her shuffling through the
streets to her customary hotel lunch in a red wig, one of a selection of moth-eaten fur coats and the same pair of shabby old
shoes. They did not give her a second glance, and certainly not a
smile of recognition. 'Most people were a rat or a guttersnipe to

her,'[10] claimed one of her former trainers, and an ex-secretary, whom she had accused of being a spy, spoke of her as a quarrelsome and unpleasant old woman.

A 26-year-old stableman was charged with her murder. At his trial he was sentenced to ten years' imprisonment on the lesser charge of manslaughter. His action – striking her with an iron bar – was deemed to have been provoked. The woman had reacted to his asking for two weeks' holiday pay by screaming at him and hitting him repeatedly with her handbag. He simply lost his temper.

His victim was well known to the police; she used to telephone them regularly, insisting that she could hear burglars breaking in to steal her precious belongings. They knew that she had inherited £840,000 on her father's death in 1931 (unimaginable riches, with the spending-power of about £38 million today) and was one of the wealthiest – and possibly least generous – people in the country. After her death, rumours emerged that an unfaithful French lover had stolen her sanity years before; more sympathetic souls blamed her bizarre behaviour on the lack of a suitable outlet for her undoubted intellectual and physical energies. She had once been beautiful, and had inherited her father's acumen as well as his fortune. He was the inventor of the steam turbine, Charles Parsons; she was the founder – with her mother Katharine of the Women's Engineering Society, the brilliant Rachel Parsons.

Her obituary in *The Woman Engineer* is brief, unlike that of her peer Dame Caroline Haslett, who died later the same month. But it does at least mention that she was once a pioneering engineer in her own right, which is a dignifying fact omitted from almost every other publication. No one really knows what went wrong with Rachel's life, but her legacy remains: the WES is still going strong. Rachel gave the women of her profession a collective voice, and the confidence to use it.

Now is a good time to talk about legacies, as this narrative of enterprising women draws to a close. It is often said that those who do well in life are standing on the shoulders of giants. Few of the women we have met here were giants. With one or two exceptions, they were not distinguished by physical strength or imperious personality; nor were they the sort of people to trample down the opposition. The majority did not even seek to be pioneers. Personal glory was not the object of the exercise – though a gratifying number did receive honours along the way. Giants are taller than the rest of us, and see further; the women I have been writing about had to climb, by their own efforts and in the teeth of a gale of opposition, to reach success. I prefer to think of them as something like fairy godmothers. Not the twinkly, Disneyesque kind who sprinkle wish-fulfilment like stardust from their wands, but the kind who bestow gifts which really matter: the fruits of their experience. Rachel Parsons' story does not seem quite so sad if we accept what she offered us at the height of her career.

Of her colleagues, electrical engineer Margaret Partridge died in 1967, some twenty years after retirement. Her ashes rest with those of her partner Dorothy Rowbotham in the churchyard of their village in Devon. There's a blue plaque on their house in Miss Partridge's honour. It would be nice if a neat but powerful electric light were trained on it at night, just to make the two of them feel at home.

Annette Ashberry's foundation of her all-female business, Atalanta Engineering, provided both encouragement and employment to her sister professionals. After giving that up she embarked on another chapter in a surprising career, reinventing herself as an authority on miniature gardening. A 1952 Pathé newsreel shows her (looking very feminine and accompanied by a kitten) snipping at bonsai-like Alpine plants and tiny rose bushes. She ran a business designing and selling 'out-of-the-ordinary window-boxes' for people who, like Gertrude Leverkus and Enid Rosser

Locket, lived in small flats or bedsits and hankered after a garden. She even made one for Princess Elizabeth, presumably for a doll's house or something similar. Annette died in 1990, well into her nineties.

Tilly Shilling passed away the same year. After the war, and flushed with the success of her 'Orifice', she remained at the RAE in Farnborough with her husband, eventually retiring in 1969. She enjoys the unusual accolade of having a local pub named after her, and a small collection of racing memorabilia from her motor-cycling glory days is kept in the museum at Brooklands. Amy Johnson famously perished when a plane she was delivering dur-ing the war went down in bad weather over the Thames in 1941. She was only thirty-seven. Her predecessor as president of the WES, construction engineer Laura Willson, moved from York-shire to Surrey with her husband in 1927 and continued to build relatively affordable houses there; by now she had been appointed the first female member of the Federation of House Builders. When she died at the age of sixty-four, she bequeathed to her family 185 houses, most let to tenants, worth about £3 million in today's terms. Many of those tenants blessed Laura for the practi-cality and unfussy elegance of their homes. She understood at first hand what modern women needed to make life richer: inter-esting work, a comfortable home and, if possible, a loving family with whom to share it.

Dr Ida Mann was convinced when she was young that family life was not for her. One husband and three stepchildren later, she died in Australia, where she and Bill had settled in 1949. She ran a private practice there and travelled widely through Australasia and Oceania studying vernacular ocular disease. The Nuffield Laboratory of Ophthalmology, created for her in Oxford, still functions as a crucible of ophthalmic research, and her memory is very much alive in the corridors of Moorfields Hospital, where one can still imagine her marching briskly ahead, just out of sight.

Her life proved that it is possible for a female pioneer in the élite professions to be coruscatingly clever, yet happy and unobjectionable too – if a little daunting. In the world of eye-doctors, Ida is a legend.

Dr Lulu Martindale passed away twenty years after her beloved Ismay, in 1966. She was ninety-three, busy and cheerful to the end, assuring friends that she had had her full share of love and happiness, and was content. Because of her comfortable personality one is apt to forget the stellar nature of her career as the first female GP in Brighton, the first woman on the council of the Royal College of Obstetricians and Gynaecologists, an early woman magistrate, and a leading light in the treatment of cervical cancer. There was not an ounce of stridency in her, nor of resentment at the institutional prejudice she faced throughout her life. In fact, very few of these women appear to have been resentful, preferring instead to spend their energy on deconstructing that crystal ceiling, not just for themselves, but – whether consciously or not – for the generations of working women to come.

In later life Dr Martindale's neighbour Octavia Wilberforce touchingly ran, at a farmhouse near Brighton, a convalescent home for burnt-out professional women and overworked housewives, while maintaining her general practice in the town. She cared deeply for the well-being of her contemporaries, and always regretted that she had been unable to save her friend Virginia Woolf from suicide. After retirement in 1954, she spent her time looking after her Jersey cows, making social visits and volunteering for the local council. She died in 1963 at the New Sussex Hospital for Women and Children, founded and supported by old allies Dr Lulu Martindale, Gordon Holmes, Lady Rhondda, Dr Louisa Aldrich-Blake – and herself.

Dr Peggy Kenyon and her friend Dr May Du Buisson both travelled after their marriages, Peggy in what is now Pakistan and May all over the world. Peggy gave up medicine while trying to manage a young family and a troubled marriage, but, like so many of her colleagues, returned to it in later life. May carried on working abroad, using the experience of those five weeks in 1923 with the hop-pickers in Kent to inform an influential career at the front line of public health. I have much for which to thank her personally: without May, I should not have met my husband. Her younger son, William, went on to have a daughter of his own, a friend of mine who introduced me to Bruce when I was twenty. Bruce was a medic, I an English student; it is vanishingly unlikely that our paths would have crossed otherwise. May (and family): I can't thank you enough.

Elisabeth Scott was no longer famous when she died in 1972, and was usually referred to – if at all – rather tortuously as 'grand-daughter of Sir George Gilbert Scott's brother John' rather than as a leading architect in her own right. She peaked too soon, perhaps, with her design for the Shakespeare Memorial Theatre at Stratford. But the pursuit of fame did not loom large as a motivation for many of these pioneering women. Elisabeth married, her temporary celebrity tempting the press to comment on what was considered an unsuitable match. (Her husband declined to work for a living, apparently. But why should he, as a breadwinner's spouse?) She quietly got on with life, working in the borough architect's office in her home town of Bournemouth, designing the pavilions at the heads of Boscombe and Bournemouth piers and enjoying the collegiate aspect of her occupation. 'Elisabeth was gentle, unassuming, determined,' wrote an obituarist, 'with a personal integrity that acknowledged her associates' help.'[11] That sort of generosity was a hallmark of those who campaigned – as she did – to make the terms of the SDRA a reality for working women.

The Charles sisters practised together as domestic architects and designers in the home counties and in Cornwall. Ethel was the more conspicuously successful, designing houses for Letchworth Garden City and in 1909 winning an international competition to build a church in Germany. As unmarried daughters, however, they accepted the traditional role of domestic helpmeet for other members of the family, keeping house for a brother in Surrey after the First World War. This must surely have curbed their professional ambitions. Bessie died in 1932; Ethel thirty years later.

Gertrude Leverkus lived until 1989; having spent twenty-nine years after her retirement in Brighton, she eventually moved into a nursing home in Hove. To most of us the phrase 'a nursing home in Hove' conjures an image of quiet gentility, with residents resting in high-backed floral armchairs, reflecting on the past while waiting for lunch at noon. For Gertrude, it appears to have been no such thing: proactive all her life, she was obviously frustrated by the thought of sitting still for the rest of her days – even well into her eighties. What could she do to allay the boredom? Well, what had she done all her life? She took paper, a pen and her drawing-board, and completed a detailed architectural plan of the building. It is beautiful and strangely moving. Once an architect, it seems, always an architect.

Gertrude left a legacy beyond concrete and steel. Her type-written memoirs, compiled for her wider family, are sprightly and engaging. They document the story of her career, from the moment her father suggested she become what was then a highly exotic creature. What began as a speculative adventure quickly developed into a vocation. The memoirs close with this heartfelt tribute.

Architecture is one of the best professions in the world for those whose minds work constructively and tidily. It is an outdoor life – on jobs – and an indoor life – in studios and drawing-offices. It is human, with contacts not only with clients and business men, but also with working builders and operatives. It is practical to the last degree – all one's thinking is on lines of efficiency. It is an Art, since one is designing and visualising shapes and colour and form. It requires logical and mathematically correct thinking. It takes one up into the clouds on delightful occasions, but it is tied up with money, costing, and the right choice of materials, so that one's feet are kept firmly on the ground. It is done with a pencil on the drawing-board, but also with the tact of a diplomat. In other words, Architecture is the best profession in the world.[12]

How cruel it would have been to deny Gertrude that level of career satisfaction because of her sex. And how many women before her, or with less enlightened parents, might have flourished as she did, had they been allowed the freedom to choose?

As for women in the Church: to a certain extent, as it was in the beginning, so it is now. Roman Catholics have no women priests, nor even any clergy wives, except in the isolated cases of married Anglican vicars who have converted and continued their ministry. Things did not begin to change materially in other denominations, including Methodism and the Church of England, until the end of the twentieth century. They are still evolving, slowly, with the spirit of women like Maude Royden at the heart of what remains a controversial and divisive progression. Maude – the first woman to have been granted the honorary degree of Doctor of Divinity, which she added to a clutch of other awards – passed away in her eightieth year, in 1956. She died as she had lived, with grace and humility, uncomplaining after a coronary thrombosis she had assumed was indigestion, and 'longing to go'.[13] Never one for sanctimoniousness, she cheerfully requested 'lots of flowers' at her funeral. Her adopted daughter Helen survived her, as did her colleagues Constance Coltman (d. 1969), Edith Picton-Turbervill (d. 1960) and the first female Baptist pastor Edith Gates (d. 1962).

Like Dr Louisa Martindale and Gertrude Leverkus, Maude

appreciated the opportunity to live life on her own terms. Though she never achieved an over-arching ambition to be ordained, and presumably never consummated the love of her life, it was not in her nature to be regretful. It was a privilege to be a pioneer, according to her. 'We had our work – work we loved – and were neither crippled nor repressed by the discipline we accepted. No-one can have everything in this life.'[14]

Although people generally take their teachers for granted, some stand out. I remember the primary schoolmistress, for example, who took me aside one day after I had proudly presented her with yet another chaotic masterpiece of colouring-in, and suggested I try making a picture out of words instead; the poor man who tried to teach me maths and navigated me through three failed O-level attempts to my ultimate grade C triumph; the sixth-form staff who encouraged me to try for university. The rest – the patient architects of my education – are almost forgotten. I was fortunate: they all expected me to do well (apart from the careers adviser and that long-suffering mathematician), and were unfailingly but unremarkably supportive. I am willing to bet, however, that many of the pioneers attributed their success to individual teachers who believed in them against the odds, and set them on the path to a profession.

The vast majority of girls during the period between the wars were taught by maiden ladies, many of whom sacrificed hopes of marriage in order to equip their students for a brighter future. This was the case at university level as well as at school. Enid Starkie, Maria Czaplicka, her mentor Emily Penrose, Professor Edith Morley, headmistress Lilian Faithfull: they and relatively prominent academics like them deserve recognition; and behind these unsung heroines are crowds of even more obscure women, propelling their protégées forward into the light. At Gwyneth Bebb Thomson's old school in London, they held a collection after her untimely death and commissioned a stained-glass window to remember her by: a pupil–teacher relationship could work both ways. The success of alumnae like Gwyneth enriched the lives of everyone involved.

Enid Starkie's biography was written by one of her former students. It describes with affection and a measure of astonishment how Enid lived out her days in Oxford, occasionally leaving for foreign lecture tours or visiting professorships, losing none of her flamboyance and making no concessions to advancing years. She died of lung cancer in 1970, at the age of seventy-two. Her scholarship was important, but it was her originality which marked her out, and proved that not all female academics were the distrait, slightly gravy-stained spinsters of popular imagination. Enid was doughty, colourful and undaunted.

Helena Normanton carried on working as long as she was able. She never lost the habit of outspokenness and opportunism which – along with her gender – marked her out as 'not one of us' in the legal profession. 'Opportunism' sounds a pejorative word today; in Helena's case it simply meant grasping the chance to work whenever it was offered. Others might have resorted to an inherited silver spoon to sustain them in lean times; Helena did not have that option. It would not have occurred to her, I think, to rely on her accountant husband's earnings. Besides, he died in 1948 and she had nine years of widowhood to support.

In 1952 Helena resigned as president of the Married Women's Association (MWA) after publicly declaring, on its behalf, her support for a putative government scheme to pay wives a formal allowance from the family income for housework. She suggested that if wives did not do the housework for which they had been paid satisfactorily, they should be retrained or punished. Unfortunately, before doing so she had neglected to consult the membership of the MWA, many of whom derided the idea as nothing better than giving pocket money to a child, and then metaphorically sending it to the naughty-step if it transgressed. Helena's brand of feminism was fierce, but rooted in a strong sense of duty, which could complicate matters for more modern campaigners.

It was partly from that sense of duty that Helena – having no children of her own – bequeathed money shortly before her death to help found the University of Sussex in Brighton. She was the first to sign up when an appeal for donors went out, explaining that Brighton had educated her, as a fatherless child; now she owed it to her community to repay it. In 2017, two Helena Normanton Research Fellowships were established in her name. If the recipients know her story, and think of her sometimes, they will surely be inspired by her commitment and extraordinary bravery.

Enid Rosser Locket passed her Bar finals in 1927. She did not embrace her new profession. She felt uncomfortable in the uniform. Collars were awkward: they needed to be stiff enough to support the white bands worn by barristers, yet comfortable enough to last the day without chafing. Her solution was to commission the fashionable department store Harvey Nichols to make her some white linen vests with an integral collar she could strengthen with starch. That worked. She worried (as Helena seldom did) that women lawyers were figures of fun, only accepted in court for the purposes of light relief. She found it hard to win briefs, though female solicitors were supportive, and could not survive on Poor Persons work alone. Her father helped her out, but that was humiliating. The biggest surprise – and drawback – of her professional career was its emotional cost. Making heartfelt appeals to a jury was unbearably stressful unless one was a skilful actor, and for each triumph in court there was bound to be a corresponding failure. Every day was upsetting. So Enid made a decision: in 1933 she left the courtroom for commerce, working happily for the next twenty years as a legal adviser to Mr John Spedan Lewis, founder of the retail business which still bears his name. Her gift to those who followed is the courage to change direction, despite years of training and investment, if that is what feels right. Life is too short to be constantly swimming against the tide.

Nancy Nettlefold also gave up the law after qualification. She joined and eventually ran her family's wholesale ironmongery business; became heavily involved in local politics; emigrated to South Africa, where she joined the anti-apartheid movement; and died in Cape Town in 1966. Nancy had been one of the original four women, with Gwyneth Bebb Thomson, involved in the case against the Law Society in 1913. Of the remaining two, Ray Strachey's sister Karin Costelloe trained not as a solicitor, in the end, but as a doctor. She specialized in psychiatry, married Virginia Woolf's brother and, sadly – like her sister-in-law – took her own life. She died in 1953, a victim of progressive deafness and what was then called manic depression. Maud Crofts was the only one of the quartet to stick with the idea of being a solicitor. She and her husband went into practice together; she specialized in issues affecting women and made sure that she could leave work every day to collect the children from school, insisting on a smaller share of the practice profits because of her shorter hours. She also acted as legal adviser to Lady Rhondda's Six Point Group. When she retired at the age of sixty-six, some of her old Girton friends, who were clients, took their business elsewhere. No offence, they explained to the other partners; it was just that they didn't feel comfortable being represented by a man. That was Maud's legacy: turning the professional world upside down within a generation, so that in her corner of it at least, women became the norm and men the unwelcome exception.

And what of the women who accompanied Nancy and Gwyneth to that dinner at the House of Commons in 1920? Ray herself died in 1940, aged fifty-three, of complications following routine surgery. She was busy all her life, always keen to work not just for her own needs – financial and personal – but to improve the lot of others like her. Virginia Woolf remembered her as a restless soul, never still, 'as if always trying to get what she could not'.[15] Millicent Fawcett lived to witness universal suffrage, dying the year after it was finally achieved, in 1929. Lady Rhondda kept going, more or less full tilt, until 1958 when she was seventy-five. For the last few years of her life she suffered from cancer, but refused treatment in case it clouded her mind. She insisted that as editor of *Time and Tide* she had a duty to stay sharp.

So it goes on. I could list all the names in this narrative, themselves representatives of scores of others, and each would have something to offer to today's working women. The degrees of separation between them all were surprisingly few: it must have felt a little like being part of an extended family when they stepped out together – like the women in my imaginary procession, arms linked and chins held high – into the uncharted territories of the male Establishment. They did what they did for a variety of reasons: for the good of society, of their souls, of their purses; to fulfil a personal ambition or perform a duty; because they had to, or because they could. Collectively they left us an environment more likely to accept women at its heart; they enlightened male colleagues; they showed us that marriage and motherhood can enhance one's career rather than spelling its end; and they gave us a heightened awareness of discrimination (if not yet freedom from it: that's up to us). Best of all, they bought for us the luxury of precedent.

Every working woman today can tell her own tale of discrimination. Barrister Nemone Lethbridge recently gave an interview in which she recalled her early career.

> When I got my first tenancy in Hare Court they put a Yale lock on the lavatory. And all the men in Chambers were given a key, but I wasn't, and I was told to go up Fleet Street and use the Kardomah [café].[16]

Another lawyer told me that she was issued a set of rules when she joined Chambers:

1) Never be upset if you're not briefed because you're a woman.

2) Always buy your round of drinks. (Pay for them, that is; give your money to a male colleague because you mustn't go to the bar yourself. That's vulgar.)

3) Never go to bed with anyone in your own Chambers.[17]

At an academic conference in 2018 I listened to endless tales of under-representation and breathtaking gender bias. Naïvely, I was shocked to hear that females seeking university tenure or research funding assume non-gender-specific names to improve their chances: Alex, Chris, or something so unfamiliar that few realize it is feminine. It comes too easily to us to think generically of architects, engineers and consultant surgeons as male. And senior women at the Inns of Court are *still* called 'Master'.

When I was once interviewed for a job with a well-known firm of antiquarian booksellers, I was asked to *prove* to the men on the other side of the desk that employing me would not be a waste of time and money, given that I was 'likely' to get pregnant. Though I thought of plenty of scathing answers afterwards, at the time I was dumbstruck – and did not get the job. There was much consternation when the principal of a women's college in Oxford announced to the governing body that she would like to get married. No one had thought to change the statutes since the place was founded in 1879, when principals didn't – couldn't – marry while in post. She was obliged to resign as a 'Miss' before her wedding day, and then reapply a fortnight afterwards as a 'Mrs'. She *did* get the job. This was not in the 1930s or even the 1950s: it was in 1991. It was not until 2016 that a major firm of solicitors in the City changed its customary form of address on letters from 'Dear Sir' to Dear Sir/Madam' . . .

But this apparent lack of progress should not imply that our pioneers' achievements meant nothing. There is a lovely little anonymous poem in a Gray's Inn publication of 1960, about a '*Mère de Famille* Reading for the Bar':

> *Everybody works but mother;*
> *She reads law all day —*
> *Wills and wives and wreckage*
> *And all the Law Lords say.*
> *Grandma does the housework*
> *Helped by grand pa pa,*
> *Everybody works in our house*
> *But our dear ma.*[18]

Throughout the century since the passing of the SDRA, admiring families up and down the country have quietly supported daughters, sisters, wives and mothers seeking to realize their potential in the professional workplace. Their numbers have increased and continue to do so, both in real terms and in proportion to their male counterparts (though it's unlikely the people in this book would congratulate us on the pace of change). In 2019, more than half the medical students in Britain were women, as were more than half of solicitors in practice. Role models are desperately important to us as individuals, because they challenge received wisdom and show us how important it is to strive for things we assume are beyond reach. Gradually, person by person and institution by institution, habits alter and expectations grow. Our reach extends as our grasp becomes stronger and more assured. The quest for equality is a long game, and we are playing it still, but it's much easier to join in with things than to start them; to be a participant, than a pioneer.

To keep us going, we now have the proof of something the pioneers could never be quite sure of, because they hadn't done it yet: ladies *can* climb ladders — as high as they like.

Chronology

'Firsts' and significant dates for women in the traditional professions (with international milestones in italics).

1849
British-born Elizabeth Blackwell graduates in medicine in the United States.

1865
Elizabeth Garrett (Anderson) qualifies as a doctor in the UK, the first woman in Europe to do so.

1869
Girton College, Cambridge opens: the first residential university college for women.

Arabella Mansfield is admitted to the Iowa Bar.

1870
Women are employed in the British Civil Service, as telephonists and telegraphers.

The Married Women's Property Act is passed, making married women legally entitled to hold money and/or property in their own names.

1872
Federal employees in the US are legally entitled to equal pay for equal work.

1874
The London School of Medicine for Women opens.

1881
Louise Blanchard opens an architectural partnership with her husband in the US.

Women are awarded degrees in the UK (at the University of London).

1886
Indians Anandi Gopal Joshi and Kadambini Ganguly graduate from medical school.

1888
A resolution for equal pay for men and women is secured at the Trades Union Congress.

1895
Dentist Lilian Lindsay qualifies
in the UK.

1898
Ethel Charles becomes an
associate member of the Royal
Institute of British Architects
(RIBA). Her sister Bessie is the
second (in 1900) but there are no
women Fellows until 1931.

1900
Olga Petit and Jeanne Chauvin
practise as qualified lawyers in
France.

1903
Adolphine Kok practises as a
qualified lawyer in the Netherlands.

1904
Elise Sem practises as a qualified
lawyer in Norway.

1908
Edith Morley is appointed
professor (at Reading University).

1911
Eleanor Davies-Colley is elected
a Fellow of the Royal College of
Surgeons, London.

1917
The Medical Women's
Federation is founded.

1918
The Representation of the
People Act is passed, allowing
women aged thirty and
over to vote (subject to
property or educational
qualifications).

1919
The Women's Engineering
Society is founded.

Nancy Astor takes her seat as a
Member of Parliament.

The Sex Disqualification
(Removal) Act is passed.

1920
Scot Madge Easton Anderson
qualifies as a solicitor.

Oxford University awards
degrees to women.

Female jurors are sworn in.

1922
Dr Ivy Williams is called to
the Bar.

Carrie Morrison, Maud Crofts,
Mary Sykes and Mary Pickup
qualify as solicitors in
England.

Maria Otto practises as a qualified
lawyer in Germany.

Veterinary surgeon Aleen Cust
qualifies.

1924

Ethel Watt becomes a chartered accountant.

1928

The Representation of the People (Equal Franchise) Act is passed, reducing the voting age for women to twenty-one and removing the property or educational qualification.

1934

Helen Mackay is elected a Fellow of the Royal College of Physicians, London.

1944

The marriage bar is removed (except in the Civil Service, where it is lifted in 1946 for home civil servants, and in 1973 for Foreign Office personnel working overseas).

1945

Sibyl Campbell is appointed to a full-time professional post in the British judiciary, as a stipendiary magistrate.

1948

Lillian Penson is appointed Vice-Chancellor of the University of London.

Margaret Kidd takes silk in Scotland.

Cambridge University awards degrees to women – the last UK university to do so.

1963

The Equal Pay Act is passed in the US.

1965

Elizabeth Lane is appointed a High Court judge, after sitting as the UK's first female county court judge in 1962.

1970

The British Women's Liberation Movement is founded.

The Equal Pay Act is passed.

1973

Women are admitted to the floor of the London Stock Exchange.

1975

The Sex Discrimination Act is passed.

Jackie Tabick becomes a rabbi.

Women can be considered for mortgages on their own account.

1980

Women do not need a male guarantor to open a credit agreement (hire purchase etc.).

1984
Brenda Hale is appointed to the
Law Commission and in 2004 is
appointed the first woman Law
Lord.

1986
Statutory maternity pay is
introduced.

1990
Married women are taxed
independently.

1994
Thirty-two women are ordained
as Church of England priests.

1998
Heather Hallett is elected chair
of the Bar Council.

2002
All-women shortlists for
employment purposes are
legalized.

2009
Ruth Reed is elected president of
RIBA.

2015
Libby Lane is ordained bishop in
the Church of England.

2018
All combat roles are opened to
women in the British Army.

According to recent figures:
- 12 per cent of the UK's engineering workforce is female;
- more than 50 per cent of current medical students are women;
- more than 50 per cent of practising solicitors are women, as are around 38 per cent of barristers;
- 20 per cent of chartered architects are female, as are almost 50 per cent of architecture students;
- around 45 per cent of academics employed in higher education (but only 25 per cent of professors) are women;
- 29 per cent of active clerics are female, as are around half the candidates in training.

Dramatis Personae

A brief guide to some of the individuals featured in this book. Further biographical details will be found within the text and by exploring the bibliography.

Academia

Czaplicka, Maria (1884–1921). An anthropologist, born in Warsaw to a working-class family of noble descent. Following a hard-won education at home she gained a scholarship to study in London in 1910. She progressed to Oxford and in 1914 undertook a major expedition to Siberia. After the war she found it increasingly difficult to find funding and academic support for her work, even though she was acknowledged to be brilliant. Defeated, she took her own life at the age of thirty-six.

Faithfull, Lilian (1865–1952). The best kind of head teacher is kindly, astute, authoritative yet accessible. Lilian Faithfull, suffragist and humanitarian, was all of these. Having read English at Oxford, she spent her working life cheerfully influencing women's secondary and higher education. She was appointed Vice-Principal of King's College London (Ladies' Division) in 1894 and was headmistress of Cheltenham Ladies' College for fifteen years. In 1926 she was appointed CBE.

Miller, Margaret Stevenson (1896–1979). Having taken a first degree from Edinburgh University and a PhD in London, she joined the academic staff of Liverpool University as a lecturer specializing in Soviet economics, a subject on which she published widely. In 1932 she married a colleague, Douglas Campbell, thereby prompting the university authorities to institute a marriage bar on women academics. She and her friend Dr Jean Wright were catalysts of a feminist campaign against the bar, which was not generally lifted until 1944.

Morley, Edith (1875–1964). A suffragette and a literary scholar, Edith enjoyed the distinction – *really* enjoyed it – of being the first female to be appointed professor at a British university (Reading, in 1908). She was awarded the OBE in 1950 for her work supporting Belgian refugees during the Second World War.

Murray, Margaret (1863–1963). Archaeology was a relatively new academic discipline when she was appointed a Fellow of University College London in 1922. She had always wanted to be a nurse, but at 4 feet 10 inches was too small to qualify. Egyptology was a strange alternative to choose, but she flourished, becoming a passionate and highly respected authority in her chosen field.

Penrose, Emily (1858–1942). Though largely self-educated, she was admitted to Oxford in 1889, at the age of thirty-one, to read Classics. She was the first female to achieve the standard for a first-class degree in the subject. Being a woman, she was ineligible to graduate until 1920, when, as Principal of Somerville College (where she was Maria Czaplicka's mentor), she steered to victory the campaign to admit women to full membership of the university. In 1927 she was appointed DBE.

Starkie, Enid (1897–1970). Irishwoman and perpetual eccentric Miss Starkie spent most of her professional life teaching French literature to bedazzled undergraduates. She was a prolific academic author and the first woman to be awarded a doctorate of letters in modern languages at Oxford. In 1967 she was appointed CBE.

Architecture

Charles, Bessie (1869–1932) and **Ethel** (1871–1962). The Charles sisters were the first women to be elected associate members of the Royal Institute of British Architects (RIBA), in 1900 and 1898 respectively. Forbidden to train at the Architectural Association's school because of their gender, they joined a practice in London in

1892 and learned on the job, working professionally (though sporadically) before the First World War.

Drew, Jane (Joyce) (1911–96). When Jane Drew entered the Architectural Association's school in 1929, only twelve of its one hundred pupils were women. She married before qualifying, and set up in practice with her first husband. Later, in 1939, she established a women-only practice of her own, and was instrumental in encouraging mothers (like herself) back into professional life after maternity leave. One of the most distinguished architects – male or female – of her generation, she was appointed DBE in the year of her death.

Gray, Eileen (1878–1976). Trained at the Slade School of Art in London, she worked initially as an interior designer, turning to architecture only after moving to France in 1920. Her influence on modernists such as Le Corbusier was palpable, and though her fame dimmed after the Second World War, retrospective exhibitions in London and Paris in the 1970s restored her professional reputation.

Hughes, Edith Burnet (1888–1971). Born in Scotland, she studied garden design at art school in Aberdeen before switching to architecture. She qualified in 1914, and taught her subject at her alma mater and in Glasgow before opening an architectural practice of her own in 1920. Her success did not guarantee Fellowship of RIBA; when she was proposed in 1927, there was a flat refusal to elect her. She was simply the wrong sex.

Leverkus, Gertrude (1898–1989). The third woman to be elected an associate member of RIBA, after the Charles sisters. She trained at the University of London, was one of the first women to earn her living as an architect and remained in the profession all her life. She was a firm advocate of granting women opportunity and responsibility in the workplace.

Scott, Elisabeth (1898–1972). Peaked early in her career, sensationally winning an international competition in 1928 to redesign the

Shakespeare Memorial Theatre in Stratford-upon-Avon, which had burned down two years earlier. She worked in architecture all her life, but never quite regained the heights of her early success.

The Church

Coltman, Constance (*née* Todd, 1889–1969). It is not easy to say who was Britain's first ordained woman minister, given the range of nonconformist groups, but Constance Coltman was certainly an important pioneer. She and her fiancé were ordained as Congregationalist ministers in 1917, having met as students at the Oxford college where they trained. After their marriage, they had joint charge of successive parishes. Mrs Coltman was also a mother, a suffragist, a pacifist and an activist for women's rights within and outside the Church.

Gates, Edith (1883–1962). What led to Edith's being given pastoral charge of a Baptist parish in Oxfordshire in 1918 is unclear. She received some training after this date at a college for deaconesses, and was a popular preacher, reputedly attracting congregations of three or four hundred to services at which her sister played as organist.

Hedger, Violet (1900–92). Baptist Miss Hedger began her preaching career on a soapbox in London at the age of fourteen. She was the first woman to enter Regent's Park College for formal training, and though discouraged because of her gender, passed the necessary exams and was eventually appointed to parishes in Yorkshire, Kent and London.

Kenmure, Vera (1904–73). Realizing her vocation while studying Classics at Glasgow University, she was ordained in 1927 and became the first woman to be given pastoral charge of a mainstream church in her native Scotland. Famous for her eloquence, she attracted controversy by insisting that full careers as a mother and a parish minister were *not* mutually exclusive.

Von Petzold, Gertrude (1876–1952). Prussian-born Miss von Petzold was the first woman to qualify from Manchester College in Oxford (a nonconformist theological training college at the time), and the first in Britain to be appointed a minister in the Unitarian Church. Her application for British naturalization was refused during the First World War, prompting her to emigrate to the United States.

Picton-Turbervill, Edith (1872–1960). She received little formal education, beyond a succession of governesses and a short period at school. After acknowledging a vocation in 1895, she worked for the Young Women's Christian Association at home and abroad. She was a natural activist, campaigning for the rights of women in the Church, in other professions and in Parliament, where she sat as a Labour MP from 1929 to 1931.

Royden, Maude (1876–1956). Maude Royden's life was rich and complex. She was a small, physically disabled woman whose presence loomed large; a gentle iconoclast; a celibate who publicly – and apparently without censure – advocated the joy of sex. She is acknowledged as an influential Church of England preacher, yet was never ordained. Her influence is at the heart of this book.

Engineering

Ashberry, Annette (1894–1990). Born Hannah Annenberg to a family of Jewish immigrants in London's East End, she learned her skills during the First World War, and afterwards founded Atalanta Engineering Ltd, run by women. She was a prominent member of the Women's Engineering Society (WES) and in 1925 became the first woman elected to membership of the Society of Engineers.

Drummond, Victoria, MBE (1894–1978). This debutante was not destined for life as a ship's engineer; born in a Scottish castle, she was a god-daughter of Queen Victoria, educated at home. Like so many women engineers, she trained for her profession during the First

World War, eventually serving as a chief engineer in the merchant fleet. In 1941 her courage at sea was recognized with the award of the MBE.

Haslett, Caroline (1895–1957). Beginning her career in electrical engineering at an office desk in 1913, working as a secretary, she rapidly became bored and transferred to the workshop floor. Here she flourished, becoming a founder member of the WES and editor of its journal. She also founded the Electrical Association for Women in 1924. Her mission was to use electrical equipment to make domestic life easier for women. She was appointed CBE in 1931 and DBE in 1947.

Parsons, Katharine (1859–1933) and **Rachel** (1885–1956). Encouraged by her mother Katharine, Lady Parsons, Rachel became the first woman to read Engineering at Cambridge, and joined her father Sir Charles's business manufacturing and designing steam turbines. In 1919 Rachel became the first president of the WES, which she co-founded with Katharine. After her parents' death, Rachel inherited vast amounts of money, some of which she spent on a string of race-horses. She died in eccentric isolation, murdered by a former employee.

Partridge, Margaret (1891–1967). Margaret was a pioneer of electrical engineering, bringing power to entire towns and villages. She was inspired by her work during the First World War, and went on to serve as the president of the WES, even though she was based in Devon. She was evangelical in her insistence that women should be taken seriously in the professions. Margaret and her partner (in business and life) Dorothy Rowbotham are buried together in a small Devon churchyard.

Shilling, Beatrice 'Tilly' (1909–90). A schoolgirl with a penchant for motorcycling when she answered Margaret Partridge's advertisement for an apprentice engineer, she got the post and went on to study engineering at Manchester University. She spent most of her working life at the Royal Aircraft Establishment, where she invented a fuel device crucial to aerial success in the Second World War, affectionately known as 'Miss Shilling's Orifice'.

Willson, Laura (1877–1942). The same fervour that landed her in Holloway Prison as a militant suffragette fuelled a lifelong determination to improve conditions for housewives, through her designs, and for professional women, through campaigning via the WES. She was a construction engineer, whose affordable houses were built to improve families' quality of life.

The Law

Morrison, Carrie (1888–1950). A Girton alumna who in 1922 became the first woman to qualify as a solicitor in Britain, after working in Intelligence during the war. She practised both alone and in partnership with her husband, whom – unusually – she later divorced. She had a particular interest in the precursor of the legal aid scheme.

Normanton, Helena, KC (1882–1957). The first woman to be admitted to the Inns of Court to read for the Bar in Britain (on 30 December 1919) and, with Rose Heilbron, one of the first two in England to take silk, becoming a King's Counsel (KC) in 1949. She came from a humble background; this and her gender made briefs hard to come by, so she supplemented her salary by writing and public speaking. She married in 1921, but refused to take her husband's name.

Rosser, Enid (Mrs Locket, 1899–1990). Studied at Oxford and London Universities before being recruited to work in the Lord Chancellor's office as an administrative assistant. In 1922 she began reading for the Bar part-time, and practised as a barrister until joining the department store John Lewis, where she worked as a legal adviser until retirement in 1953.

Sorabji, Cornelia (1866–1954). Despite a litany of 'firsts' (she was the first woman to graduate from university in western India; the first to sit the Bachelor of Civil Law exam at Oxford; the first to practise as a lawyer in India), Cornelia Sorabji's success was doubly limited by her race and gender. She was never able to practise in the law courts unhindered, and contented herself with campaigning for the legal status of women in Britain and her native India.

Thomson, Gwyneth (*née* Bebb, 1889–1921). Had Oxford University awarded women degrees at the time she completed her studies in Jurisprudence, she would have got a first. In 1913 she was plaintiff in a test case against the Law Society for refusing to admit women to train as solicitors. During the war she worked for the Ministry of Food, for which she was appointed OBE. She was accepted by Lincoln's Inn to read for the Bar on Christmas Eve 1919, the day after the Sex Disqualification (Removal) Act was passed – and the day after giving birth to her daughter. She was admitted the following month, and did well. However, Gwyneth never qualified. She died after complications following the birth of her second child.

Williams, Ivy (1877–1966). Already in her early forties when she was admitted to Inner Temple to read for the Bar, she was the first British woman to be called; but, rather than practising as a barrister, she returned to her old college at Oxford to become the university's first female tutor in Law. She was awarded an honorary doctorate (DCL) in 1923.

Medicine

Aldrich-Blake, Louisa (1865–1925). A surgeon and an engine of progress in the campaign for equal opportunities for women doctors. She trained at the London School of Medicine for Women (LSMW, where she served as dean from 1914) and was the first woman to qualify as a Master of Surgery, in 1895. She rose up the ranks of her profession as though she were a man, inspiring by example rather than by political activism. She was appointed DBE in the year of her death.

Boyle, Helen (1869–1957). Specialist in the unfashionable – at the time, almost unrecognized – field of psychiatry. In 1905 she helped found the Lady Chichester Hospital for Women with Nervous Diseases in Brighton, which soon earned a nationwide reputation for good practice, and was a co-founder of the Medical Women's Federation (MWF) in 1917.

Du Buisson, Helen Mary 'May' (Lady Twining, 1896–1976). A pioneer of public health, especially for women and children, she trained at King's College, London, and qualified as a Member of the Royal College of Surgeons after working as a volunteer nurse during the First World War. Most of her working life was spent on postings with her husband in Africa, the Caribbean, Mauritius and North Borneo.

Hoggan, Frances (*née* Morgan, 1843–1927). British women were not allowed to qualify as doctors in her youth; she was forced to study on the Continent before establishing the first husband-and-wife general practice in Britain. Despite the twin handicaps of being female and having an illegitimate child, Dr Hoggan was a well-loved and highly respected professional.

Jex-Blake, Sophia (1840–1912). In 2019, seven women were posthumously awarded medical degrees at Edinburgh University, in honour of their pioneering efforts to make the profession of medicine accessible to women. They were originally nicknamed 'the Edinburgh Seven' and Sophia Jex-Blake was at their head. Forbidden to graduate in medicine from Edinburgh in 1873, the following year she helped found the LSMW, responsible for training the first cohorts of British women doctors. She eventually obtained her medical degree from Bern in Switzerland in 1877.

Mann, Ida (Mrs Gye, 1893–1983). An ophthalmologist who practised at the top of her profession in England and in Australia, her adopted home, where she was appointed CBE in 1951 and DBE in 1980. She trained at the LSMW, qualified in 1920 and within seven years had been appointed senior surgeon at Moorfields Eye Hospital in London. She was the first woman to be given a professorial chair at Oxford and was globally respected as an innovator, a researcher and a fine technician.

Martindale, Louisa (1872–1966). Yet another alumna of the LSMW and a friend of Louisa Aldrich-Blake and Helen Boyle, who ran a general practice in Brighton while specializing in gynaecology. Appointed CBE in 1931, she was the first woman elected to serve on the council of the Royal College of Obstetricians and Gynaecologists and was president of the Medical Women's International Federation from 1937 to 1947.

Wilberforce, Octavia (1888–1963). Her mother was appalled when she announced her intention, at the age of twenty-three, to study medicine. But Octavia was stubborn, begging an education and eventually qualifying – after seven years – in 1920. Like her friend Louisa Martindale she settled in Brighton as a GP, also working as a physician at Helen Boyle's Lady Chichester Hospital and at the Marie Curie Hospital in London.

General

Holmes, (Beatrice) Gordon (1884–1951). An endlessly energetic and ambitious woman who virtually educated herself to become a wealthy businesswoman, stockbroker and entrepreneur. Her suffragette heritage prepared her well for a life of public activism for women's rights. She was a vociferous campaigner for gender equality, determined to rescue ambitious women from the limitations of domestic life.

Martindale, Hilda (1875–1942). She chose a different path from her elder sister Louisa, joining the Civil Service in 1901 as a Home Office factory inspector and rising to the rank of Director of Women's Establishments in the Treasury in 1933. In 1935 she was appointed CBE. Luckily, she never married; that would have meant dismissal, and deprived the Civil Service of one of its true pioneers.

Matheson, Hilda (1888–1940). Had a varied career before joining the BBC as Director of Talks in 1926. After reading history at Oxford she worked as a scholarly amanuensis, in wartime Intelligence and as political secretary to Lady Astor MP. Her short but stellar career at the BBC lasted from 1926 to 1931; following her resignation she worked as a high-profile writer and researcher. In 1939 she was appointed OBE.

Rhondda, Viscountess (Margaret Mackworth, *née* Thomas, 1883–1958). A suffragette in her youth who went on to be a tireless supporter of professional and business women and herself a director of several companies, a politician (founding the Six Point Group in 1921) and the founding editor of *Time and Tide*, a feminist periodical published from 1920 to 1966. She ran a personal campaign after her father's death to be allowed to take her rightful place in the House of Lords as an hereditary peeress; that battle was not won until the passing of the Peerage Act in 1963.

Somerville, Mary (1897–1963). An Oxford graduate and the first woman to be appointed Controller at the BBC. She joined in 1925, straight from university, and spent her burgeoning career in the education department, laying the foundation of schools broadcasting: a BBC flagship enterprise. In 1935 her efforts were rewarded with the OBE. Twice married, and a mother, she exasperated and endeared herself to her colleagues in equal measure.

Strachey, Ray (1887–1940). The suffrage movement's historian (writing *The Cause* in 1928) and one of its most committed activists, transferring her energies after the vote was won to bettering the lot of educated women through political engagement and writing. She had a keen interest in electrical engineering and a practical bent for architecture, designing and building a house in Sussex for her somewhat dysfunctional family.

Notes and References

For full details of sources quoted, please see the Select Bibliography, pages 323–33.

Introduction

1 Woolf, 'Professions for Women', unpaginated.
2 The esteemed medic Sir Almroth Wright declared that the mind of woman was so seriously corrupted by 'the reverberations of her physiological emergencies', that is, her periods, that it was practically useless.

1 The Society of Outsiders

1 Graduate Gwendolen Freeman remembering the response to her job application to a publishing firm in 1929. See Robinson, *Bluestockings*, p. 213.
2 The sobering statistic about teachers is from Lang, *British Women*, p. 19. Edith Morley was appointed Professor of English Language at Reading in 1908, and Professor of English Literature there four years later. Winifred Cullis was awarded the Chair of Physiology at the University of London in 1919.
3 Descriptions of the evening can be found in the suffrage journal *Common Cause*, 12 March 1920; in contemporary local and national newspapers; and in Helena Normanton's papers at the Women's Library collection at LSE Library (7HLN/A/02).
4 Comments from a letter to Gwyneth Bebb Thomson's sister Catherine, 23 May [1920], reproduced by kind permission of Gwyneth's grandchildren Martin Tomlins and Anne Tickell. Copies of Bebb Thomson's papers are lodged in the archives at St Hugh's College, Oxford.

5   Charles, 'Development', p. 180.

6   The Diary of Edith Hughes, 1884, Cadbury Research Library:
    Special Collections, University of Birmingham (MS6).

7   Edith Barnett, *Penny Cookery Book* (London: Allman & Son for
    the National Health Society, 1884).

8   Quoted in McIntyre, 'Britain's First Medical Marriage', p. 112.

9   *Cambrian News and Merioneth Standard*, 15 Jan. 1886.

10 Unattributed newspaper cutting, early 1930s, in a scrapbook at the
    Women's Library collection at LSE Library (10/37).

11 *Exeter and Plymouth Gazette,* 26 Aug. 1921.

12 *Yorkshire Post*, 29 Apr. 1927.

13 *Woman Engineer,* vol. 1, no. 15 (June 1923), p. 251. Available
    online via the Women's Engineering Society and IET Archives:
    https://www.wes.org.uk/content/journal-archive.

14 Ibid., p. 252.

15 *Woman Engineer,* vol. 1, no. 12 (Sept. 1922), p. 180.

16 Fletcher, *Maude Royden,* p. 6.

17 Obituary by Royden's lifelong friend Dame Kathleen Courtney,
    written for alumnae of Lady Margaret Hall, in the Women's
    Library collection at LSE Library (7AMR/01/42).

18 Robinson, *Bluestockings,* p. 152.

19 Richardson, *Enid Starkie,* p. 93.

20 Starkie, *A Lady's Child,* p. 20.

21 Enid Starkie herself earned £400 per annum when first engaged
    by Somerville College.

22 Leverkus, *Auntie Gertrude's Life,* unpublished manuscript, in the
    Women's Library collection at LSE Library (7GLE), p. 14.
    Reproduced by kind permission of the Leverkus family.

23 Private interviews with the author.

24 Reported in *The Times,* 1 Sept. 1910. The competition was
    administered by the Royal Drawing Society.

25 Chancery Division Law Reports [1913], Law Society Library, p. 299.

26 Ibid. [1914], p. 356. Judge and politician Sir Edward Coke (1552–
    1634) was Lord Chief Justice to King James I, prosecutor of the
    Gunpowder Plotters and, ironically, an ancestor of Gwyneth Bebb
    Thomson.

27 From a letter to Gwyneth's sister Catherine, 26 July [1921],
    reproduced by kind permission of Gwyneth's grandchildren
    Martin Tomlins and Anne Tickell. Copies of Bebb
    Thomson's papers are lodged in the archives at St Hugh's College,
    Oxford.

2 England is a Gentlemen's Club

1   Waterhouse, *Insignia Vitae*, pp. 276–7.
2   *A Medical Medley: Student Verse 1921–30*, University of
    Birmingham Medical Society, 1930, Cadbury Research
    Library: Special Collections, University of Birmingham (UBSoc
    3/c/1), p. 77.
3   *Lancet*, 30 Aug. 1873, p. 308.
4   By poet William Henley, quoted in Crowther, 'Why Women
    Should be Nurses'.
5   Quoted in Robinson, *Pandora's Daughters*, p. 17, from a book by
    Elizabeth Mason-Hohl on Trotula.
6   The word 'feisty', often used admiringly to describe
    outspoken and independent women, derives from a Middle
    English term for 'farting dog'. Mongrels were famed for their
    flatulence, apparently; they were also supposed to be aggressive –
    just like quarrelsome women. Quarrelsome women are outspoken
    and independent: so there we are.
7   Letter dated 28 Oct. (no year) from Blackwell to Barbara
    Bodichon, Rare Book & Manuscript Library, Columbia
    University in the City of New York (MS 0124).
8   *Lancet*, 7 May 1870, p. 673.
9   *The Times*, 28 July 1869. The letter was also published in *The
    Scotsman*.
10 Quoted in Blake, *Charge of the Parasols*, p. 126.
11 *Scotsman*, 21 Nov. 1870.
12 *St Stephen's Catholic University Magazine*, Dublin, 1902, p. 93;
    quoted in Kelly, *Irish Women*, p. 79.
13 *Englishwoman's Year Book* (1882 edn), p. vii.
14 Ibid., p. 3.
15 Ibid., p. 4 of the final advertisements.

16   Frankenberg, *Not Old*, p. 86.
17   *Englishwoman's Year Book and Directory* (1915 edn), p. 98.
18   Ibid., p. 105.
19   *Dundee Evening Post*, 4 Dec. 1903.
20   Ibid. Miss Cave's case was widely covered in the press. The following year her appearance in court, dressed in cap and gown, was also reported. On that occasion she was acting as a witness in a case involving her father and a bicycle, and was accused of pretending to be his legal counsel. In 1904 she applied to the Law Society, as Gwyneth Bebb Thomson was later to do, but with a similar lack of success.
21   ASLEF Minute Book, 1916, Sheffield City Council, Libraries Archives and Information: Sheffield City Archives (ASLEF/1b).
22   Baumann, 'The Future of the Bar', p. 630.
23   Holmes, *In Love With Life*, p. 64.
24   Kim Wilson, womenofeastbourne.co.uk/wp-content/uploads/2017/08/Emily-Phipps-the-full-story.pdf.
25   Louisa Martindale, *A Woman Surgeon*, p. 33.

3   Working Girls

1   Mackworth, *This Was My World*, p. xi.
2   *Time and Tide*, 23 Jan. 1924, p. 91. The immediately following quotations are from the same source.
3   Statistics extrapolated from *A Vision of Britain through Time*, visionofbritain.org.uk/census/EW1921GEN/8.
4   Quoted in Zimmeck, 'Strategies and Stratagems', p. 905.
5   Stanley Leather, quoted in Summerfield (ed.), *Women, Education and the Professions*, p. 3.
6   Quoted by Meta Zimmeck, 'We are All Professionals Now: Professionalization, Education and Gender in the Civil Service, 1873–1939', in Summerfield (ed.), *Women, Education and the Professions*, p. 67.
7   Quoted in Holcombe, *Victorian Ladies*, p. 163.
8   Berry and Bishop (eds), *Testament of a Generation*, p. 61.
9   Hilda Martindale, *Women Servants*, p. 178.

10 They were described as such in a Treasury memo in 1918, quoted in Zimmeck, 'Strategies and Stratagems', p. 905.

11 'Miss Fluffy Femininity carries off the prizes', an article in *Woman's Life*, 10 Jan. 1920, quoted in White, *Women's Magazines*, p. 99.

12 Undated newspaper cutting from the *Daily Herald*, author's collection.

13 Holcombe, *Victorian Ladies*, p. 146.

14 Hilda Martindale, *Women Servants*, p. 25.

15 Bennett, *Our Women*, p. 124.

16 Burstall, *Retrospect*, p. 104. Headmistress Miss Burstall is quoting a colleague.

17 Cunningham and Gardner, *Becoming Teachers*, p. 176.

18 Ibid., p. 200.

19 Barlow, *Seventh Child*, p. 56.

20 This and subsequent quotations from Miss Faithfull's autobiography, *In the House of my Pilgrimage*.

21 Sidgwick, 'The Place of University', p. 22.

22 Bateson, *Professional Women*, p. v.

23 Ibid., p. 133.

24 *Daily Herald,* 4 March 1933.

25 The National Archives (TNA), LAB 2/1783/E3140/1920.

4 Biggish Women

1 *Woman Engineer,* vol. 1, no. 6 (March 1921), p. 59.

2 Quoted in Lang, *British Women*, p. 115.

3 Wilberforce, *Eighth Child*, p. 74.

4 For information on early solicitors I am indebted to legal historian Elizabeth Cruickshank, who gave me an unpaginated offprint of her article 'Follow the Money: The First Women Who Qualified as Solicitors 1922–1930'.

5 Wilberforce, *Eighth Child*, p. 27.

6 Ibid., p. 59.

7 Mann, *The Chase*, p. 27.

8 Ibid.

9 Bryson, *Look Back*, p. 54.

10 See note 4.

11 These statistics were extrapolated from a questionnaire sent out to its members by the Medical Women's Federation, quoted in Lang, *British Women*, p. 73.

12 Mann, *The Chase*, p. 51.

13 Ibid., p. 60.

14 Ibid., p. 62.

15 This and subsequent quotes are from an unpublished memoir kindly lent to me by Peggy Kenyon Taylor's family. Taylor, *Memoir*, p. 118.

16 Ibid., p. 132.

17 Ibid.

18 From a letter from Gwyneth Bebb Thomson to Lincoln's Inn, 27 Dec. 1919, reproduced by kind permission of Gwyneth's grandchildren Martin Tomlins and Anne Tickell.

19 Extracts printed in *Graya* (the journal of Gray's Inn), vol. 89 (1985–6), pp. 39–43. Reproduced by kind permission of the Masters of the Bench of the Honourable Society of Gray's Inn.

20 Ibid.

21 *Woman Engineer*, vol. 1, no. 1 (Dec. 1919), p. 6.

22 Ibid., no. 2 (March 1920), p. 9.

23 Quoted in Clarsen, *Eat My Dust*, p. 58. From the house magazine of the Arrol-Johnston plant at Tongland, Kirkcudbright, *The Limit* (Christmas 1919; original not seen). To confuse matters, the engineers' house magazine of Loughborough Technical College was also called *The Limit*.

24 From an album in the archives of the University Women's Club entitled *Some Distinguished Members*.

25 *Builder*, 22 Feb. 1902, pp. 179–83.

5 Those Charming Impostors

1 Woolf, 'Professions for Women', title-page. The phrase 'charming impostors' in the chapter title is taken from a conversation with a lawyer who remembered the people in her chambers describing women as such when she started training.

2 From a letter to Gwyneth Bebb Thomson, 12 Oct. 1911, reproduced by kind permission of Gwyneth's grandchildren Martin Tomlins and Anne Tickell.

3   Quoted in Doughan and Gordon, *Women, Clubs and Associations*, p. 16.

4   Crawford, *The Women's Suffrage Movement*, pp. 124–5.

5   McIntyre, *How British Women Became Doctors*, p. 170.

6   *Woman Teacher*, 5 March 1920.

7   Ibid., 31 Dec. 1930.

8   MWF newsletter, Nov. 1930, Wellcome Collection, London (B 2/1).

9   Ibid., Nov. 1923.

10 Ibid., July 1926.

11 Quoted in the catalogue record of the Provisional Club archives, in the Women's Library collection at LSE Library (5WPV).

12 Czaplicka, *My Siberian Year*, p. 25.

13 *Common Cause*, 3 June 1921.

14 Reproduced in Bryceson et al. (eds), *Identity and Networks*, p. 153.

15 Inner Temple Admissions Database: http://www.innertemplearchives.org.uk/search.asp. Alice was first admitted in 1936, so one of the lacunae in her record could be explained by the Second World War.

16 Cole, *The Road to Success*, p. 33.

17 Locket, *Ramblings*, p. 114.

18 Lang, *British Women*, p. 22.

19 *Time and Tide*, 25 Nov. 1927.

20 For information about the redoubtable Maria Nickel, see Hart, *Ask Me No More*, p. 18, and the Downe House magazine *Cloisters*, no. 6, 2013.

21 Autograph Book, in the Women's Library collection at LSE Library (7HLN/A/11).

22 Locket, *Ramblings*, p. 275.

23 Mann, *The Chase*, p. 66.

24 Wilberforce, *Eighth Child*, pp. 121–2.

25 Smith, *Ad Vitam*, pp. 71–2.

26 Murray, *My First Hundred Years*, p. 159.

27 Wauchope, *The Story of a Woman Physician*, p. 45.

28 Lincoln's Inn Black Books, vol. 6 (1914–65), p. 189.

29 *Builder*, 6 Feb. 1920, p. 161.

6 Not Quite Nice

1 *Times Educational Supplement*, 22 April 1933, quoted in Partington, *Women Teachers*, p. 36.

2 Lady Justice is traditionally considered to be blind, meaning impartial. However, the famous statue at the Old Bailey in London does not provide her with a blindfold, as is popularly supposed.

3 Quoted in Wade, *The Justice Women*, p. 16.

4 Haynes, *Much Ado about Women*, Law Society Library (CAR 16/2).

5 Ibid., p. 18.

6 Bryson, *Look Back*, p. 150.

7 Richardson, *Enid Starkie*, p. 95.

8 *Manchester Evening News*, 2 Oct. 1936.

9 *Daily Mirror*, 25 April 1938.

10 *A Medical Medley. Student Verse 1921-30*. University of Birmingham Medical Society, 1930, Cadbury Research Library: Special Collections, University of Birmingham (UBSoc 3/c/1), p. 8.

11 Quoted in Lang, *British Women*, p. 148.

12 *Illustrated Police News*, 2 Dec. 1926.

13 This and subsequent quotes are from 'Correspondence about students with the Senior Tutor for Women Students 1926–47', Cadbury Research Library: Special Collections, University of Birmingham (UC 3/vi/7 – 3/vii/2), uncatalogued in Dec. 2018.

14 *Woman Engineer*, vol. 3, no. 3 (June 1930), pp. 41–2.

15 Helena Normanton's papers, in the Women's Library collection at LSE Library (7HLN/A/35).

16 *Law Society Journal*, Dec. 1928, p. 28.

17 Statistics from *A History of Women in the UK Civil Service*, civilservant.org.uk/library/2015_history_of_women_in_the_ civil_service.pdf.

18 This and subsequent quotes are from The National Archives (TNA T199/57).

19 *Daily Express*, 31 Oct. 1935.

20 *Miss Modern*, no. 1 (Oct. 1930).

21 *Daily Herald*, 2 June 1938.

22 https://www.legalcheek.com/2015/10/1920s-cartoon-predicts-
    that-first-women-barristers-would-hilariously-modify-their-wigs/.
23 M. S. Miller, 'Women in the World of Commerce', paper in the
    Women's Library collection at LSE Library (7MSM).
24 Fawcett, *What the Vote Has Done.*
25 Lang, *British Women*, p. 20.
26 Berry and Bishop (eds), *Testament of a Generation*, p. 141.
27 Holtby, *Women*, p. 17.

7 Dynamite in Curlers

1   *Morning Post*, 4 June 1936.
2   Available online via the Women's Engineering Society and IET
    Archives: https://www.wes.org.uk/content/journal-archive.
3   *Woman Engineer*, vol. 4, no. 10 (March 1937), p. 150.
4   Ibid., vol. 3, no. 19 (June 1934), p. 303.
5   Wilberforce, *Eighth Child*, p. 240.
6   Sacks, *Uncle Tungsten*, p. 240.
7   Wellcome Collection, London (SA/MWF/C57).
8   Mann, *The Chase*, p. 90.
9   See Cadbury Research Library: Special Collections, University of
    Birmingham (UC 3/vi/7 – 3/vii/2), uncatalogued in Dec. 2018.
10 Fletcher, *Maude Royden*, p. 200.
11 *Scotsman*, 8 April 1929.
12 *Dundee Evening Telegraph,* 21 Jan. 1939.
13 Walker, *Golden Age*, p. 19.
14 The two doctors were Dr Ethel Bentham (Labour, elected in
    1929) and Dr Edith Summerskill (Labour, 1938); the two
    academics were Marjorie Graves, who later worked in the Civil
    Service (Conservative, 1931) and Dr Marion Phillips (Labour,
    1929); the teacher was Jennie Lee (Labour, 1929) and the preacher,
    Edith Picton-Turbervill (Labour).
15 Berry and Bishop (eds), *Testament of a Generation*, p. 60.
16 Quoted in Bingham, *Gender*, p. 51.
17 Burstall, *Retrospect*, p. 234.
18 This and subsequent quotes are from Malcolmsons (eds), *A
    Free-Spirited Woman*, pp. 4, 30.

19   Mitch et al. (eds), *Origins*, p. 217.
20   Miss Q and Miss B are featured in an undated (but very art deco) careers pamphlet in Cadbury Research Library: Special Collections, University of Birmingham (UC 3/vi/7 – 3/vii/2), uncatalogued in Dec. 2018.
21   Women who had paid the appropriate level of insurance were eligible for unemployment benefit commensurate with their (generally lower) wage-earning potential until 1931, when the 'Anomalies Regulations' were introduced. These deemed an unemployed married woman to be dependent on her husband's income, and therefore entitled to fewer benefits.
22   Eyles, *Careers for Women*, p. 184.
23   Beddoe, *Back to Home and Duty*, p. 79.
24   Perrone, *University Teaching*, p. 22.
25   Lang, *British Women*, p. 165.
26   Mabel Lindsey's Scrapbook, 1916–40, in the Greater Manchester County Record Office (with Manchester Archives) (ref. 58742), p. 21.
27   Zimmeck, *Strategies and Stratagems*, pp. 921–2.
28   *The Times*, 8 Apr. 1932.
29   BBC Written Archives Centre (L2/195/1). BBC copyright content reproduced courtesy of the British Broadcasting Corporation. All rights reserved.
30   Ibid.
31   Ibid.
32   Woolf, *Three Guineas*, p. 135. Reproduced courtesy of the Society of Authors as the Literary Representative of the Estate of Virginia Woolf.

8   Wives or Workers?

1   Rose Macaulay, writing in *Good Housekeeping*, Dec. 1923, p. 69.
2   By courtesy of the University of Liverpool Library, Special Collections (P822/1), 1 Nov. 1932.
3   Letter dated 17 May 1920, Cadbury Research Library: Special Collections, University of Birmingham (UB/COU/1/14).
4   Holtby, *Women*, pp. 143–4.

5   Partington, *Women Teachers*, p. 29.
6   *The Times*, 6 Jan. 1922.
7   Eyles, *Careers for Women*, p. 85.
8   Hamilton, *Marriage*, p. 185.
9   Woolf, *Three Guineas*, p. 13.
10 Austen, *Pride and Prejudice*, ch. 22. The author is explaining how Charlotte Lucas can bring herself to accept Mr Collins's slightly oily hand in marriage.
11 Elsie Fisher, quoted in Oram, *Women Teachers*, p. 197.
12 *Alexandra College Magazine* (1899), pp. 374–5.
13 Quoted in Oram, *Women Teachers*, p. 56.
14 *Ariel*, March 1938, p. 57.
15 Quoted in Oram, *Women Teachers*, p. 190.
16 Malcolmsons (eds), *A Free-Spirited Woman*, p. 28.
17 BBC Written Archives Centre, Staff Files (L2/195/1). BBC copyright content reproduced courtesy of the British Broadcasting Corporation. All rights reserved.
18 Ibid., Married Women Policy File 1, 1928–35 (R49/371/1), memo dated 23 Sept. 1932.
19 Ibid., memo dated 20 Apr. 1933.
20 Ibid., undated memo; memo dated 25 Oct. 1932.
21 'Motherhood Means Dismissal', *Daily Mirror*, 28 Aug.1933.
22 See Murphy, *Behind the Wireless*, for an excellent discussion of the marriage bar at the BBC.
23 This and previous comments are from BBC Written Archives Centre, Married Women Policy Tribunals, 1934–37 (R49/371/1). BBC copyright content reproduced courtesy of the British Broadcasting Corporation. All rights reserved.
24 Ibid., 6 March 1935.
25 Cairns, *Careers for Girls*, p. 64.
26 Brittain, *Women's Work*, p. 66.
27 Muriel St Clare Byrne collection, Somerville College, Oxford (MSB Add. Mss. 7/1).
28 Locket, *Ramblings*, p. 182.
29 Royden, *A Threefold Cord*, p. 17.
30 Ibid., p. 25.

31 Carney, *Stoker*, p. 50.
32 Mann, *The Chase*, p. 58.
33 Ibid.
34 Ibid., p. 133.
35 Buckley and Potter (eds), *Ida and the Eye*, p. xvii.

9 Butterfly's Wings with Blue Stockings

1   Bennett, *Our Women*, p. 125.
2   *Woman's Life*, 10 Jan. 1920, quoted in White, *Women's Magazines*, p. 99.
3   *Good Housekeeping*, Mar. 1922, p. 11.
4   On one occasion Helena Normanton caused *Good Housekeeping*'s proprietors and printers to be sued by a man claiming she had implied that he was guilty of murder, when discussing a recent case in an article about the death penalty. The magazine lost the case but was only required to pay nominal damages to the plaintiff. See *The Times*, 30 Nov. 1928.
5   Since you ask: Bismarck herrings are pickled fish from the Baltic Sea.
6   *Miss Modern*, Oct. 1930, p. 42.
7   *Good Housekeeping*, June 1923, p. 32.
8   *Daily Herald*, 28 Oct. 1924.
9   Memoirs of Myfanwy Gipson (private collection).
10 Woolf, *Three Guineas*, p. 36.
11 Forester, *Success through Dress*, p. 131.
12 Holtby, *Women*, p. 118.
13 Smith, *Ad Vitam*, p. 120.
14 Statistics from Pugh, *We Danced*, p. 229, and Linda Wood, 'British Films 1927–1939', available on the British Film Institute website: https://www.bfi.org.uk/sites/bfi.org.uk/files/downloads/bfi-british-films-1927-1939.pdf.
15 See Lancaster, *Department Store*, for these references and more on the social history of shopping.
16 Adam, *Eileen Gray*, p. 19.
17 Quoted in Fletcher, *Maude Royden*, p. 117.
18 *Daily Express*, 2 May 1923.

19   *Radio Pictorial*, 3 Jan. 1936.

20   *Ariel*, Oct. 1937.

21   May Du Buisson Twining family papers (private collection, parts of which are lodged in the manuscript collections of the Bodleian Library, Oxford, but were uncatalogued at the time of consultation, Apr. 2019).

22   Leta Jones papers (D452/7), courtesy of the University of Liverpool Library, Special Collections and Archives.

10   Modern Women

1   Hamilton, *Marriage*, p. 24.

2   Quoted in *The Impact of World War II on Women's Work*, striking-women.org/module/women-and-work/world-war-ii-1939-1945.

3   *Woman Engineer*, vol. 5, no. 1 (Dec. 1939), p. 14.

4   Quoted in https://www.bbc.co.uk/history/ww2peopleswar/stories/53/a3890153.shtml.

5   This was Florence Li Tim-Oi, consecrated in Jan. 1944.

6   Williams, *The New Democracy*, p. 54.

7   Marking (ed.), *Oxford Originals*, p. 68.

8   Reproduced in Aiston, 'A Good Job for a Girl?', p. 367.

9   Ibid., p. 381.

10   *Newcastle Journal*, 4 July 1956.

11   *Architects' Journal*, 12 July 1972, p. 68.

12   Leverkus, *Auntie Gertrude's Life*, unpublished manuscript, in the Women's Library collection at LSE Library (7GLE), p. 66.

13   Maude Royden papers, in the Women's Library collection at LSE Library (7AMR/02/09).

14   Royden, *A Threefold Cord*, p. 104.

15   Anne Olivier Bell (ed.), *Diary of Virginia Woolf*, vol. 5, p. 304, quoted in Holmes, *Working Woman*, p. 313.

16   Interviewed by Master Rachel Spearing for the Inner Temple's Oral History project, 2 Feb. 2018.

17   Private conversation with the author.

18   *Graya*, vol. 51 (Easter, 1960), p. 29, reproduced by kind permission of the Masters of the Bench of the Honourable Society of Gray's Inn.

Select Bibliography

Periodicals

Ariel (BBC, 1936–)
Britannia and Eve (1929–57)
Buider (1843–1966)
Common Cause (1909–20)
Good Housekeeping (1922–)
The Lancet (1823–)
Limit [Loughborough] (1918–54)
Limit [Tongland] (1918–20)
Miss Modern (1930–1)
Queen (1861–1958)
Radio Pictorial (1933–9)
Time and Tide (1920–66)
Woman Engineer (1919–)
Woman Teacher (1919–36)
Woman's Journal (1927–)

Books and Articles

Adam, Peter, *Eileen Gray: Architect/Designer. A Biography* (Farnham: Lund Humphries, 2015)

Aiston, Sarah, 'A Good Job for a Girl? The Career Biographies of Women Graduates of the University of Liverpool Post-1945', *Twentieth Century British History*, vol. 15, no. 4 (2004), pp. 361–87

Alexander, Wendy, *First Ladies of Medicine: The Origins, Education and Destination of Early Women Medical Graduates of Glasgow University* (Glasgow: Wellcome Unit for the History of Medicine, 1987)

Arscott, Christine (ed.), *The Headmistress Speaks* (London: Kegan Paul, 1937)

'A Worker', *Should Women Preach?* (London: W. C. Daniel, 1918)

Baker, Hatty, *Women in the Ministry* (London: C. W. Daniel, 1911)

Barlow, Amy, *Seventh Child* (London: Duckworth, 1969)

Bateson, Margaret, *Professional Women upon their Professions: Conversations* (London: Horace Cox, 1895)

Baumann, Arthur, 'The Future of the Bar', *Nineteenth Century and After*, March 1917, pp. 630–9

Beddoe, Deirdre, *Back to Home and Duty: Women between the Wars 1918–1939* (London: Pandora, 1989)

Bennett, Arnold, *Our Women: Chapters on the Sex-Discord* (London: Cassell, 1920)

Berry, P., and Bishop, A. (eds), *Testament of a Generation: The Journalism of Vera Brittain and Winifred Holtby* (London: Virago, 1985)

Bingham, Adrian, *Gender, Modernity and the Popular Press in Inter-War Britain* (Oxford: Clarendon Press, 2004)

Black, Clementina (ed.), *Married Women's Work. Being a Report of an Enquiry Undertaken by the Women's Industrial Council* (London: Virago, 1983 [1915])

Blake, Catriona, *Charge of the Parasols* (London: Women's Press, 1990)

Bourne, Judith, *Helena Normanton and the Opening of the Bar to Women* (Hook: Waterside Press, 2016)

Briscoe, V., *300 Careers for Women* (London: Lovat Dickson, 1932)

Brittain, Vera, *Women's Work in Modern England* (London: Noel Douglas, 1928)

Brock, Claire, *British Women Surgeons and their Patients* (Cambridge: Cambridge University Press, 2017)

Bruley, S., *Women in Britain since 1900* (London: Macmillan, 1999)

Bryceson, Deborah Fahy; Okely, Judith; and Webber, Jonathan (eds), *Identity and Networks: Gender and Ethnicity in a Cross-Cultural Context* (New York: Berghahn, 2007)

Bryson, Elizabeth, *Look Back in Wonder* (Dundee: David Winter, 1967)

Buckley, Cheryl, and Fawcett, Hilary, *Fashioning the Feminine: Representation and Women's Fashion from the Fin de Siècle to the Present* (London: Tauris, 2001)

Buckley, Elizabeth, and Potter, Dorothy (eds), *Ida and the Eye: A Woman in British Ophthalmology* (Tunbridge Wells: Parapress [1996])

Burstall, Sara, *Retrospect and Prospect: Sixty Years of Women's Education* (London: Longman, Green, 1933)

Cairns, J. A. R., *Careers for Girls* (London: Hutchinson, 1928)

Careers and Vocational Training: A Guide to the Professions and Occupations of Educated Women and Girls (London: Central Employment Bureau, 1924)

Carney, Michael, *Stoker: The Life of Hilda Matheson OBE 1888–1940* (Llangynog: privately published, 1999)

Carthew, A. G. E., *The University Women's Club: Extracts from Fifty Years of Minute Books 1886–1936* (London: UWC, 1996)

Charles, Ethel, 'The Development of Architectural Art from Structural Requirements and Nature Materials', *Builder*, Feb. 1902, pp. 179–83

Clarsen, Georgine, *Eat My Dust: Early Women Motorists* (Baltimore: Johns Hopkins University Press, 2008)

Clephane, Irene, *Towards Sex Freedom* (London: John Lane, 1935)

Cole, Margaret, *The Road to Success: Twenty Essays on the Choice of a Career for Women* (London: Methuen, 1936)

Copelman, D. M., *London's Women Teachers: Gender, Class and Feminism 1870–1930* (London: Routledge, 1996)

Cowman, Krista, and Jackson, Louise, *Women and Work Culture: Britain c 1850–1950* (Aldershot: Ashgate, 2005)

Crawford, Elizabeth, *The Women's Suffrage Movement: A Reference Guide* (London: Routledge, 2001)

Crofts, Maud, *Women under the Law* (London: National Council of Women of Great Britain, 1925)

Crowther, M. Anne, 'Why Women Should be Nurses and Not Doctors', *Women in Medicine*, 22 Dec. 2016, http://www.womeninmedicinemagazine.com/profile-of-women-in-medicine/why-women-should-be-nurses-and-not-doctors

Cruickshank, Elizabeth, 'Follow the Money: The First Women Who Qualified as Solicitors 1922–1930', paper presented at a symposium on 'First Women Lawyers in Great Britain and the Empire' (Twickenham: St Mary's University, 2016), vol. 1

— *Women in the Law: Strategic Career Management* (London: Law Society, 2003)

Cunningham, P., and Gardner, P., *Becoming Teachers: Texts and Testimonies 1907–50* (London: Woburn, 2004)

Curtis, Mavis, *What the Suffragists Did Next: How the Fight for Women's Rights Went On* (Stroud: Amberley, 2017)

Czaplicka, Marie, *My Siberian Year* (London: Mills & Boon, 1916)

Debenham, Betty and Nancy, *Motorcycling for Women* (London: Pitman, 1928)

Directory of Women Teachers (London: Year Book Press, 1917)

Dorner, Jane, *Fashion in the Twenties and Thirties* (London: Allan, 1973)

Doughan, David, and Gordon, Peter, *Women, Clubs and Associations in Britain* (London: Routledge, 2006)

Dyhouse, Carol, 'Driving Ambitions: Women in Pursuit of a Medical Education 1890–1939', *Women's History Review*, vol. 7, no. 3 (1998), pp. 321–43

— *Girl Trouble: Panic and Progress in the History of Young Women* (London: Zed, 2013)

— *Glamour: Women, History, Feminism* (London: Zed, 2010)

— *No Distinction of Sex? Women in British Universities 1870–1939* (London: UCL, 1995)

— *Students: A Gendered History* (London: Routledge, 2006)

Englishwoman's Year Book (London: Hatchard, 1882)

Englishwoman's Year Book and Directory (London: A. & C. Black, 1915)

Etherington-Wright, Christine, *Gender, Professions and Discourse: Early Twentieth-Century Women's Autobiography* (Basingstoke: Palgrave, 2009)

Eyles, L., *Careers for Women* (London: Elkin Mathews & Marrot, 1930)

Faithfull, Lilian, *In the House of my Pilgrimage* (London: Chatto & Windus, 1925)

Fawcett, Millicent, *What the Vote Has Done* (London: National Union of Societies for Equal Citizenship, 1926)

Fiell, Charlotte, and Dirix, Emanuelle, *1920s Fashion: The Definitive Sourcebook* (London: Fiell, 2012)

Fletcher, Sheila, *Maude Royden: A Life* (Oxford: Blackwell, 1989)

Ford, I. O., *Women as Factory Inspectors and Certifying Surgeons*, Investigation Papers no. 4 (Manchester: Women's Co-operative Guild, 1898)

Forester, C. W., *Success through Dress* (London: Duckworth, 1925)

Forster, Emily; Murray, Stella; and Marshall, A. C., *Lloyd's ABC of Careers for Girls* (London: United Press, 1922)

Frankenberg, Charis, *Not Old, Madam, Vintage* (Lavenham: privately printed, 1975)

Glew, Helen, *Gender, Rhetoric and Regulation: Women's Work in the Civil Service and the London County Council, 1900–55* (Manchester: Manchester University Press, 2016)

Gottlieb, Julie V., and Toye, Richard (eds), *The Aftermath of Suffrage: Women, Gender and Politics in Britain 1918 45* (London: Palgrave Macmillan, 2013)

Graves, R., and Hodge, A., *The Long Week-End: A Social History of Great Britain 1918–1939* (London: Faber & Faber, 1941)

Haldane, Charlotte, *Motherhood and its Enemies* (London: Chatto & Windus, 1927)

Hamilton, Cicely, *Marriage as a Trade* (London: Chapman & Hall, 1912)

Harrison, Jane E., *Reminiscences of a Student's Life* (London: Leonard and Virginia Woolf, 1925)

Hart, Jenifer, *Ask Me No More: An Autobiography* (London: Halban, 1998)

Haselgrove, Evelyn, *The University Women's Club: A History* (London: UWC, 1994)

Haynes, E. S. P., *Much Ado about Women* (Kensington: Cayme, 1926)

Heilbron, Hilary, *Rose Heilbron: The Story of England's First Woman QC and Judge* (Oxford: Hart, 2012)

Holcombe, Lee, *Victorian Ladies at Work: Middle-Class Working Women in England and Wales 1850–1914* (London: David & Charles, 1973)

Holden, K., *The Shadow of Marriage: Singleness in England 1914–60* (Manchester: Manchester University Press, 2007)

Holmes, Beatrice Gordon, *In Love with Life: A Pioneer Career Woman's History* (London: Hollis & Carter, 1944)

Holmes, Jennifer, *A Working Woman: The Remarkable Life of Ray Strachey* (Kibworth Beauchamp: Matador, 2019)

Holtby, Winifred, *Women and a Changing Civilization* (London: John Lane, 1934)

Hopkinson, Diana, *Family Inheritance: A Life of Eva Hubback* (London: Staples, 1954)

Howarth, J., and Curthoys, M., 'The Political Economy of Women's Higher Education', *Historical Research*, vol. 60, no. 142 (1987), pp. 208–31

Hutchins, B. L., *Women in Modern Industry* (Wakefield: E. P. Publishing, 1978 [1915])

Hutton, Isabel, *Memories of a Doctor in War and Peace* (London: Heinemann, 1960)

Kaye, Elaine; Lees, Janet; Thorpe, Kirsty; and Durber, Susan, *Daughters of Dissent* (London: United Reformed Church, 2004)

Kelly, Laura, *Irish Women in Medicine c.1880s–1920s: Origins, Education and Careers* (Manchester: Manchester University Press, 2012)

Kent, Susan Kingsley, *Aftershocks: Politics and Trauma in Britain 1918–31* (London: Palgrave Macmillan, 2008)

Kirk, Harry, *Portrait of a Profession: A History of the Solicitor's Profession 1100 to the Present Day* (London: Oyez, 1976)

Lancaster, Bill, *The Department Store: A Social History*, pb (Leicester: Leicester University Press, 1995)

Lang, Elsie, *British Women in the Twentieth Century* (London: T. W. Laurie, 1929)

Law, Cheryl, *Women: A Modern Political Dictionary* (London: Tauris, 2000)

Lee, Jennie, *This Great Journey: A Volume of Autobiography 1904–45* (London: MacGibbon & Kee, 1963)

Lloyd, Jennifer, *Women and the Shaping of British Methodism* (Manchester: Manchester University Press, 2009)

Locket, Enid, *Ramblings: The Story of Enid Rosser* (unpublished typescript in Women's Library collection, LSE Library, LOCKET)

Logan, Anne, 'In Search of Equal Citizenship: The Campaign for Women Magistrates in England and Wales 1910–1939', *Women's History Review*, vol. 16, no. 4 (2007), pp. 501–18

McIntyre, Neil, 'Britain's First Medical Marriage: Frances Morgan (1843–1927), George Hoggan (1837–1891) and the mysterious "Elsie"', *Journal of Medical Biography*, vol. 12, no. 2 (2004), pp. 105–14

—*How British Women Became Doctors: The Story of the Royal Free Hospital and its Medical School* (London: Wenrowave, 2014)

Mackworth, Margaret Haig Thomas, Viscountess Rhondda, *This Was My World* (London: Macmillan, 1933)

MacLellan, Anne, *Dorothy Stopford Price: Rebel Doctor* (Sallins: Irish Academic, 2014)

Malatesta, Maria, *Professional Men, Professional Women* (London: Sage, 2011)

Malcolmson, P. and R. (eds), *A Free-Spirited Woman: The London Diaries of Gladys Langford, 1936–40* (Woodbridge: Boydell, 2014)

Malleson, Hope, *A Woman Doctor: Mary Murdoch of Hull* (London: Sidgwick & Jackson, 1919)

Mann, Ida, *The Chase: An Autobiography* (Fremantle: Fremantle Arts Centre Press, 1986)

Marking, Stacy (ed.), *Oxford Originals: An Anthology of Writing from Lady Margaret Hall 1879–2001* (Oxford: LMH, 2001)

Martindale, Hilda, *Some Victorian Portraits* (London: George Allen & Unwin, 1948)

— *Women Servants of the State 1870–1938* (London: George Allen & Unwin, 1938)

Martindale, Louisa, *A Woman Surgeon* (London: Gollancz, 1951)

The Ministry of Women (London: Society for the Promotion of Christian Knowledge, 1920)

Mitch, David; Brown, John; and van Leeuwen, Marco H. D. (eds), *Origins of the Modern Career* (Aldershot: Ashgate, 2004)

Mitton, G. E. (ed.), *The Englishwoman's Year Book and Directory* (London: A. & C. Black, 1915)

Morgan, Herbert, *Careers for Boys and Girls* (London: Methuen, 1926)

Morley, Edith, *Before and After: Reminiscences of a Working Life* (Reading: Two Rivers, 2016)

— *Women Workers in Seven Professions: A Survey of their Economic Conditions and Prospects* (London: Routledge, 1915)

Mossman, Mary, *The First Woman Lawyers: A Comparative Study of Gender, Law and the Legal Profession* (Oxford: Hart, 2006)

Mowat, Charles Loch, *Britain between the Wars 1918–40* (London: Methuen, 1955)

Mulcahy, L., and Sugarman, D. (eds), *Legal Life-Writing* (Chichester: Wiley Blackwell, 2015)

Murphy, Kate, 'A Marriage Bar of Convenience: The BBC and Married Women's Work 1923–39', *Twentieth Century British History*, vol. 25, no. 4 (2014), pp. 533–61

—— *Behind the Wireless: A History of Early Women at the* BBC (London: Palgrave Macmillan, 2016)

Murray, Margaret, *My First Hundred Years* (London: Kimber,1963)

New Careers for Women (London: Newnes, 1917)

Normanton, Helena, *Everyday Law for Women* (London: Nicholson & Watson, 1932)

Oram, Alison, *Women Teachers and Feminist Politics 1900–29* (Manchester: Manchester University Press, 1996)

Page, Eleanor, *Careers for Girls* (London: George Allen & Unwin, 1927)

Partington, G., *Women Teachers in the Twentieth Century* (Slough: National Foundation for Educational Research, 1976)

Perrone, Fernanda, *University Teaching as a Profession for Women in Oxford, Cambridge and London*, DPhil thesis, Oxford University (1991)

Polden, Patrick, 'Portia's Progress: Women at the Bar in England, 1919–1939', *International Journal of the Legal Profession*, vol. 12, no. 3 (Nov. 2005), pp. 293–338

Pollock, Margaret, *Working Days: Being the Personal Records of Sixteen Working Men and Women* (London: Cape, 1926)

Priestley, J. B., *English Journey*, jubilee edn (London: Heinemann, 1984 [1934])

Pugh, Martin, *We Danced All Night: A Social History of Britain between the Wars* (London: Bodley Head, 2008)

Rhondda, Viscountess, *see* Mackworth, Margaret

Richardson, Joanna, *Enid Starkie* (London: John Murray, 1973)

Riddell, George, Baron, *Dame Louisa Aldrich-Blake* (London: Hodder & Stoughton, 1926)

Robinson, Jane, *Bluestockings: The Remarkable Story of the First Women to Fight for an Education* (London: Viking, 2009)
— *Pandora's Daughters: The Secret History of Enterprising Women* (London: Constable, 2002)
Robson, W. A., *From Patronage to Proficiency* (London: Fabian Society, 1922)
Rosser, Enid, *see* Locket, Enid
Rowbotham, Sheila, *Hidden from History: Three Hundred Years of Women's Oppression and the Fight Against It* (London: Pluto, 1973)
Royden, Maude, *A Threefold Cord* (London: Gollancz, 1947)
— *The Church and Woman* (London: James Clarke, 1924)
  The Great Adventure: The Way to Peace (London: Headley, 1915)
Sacks, Oliver, *Uncle Tungsten: Memories of a Chemical Childhood* (London: Picador, 2012)
Shaw, George Bernard, *Mrs Warren's Profession*, in *Plays Pleasant and Unpleasant* (London: Constable, 1898)
Sidgwick, Mrs H., *Health Statistics of Women Students of Cambridge and Oxford and of their Sisters* (Cambridge: Cambridge University Press, 1890)
— 'The Place of University in Education in the Life of Women', in *Transactions of the Women's Institute* (London, 1897)
Smedley, Constance, *Crusaders: The Reminiscences of Constance Smedley* (London: Duckworth, 1929)
Smith, Harold (ed.), *British Feminism in the Twentieth Century* (Aldershot: Elgar, 1990)
Smith, Mary Bentinck, *Ad Vitam: Papers of a Head Mistress* (London: John Murray, 1927)
Sondheimer, J. H., *History of the British Federation of University Women 1907–57* (London: British Federation of University Women, 1957)
Spender, Dale (ed.), *Time and Tide Wait for No Man* (London: Pandora, 1984)
Sphinx, A., *Journalism as a Career for Women* (London: Newnes, 1918)

Starkie, Enid, *A Lady's Child* (London: Faber & Faber, 1941)

Strachey, Ray (ed.), *Our Freedom and its Results by Five Women* (London: Hogarth, 1936)

— *Careers and Openings for Women* (London: Faber & Faber, 1935)

Summerfield, Penny (ed.), *Women, Education and the Professions*, Occasional Paper no. 8 (Leicester: History of Education Society, 1987)

Takayanagi, Mari, *Parliament and Women* c.*1900–1945*, thesis, King's College, University of London (2012)

Van Arsdel, Rosemary, *Florence Fenwick Miller: Victorian Feminist, Journalist and Educator* (Aldershot: Ashgate, 2001)

Vicinus, Martha (ed.), *A Widening Sphere: Changing Roles of Victorian Women* (London: Methuen, 1977)

Wade, Stephen, *The Justice Women: The Female Presence in the Criminal Justice System 1800–1970* (Barnsley: Pen and Sword, 2015)

Walker, Lynn, *Golden Age or False Dawn? Women Architects in the Early 20th Century*, historicengland.org.uk/content/docs/research/women-architects-early-20th-centurypdf.

Waterhouse, C. H., *Insignia Vitae, or Broad Principles and Practical Conclusions* (London: J. S. Virtue, 1890)

Wauchope, Gladys, *The Story of a Woman Physician* (Bristol: John Wright, 1963)

White, C., *Women's Magazines 1693–1968* (London: Michael Joseph, 1970)

Wilberforce, Octavia (ed. Pat Jalland), *Eighth Child: The Autobiography of a Pioneer Woman Doctor* (London: Cassell, 1989)

Williams, Gertrude, *The New Democracy: Women and Work* (London: Nicholson & Watson, 1945)

Women and the Ministry: Some Considerations on the Report of the Archbishops' Commission on the Ministry of Women (London: Church Literature Association, 1936)

Women in the Ministry: A Reader Exploring the Story of Women in Leadership and Ministry within the Baptist Union of Great Britain (Didcot: Baptist Union of Great Britain, 2011)

Woolf, Virginia, 'Professions for Women', lecture given to the National Society for Women's Service, 1931, speakola.com/ideas/virginia-woolf-professions-for-women-1931
— *Three Guineas* (London: Hogarth, 1938)
Zimmeck, Meta, 'Strategies and Stratagems for the Employment of Women in the British Civil Service 1919–39', *Historical Journal*, vol. 24, no. 4 (1984), pp. 901–24

Acknowledgements

My first thanks must go to the women in this book, and to the families and friends who encouraged them, against the odds, to pursue careers in the professions. None of them is with us any more, and though I suspect one or two might wince at the thought of such publicity, telling their stories a hundred years on from when it all began seems the right thing to do. The works, words and memories they left behind are inspiring. I admire their perseverance and capacity for joy in the face of rank prejudice, and wish I could thank them in person, not just in spirit.

There are some more corporeal acknowledgements to be made. For permission to quote from documents in their collections I'm indebted to the family of Gwyneth Bebb Thomson, particularly her grandchildren Martin Tomlins and Anne Tickell; the Cadbury Research Library: Special Collections, University of Birmingham; the BBC Written Archives Centre; the Rare Book & Manuscript Library, Columbia University in the City of New York; the Masters of the Bench of the Honourable Society of Gray's Inn; the Leverkus family (for Gertrude Leverkus's memoirs); the University of Liverpool Library, Special Collections; the Medical Women's Federation; the National Archives; Sheffield City Council, Libraries Archives and Information: Sheffield City Archives; the Society of Authors as the Literary Representative of the Estate of Virginia Woolf; the Principal and Fellows of Somerville College, Oxford; Joy Taylor (for Peggy Kenyon's memoirs); William Twining (for May Du Buisson's memoirs); John and Ruth Warren (for Myfanwy Gipson's memoirs); the Women's Engineering Society and Institution of Engineering and Technology Archives; and the Women's Library collection at the London School of Economics Library. I am particularly grateful for the generosity of the individuals associated with these collections. While every effort has been made to contact copyright holders, the publishers would be pleased to hear from any unacknowledged here.

I am also grateful for the assistance and encouragement of staff at the Bodleian Library; the British Library; Greater Manchester County Record Office (with Manchester Archives); the four Inns of Court (Gray's Inn, Inner Temple, Lincoln's Inn and Middle Temple); the Law Society; the Archives of the Royal Institute of British Architects; the Archives of St Hugh's College, Oxford; and the Wellcome Collection. These are places I visited formally; others, including some of the medical Royal Colleges and various church organizations, patiently responded to email queries and helped me if they could.

Ceridwen Lloyd-Morgan went above and beyond at the University Women's Club, as did Elizabeth Cruickshank, Beryl De Souza, Peggy Frith, Stephen Eyre, Lis Fisher, Amanda Ingram, Mark Lofthouse and Benjamin Taylor. Thanks, too, to Felicity Ashworth, Nina Baker, Katie Broomfield, Ceryl Evans, Fenella Gentleman, Henrietta Heald, Rachel Killick, Veronica Lowe, Anne Manuel, Kate O'Donnell, Senia Paseta, Albert Pionke, Sue Purver and Matthew Roper. If I've left anyone out, or made perverse mistakes despite all the expertise offered to me in the course of my research, please forgive me.

My agent, Véronique Baxter, and editor, Susanna Wadeson, are both brilliant. I couldn't do without them. Their colleagues at David Higham Associates and Transworld are unfailingly upbeat and full of good ideas, as is my copy-editor Gillian Somerscales. You would think the novelty of having a wife who puts on an apron and then disappears for the day to her study (with Captain Oates the cat) would be wearing a little thin by now, but Bruce continues to be supportive in every way. Our sons Richard and Ed are interested, interesting, and never fail to lift my spirits when the research is slow, the writing's flagging or the cat's just pressed 'send' again. The newest member of our family, daughter-in-law Tammy, is a consummate professional of whom I am extremely proud. This book is dedicated to her, with love.

Picture Acknowledgements

Every effort has been made to contact copyright holders. Any we have omitted are invited to get in touch with the publishers.

page 10: Gwyneth Bebb: photograph by Marion Neilson, reproduced with permission of Martin Tomlins and Anne Tickell, grandchildren (image courtesy of St Hugh's College Archive, Oxford)

page 22: Laura Willson, Caroline Haslett and Margaret Partridge, 1927: photograph by Photopress. The Women's Engineering Society. IET Archives and WES

page 25: Maude Royden c.1940: photograph by Elliott & Fry, Edward Gooch Collection/Getty Images

page 29: Dr Enid Starkie, photographed for *Vogue* magazine, 1951: photograph by Norman Parkinson, Iconic Images

page 33: Dr Annie McCall: reproduced by kind permission of London Borough of Lambeth, Archives Department (Image ref LMK 04704, https://borough-photos.org/lambeth/annie-mccall/)

page 37: Clapham Maternity Hospital's Christmas Party, 1922: Wellcome Collection

page 43: An anatomy lecture at Elizabeth Blackwell's Medical College for Women, New York, from *Frank Leslie's Illustrated Newspaper*, 16 April 1870: Bettmann/Getty Images

page 45: Sophia Jex-Blake: photograph by Swaine, Wellcome Collection

page 47: Matriculation Record: Edinburgh University Library (EUA IN1/ADS/STA/2)

page 50: Our Pretty Doctor, cartoon by G. du Maurier from *Punch* or the *London Charivari*, 13 August 1870: Wellcome Collection

page 68: London School of Medicine for Women: Wellcome Collection

page 70: Dr Louisa Martindale: photograph by Lafayette, Wellcome Collection

page 74: Margaret Haig Thomas c.1930: Hulton Archive/Getty Images

Index

HEARTS AND MINDS
The Untold Story of the Great Pilgrimage and How Women Won the Vote

Jane Robinson

1913: the last long summer before the war. The country is gripped by suffragette fever. Some admire these impassioned crusaders; others agree with their aims if not their forceful methods; there are those who are aghast at the thought of giving *any* female a vote.

Meanwhile, hundreds of women are stepping out on to the streets of Britain. They are the suffragists: non-militant campaigners for the vote, on an astonishing six-week protest march they call the Great Pilgrimage. Rich and poor, young and old, they defy convention, risking jobs, family relationships and even their lives to persuade the country to listen to them.

The Great Pilgrimage transformed the personal and political lives of women in Britain for ever. Jane Robinson has drawn from diaries, letters and unpublished accounts to tell the inside story, against the colourful background of the entire suffrage campaign

Fresh and original, full of vivid detail and moments of high drama, *Hearts and Minds* is both incredibly important and wonderfully entertaining.

'A brilliant, witty and moving account of women's battle to win the vote'
Shirley Williams

'Smashed windows, lobbed bombs, a fascinating book'
Daily Mail

'A story of huge courage and, most of all, immense female camaraderie . . . meticulously researched . . . a fascinating and inspiring read'
Sunday Express

Jane Robinson is also the author of *Bluestockings: The Remarkable Story of the First Women to Fight for an Education* and *Hearts and Minds: The Untold Story of the Great Pilgrimage and How Women Won the Vote*. She was born in Edinburgh and brought up in Yorkshire, before going to Oxford University to study English Language and Literature at Somerville College. She has worked in the antiquarian book trade and as an archivist, and is now a full-time writer and lecturer, specializing in social history through women's eyes. She is married with two sons and lives in Buckinghamshire. *Ladies Can't Climb Ladders* is her eleventh book.